D1105506

ESSAYS ON LOGIC AND LANGUAGE
(*SECOND SERIES*)

LOGIC AND LANGUAGE

(SECOND SERIES)

Essays by

PROFESSORS J. L. AUSTIN, DOUGLAS GASKING,
G. E. MOORE, O.M., GILBERT RYLE, J. J. C. SMART
DR. F. WAISMANN and DR. F. L. WILL
D. F. PEARS, A. M. MACIVER, G. J. WARNOCK, J. O. URMSON

EDITED WITH AN INTRODUCTION BY
ANTONY FLEW

OXFORD
BASIL BLACKWELL
1966

First printed January, 1953
Reprinted 1955
Reprinted 1959
Reprinted 1961
Reprinted 1966

PRINTED IN GREAT BRITAIN
BY THE COMPTON PRINTING WORKS (LONDON) LTD., LONDON, N.I
FOR BASIL BLACKWELL & MOTT LTD.
AND BOUND BY
THE KEMP HALL BINDERY, OXFORD

And though a philosopher may live remote from business, the genius of philosophy, if carefully cultivated by several, must gradually diffuse itself throughout the whole society, and bestow a similar correctness on every art and calling.

DAVID HUME, *Enquiry concerning Human Understanding*, Sect. I, §5.

LOGIC AND LANGUAGE
(*FIRST SERIES*)

CONTENTS

LOGIC AND LANGUAGE
(*SECOND SERIES*)

CONTENTS

ESSAYS ON
LOGIC AND LANGUAGE

INTRODUCTION

By A. G. N. Flew

THE success of *Logic and Language* (First Series) makes it possible to bring out this second and complementary volume. The aim of the former volume was a dual one – and different from that of similar collections which have appeared lately: both to provide, for the general interested and educated public, an introduction to the recent linguistic developments in philosophy; and to make available in book form, for students and specialists, some of the important articles which previously were only accessible in those libraries which take the philosophical journals. The aim of this second volume is similar: and therefore substantially the same criteria have been used for making the selection. There is no need to explain all these again; this was done in the previous Introduction. But there are four further points to be made now.

First: because this volume was designed to be complementary to the former one, extra weight has been given this time to the claims of those articles which deal with major themes which could not be touched there; and an effort has been made to avoid any overlapping between the two. Thus the papers on 'Universals' (chap. III) and on 'Categories' (chap. IV), as well as the contributions to the philosophy of history (chap. X), of mathematics (chap. XI) and of science (chap. XII), had an additional claim; because none of these subjects had been represented before. On the other hand, as always happens when multiple criteria are involved, other and conflicting claims were sometimes too strong to resist: though F. L. Will (chap. II) does deal with some of the problems of induction, others of which had already been attacked by Paul Edwards (vol. I, chap. IV); still these were for a very long time notoriously the great scandal of philosophy, and progress here deserves special prominence. And of course there are still gaps: for instance, aesthetics is entirely unrepresented.[1]

Second: while all the papers in that volume had been previously published, this contains three which have not been: namely those by Dr. Waismann (chap. I) and G. J. Warnock (chap. VI), and the second one by D. F. Pears (chap. VII). There is no need to explain or to excuse this departure: but here it can be said relevantly that 'Language Strata' (chap. I) is in effect a continuation of the same author's 'Verifiability' (vol. I, chap. VII), which particularly appealed to many reviewers; and that the other two were originally part of a series of examinations of the logical peculiarities of members of that perplexing class of sentences – to which Kant was the first to draw attention – which seem to be both synthetic and *a priori*.

Third: fearing that by this second lap many of the less strenuous and less enthusiastic laymen would have dropped out, and hoping that the remainder would now be ready for some rather harder things, the balance has been tilted slightly – but still only slightly – more in favour of the specialist. Thus the bar raised against symbolism has been lowered a little, particularly in order to admit Professor J. J. C. Smart's 'Theory Construction' (chap. XII). This contains some mathematics: but the author agrees that his main line of argument will be perfectly intelligible even to those who choose to skip the calculations. Again, several of the contributions in this second series will need much more energetic attention than anything in the first: this is certainly true of both 'Universals' (chap. III) and 'Other Minds' (chap. VIII).[2] But any reader with a taste for philosophy – and not just the student (for whom both are essential) – will be rewarded for the pains he takes on these. There is perhaps only one paper included – Professor G. E. Moore's 'Is Existence a Predicate?' (chap. V) – which can scarcely be expected to appeal to anyone but the specialist: but it would have been inexcusable not to include any

---

[1] A volume, *Essays in Aesthetics and Language*, edited by William Elton, is now in course of preparation.

[2] This is the article enigmatically, and rather remotely, mentioned by Dr. Joad. 'More recently my attention has been drawn to the doctrines of an Oxford teacher whose contribution to a certain Symposium embodied a variation of logical positivist [*sic*] doctrine which put all the others out of court. This I was assured was the very latest thing.' (*A Critique of Logical Positivism*, p. 15).

work by the *doyen* of British philosophy; and this particular piece is constantly recommended to students.

Fourth: it should be put on record that the absence of any study of the logical peculiarities of any language other than English has been noted and regretted: but extraordinarily little seems to have been done on this, at least by professional philosophers. Some logicians have put a lot of work into specifying, and even constructing, artificial languages (usually so artificial that they are much more like mathematical calculi than like any natural language). Other philosophers have learnt from Wittgenstein the value of sometimes illustrating their arguments with references to imaginary truncated languages[1] (in much the same way as treatises on mechanics are illustrated by schematic diagrams). Others again have realized keenly how different the world may look to those whose languages are radically different; for instance, one of our contributors, Dr. Waismann (vol. I, chap. VII) has noticed how differently a person regards colour if his language expresses it by a verb — in Russian 'the sky blues' — rather than as English does by an adjective. But all this is very far from constituting a study of the logical peculiarities of exotic natural languages.[2] There seems to be a lot of room here for useful team work between anthropologists, sinologues, philologists and philosophers: to examine Nietzsche's neglected dictum that 'by the grammatical structure of a group of languages everything runs smoothly for one kind of philosophical system, whereas the way is as it were barred for certain other possibilities'.

These four points — taken together with those made in the previous Introduction — should show the principles followed in making this second selection. This time it is unnecessary to compose a prefatory manifesto: for though manifestoes have their place — sometimes even in philosophy — to demand attention for the neglected or to proclaim a programme; these func-

---

[1] For Wittgenstein's methods it is now possible to refer to his *Philosophical Investigations* which is, since the author's death, at last to be publicly published (With an English translation: Blackwell, 1953).

[2] Some references might be useful: see, for example, I. A. Richards *Mencius on the Mind*; Arthur Waley, *Three Ways of Thought in Ancient China* and 'The Language Crisis in Ancient China' (which appeared in *Polemic 4*); (C. Kluckhorn and D. Leighton, *The Navaho* (Harvard U.P., 1947: the chapter on the Navaho language); and — a paper I wish I could have included in this collection — D. D. Lee, 'Conceptual Implications of an Indian language' (in *Philosophy of Science* for 1938).

tions are finished when the attention has been granted and some of the performance, not merely the programme, is there to be judged. Reasoned discussion cannot be conducted at the top of one's voice: and an atmosphere of party conflict or of clique feud obstructs the progress of philosophy.

But one or two points, which it would be worth remarking on here, arise from comments on the former volume. *First*: people – especially those unsympathetic to recent developments – are inclined to give the name 'Logical Positivism' to any philosophizing in which the use of words, expressions and sentences is mentioned prominently. This is a very loose usage: and unfortunate because it generates heat and confusion. The term was originally coined to describe the views of the Vienna Circle, a group of scientists and philosophers which formed round Moritz Schlick in Vienna in the 'twenties.[1] The Vienna Circle were interested primarily in logic and scientific method: indeed many of them had been trained originally in natural science – usually physics – rather than in philosophy. At least in their published writings they often appeared narrow, dogmatic, philistine, uninterested in traditional philosophy, and militantly secular. In England they found a devastatingly iconoclastic spokesman in Professor A. J. Ayer. His brilliant and powerful statement of the Logical Positivist position (*Language Truth and Logic*: 1st edition 1936, 2nd edition with an important new Introduction 1946) deservedly became a classic, and the centre of passionate controversy: and it is mainly because for British readers the term 'Logical Positivism' suggests the position of that book, that it is so confusing to use it loosely to cover the very different and very various views of our contributors. Though they may be wrong in this – guilty of a peculiarly vicious sort of parochialism – most of these do not think of themselves as members of any school or movement; but simply as philosophers.[2]

Second: it is felt that an inquiry, in so far as it is in any sense verbal, about words, must to that extent be trivial; and hence that

---

[1] For an account of the history of the Vienna Circle and associated groups see the Introduction to *Modern Science and its Philosophy* by Philipp Frank (Harvard U.P., 1949).

[2] The refusal to coin, and reluctance to accept, a party name is deliberate: cf. G. Ryle, 'Taking Sides in Philosophy' in *Philosophy* for 1937. Most of his colleagues would, I think, agree with him in insisting that party banners and school loyalty have no place in philosophy.

philosophers who talk about the use of words must — as one reviewer vigorously phrased it — 'be selling their truthright for a mess of verbiage'. Some verbal disputes are trivial and idle: it would indeed be trivial to criticize the same reviewer for using the word 'verbosopher', because it is a mongrel from mixed Latin and Greek parents. But other disputes about words are not trivial at all: sometimes even when all the facts are agreed much may depend on the decision as to which word to use: and much may reasonably be said for and against. Can it or can it not be called the action of a reasonable man? Are we to say he is sane or that he is insane? So not all disputes about words are 'mere disputes about words'.

The idea that modern linguistic insights and interests must involve a trivialization, or even a betrayal, of philosophy has been crystallized in and encouraged by a favourite saying of the Logical Positivists: 'Philosophical questions are not problems to be solved but (pseudo-problems or) puzzles to be (dis)solved'. This saying had its value as a slogan against those who thought of philosophy as a sort of super-science (a usurper Queen of the sciences) or as a non-experimental para-science (science from an easy chair):[1] for it emphasized that philosophy is not science, nor yet super-science nor para-science. Yet philosophical problems are no more pseudo-problems because they are not scientific problems, than Americans are pseudo-Englishmen because they are not English-men. And the implicit suggestion that philosophy must needs be trivial, just because it cannot be science, is grossly philistine. It is a disreputable relic of the old Logical Positivist campaign to glorify natural science, especially physics, at the expense of every other intellectual discipline.

But there are other sources of this anxiety about trivialization. One is, of course, that philosophers are no more exempt than are other academics from the misconception that, because much research which is not obviously important has various kinds of value, any or only research which is obviously unimportant can be properly pursued in universities: and hence work is often done which really is trivial. Another — more fundamental and less avoidable — is the fact that once anyone has seen how to dissolve

---

[1] Compare Ezra Pound, 'After Leibniz's time a philosopher was just a guy who was too damn lazy to work in a laboratory'.

a philosophic muddle or has achieved a philosophic insight it becomes hard for him any longer to understand how he or anyone else could ever have failed to see what now to him seems so obvious. Philosophy has indeed been defined as 'the discovery of the obvious'. Yet to deny the existence of a problem, to speak of pseudo-problems, where considerable men may have been perplexed, just because you believe that you know the way out, is surely either excessively arrogant or excessively modest. In so far as linguistic analysis has shown that, and also how some classical philosophical problems consisted wholly or partly in muddles and confusions, it has done something to *solve* those problems.[1] To clear up an ancient confusion is not a trivial achievement; not at least for 'those who have the wish to understand, to escape from intellectual bewilderment':[2] and, as Russell was saying when he wrote this, it is in any case only to them that philosophy has anything to offer.

Third: sometimes people coin or seize on epigrammatic statements of what philosophy is; and proceed to rejoice or deplore that this is all that it comes to. This must always be mistaken: if only because 'philosophy' is one of those words (like 'poetry', 'nation', or 'genius') the whole meaning of which cannot be given in a definition. When Professor Ryle writes of philosophy as 'the detection of the sources in linguistic idiom of recurrent misconstructions and absurd theories' (Vol. I, chap. II *ad fin.*) or Professor Price claims that 'all the great philosophical discoveries are discoveries of the obvious',[3] they are to be taken as coining epigrams or slogans to draw attention to aspects of philosophical inquiry which had been neglected or overlooked. Compare the case of the man who says that he 'would define a tank as mechanized and armoured fire-power':[4] as a formal definition of 'tank' this will not do; but it is a very good epigram for the purpose for which it was coined — to draw attention to the fact that British tanks in World War II were chronically undergunned.

---

[1] Though in the advertisement 'the problem is not a problem at all' to the advertiser who has the product which will solve it. We do tend to speak of a solved problem as something which no longer exists.

[2] Bertrand Russell, *Our Knowledge of the External World*, p. 28.

[3] 'The Permanent Significance of Hume's Philosophy' in *Philosophy*, 1940. This passage comes at p. 12 of this most relevant and excellent article.

[4] E. T. Williams in a broadcast review of the fourth volume of Mr. Churchill's war memoirs.

Or compare the things people say about the nature of poetry, or nationality, or genius: poetry is emotion recollected in tranquillity; a nation is a society united by a common error as to its origins and a common aversion to its neighbours; genius is an infinite capacity for taking pains. As definitions of 'poetry', 'nation', or 'genius' none of these will do at all: they are obviously both in some ways far too narrow and in others far too comprehensive. But as epigrams about poetry, nations, and genius they all have value: there is a lot in each of them: they would all on occasion be good things to say.

But the whole idea that there is or should be some real essence of philosophy which has been or could be expressed in a single, final, comprehensive, 'true definition' is radically misguided. 'Philosophy' has not been in the past, and we should not now try to make it, that sort of word. It has been used to refer not to some wholly homogeneous investigation or series of investigations, but to a family of related but various inquiries and activities. If we introduced a standard definition we should have by it to exclude many activities which have a perfect right to the name 'philosophy'. Uniformity can be achieved – here as elsewhere – only at the cost of wholesale suppression and expulsion. If we were to insist that philosophy must be purely and exclusively a conceptual investigation – a study of the 'logic of our language' – we should find ourselves committed to excluding almost everything that had previously been called political philosophy: for only the most heroic and extreme measures of reinterpretation could fit Hobbes, Locke, Rousseau and Burke to this mould. We should also inevitably find that we had encouraged the narrow-minded, bureaucratic departmentalism which is already too common in what ought to be the loose association of the 'republic of letters'. A tight definition of 'philosophy' might perhaps inhibit possible future developments, and it would certainly encourage philosophers to neglect and despise worthy activities which could, on a broader usage of the term, be properly called philosophical; for unfortunately professional philosophers are not immune from the temptations which beset all specialists.[1] Whereas a loose definition would probably include far too much; and would

---

[1] Even they need to beware the Specialist Fallacy: that of confusing 'I am only paid to know about X' with 'I am paid to know about X only' (and about nothing else).

certainly be so comprehensive as to be vacuously uninformative. So it is far better to attempt no definitions of 'philosophy': and if anyone asks what philosophy is, to answer him by pointing to various specimens; perhaps adding a few explanatory comments. The two volumes of *Logic and Language* contain a collection of characteristic specimens of the best work being done by English-speaking philosophers. But one necessary comment is to explain that they do not represent every sort of good work which could be or should be or is being done in philosophy; though no one who is concerned to do good philosophy can afford to remain unfamiliar with the new linguistic techniques and linguistic insights demonstrated by many of our contributors. (To say nothing here of their possible value and applications outside philosophy.)

Fourth: many are shocked to find philosophers so concerned about deviations from standard English (or whatever other language is being used or discussed) and the elucidation of the ordinary use of language. These conceptions have recently been the subject of considerable — often fairly heated — controversy among philosophers.[1] This is not the place to try to go deeply into the problems: but two points might usefully be added to those made in the Introduction to our first volume. First: it has been suggested that there is no such thing as ordinary or standard usage; because there is no absolute, normative, unchanging and universal standard of correctness. But this objection tries to prove too much, giving reasons which are not enough. To prove that there is never and nowhere any ordinary or standard usage of English (or any other) words it is not enough to point out, truly, that there is no universal, unchanging, normative and absolute standard of English (or any other) usage. And if it were true — which it certainly and fortunately is not — that there is no standard usage of words within any group at any time, then it would not be merely a few perverse philosophers whose position would be undermined. For though of course much of our usage is constantly changing, and does vary considerably from district to district, and from social group to social group; still it is only and

[1] See for instance K. E. Baier in *P.A.S.* 1951/52; and papers by Wisdom, Malcolm, etc., in *The Philosophy of G. E. Moore* (Northwestern U.P., Evanston, 1942). Other useful references will be found in footnotes to P. L. Heath's paper in *Philosophical Quarterly*, 1952.

precisely in so far as two people use and understand words in some accepted, standard way that verbal communication between them is possible. Thus this objection tries to prove too much. (Philosophy is not the first field in which conservatives have become the unwitting allies of a revolution of destruction.) Second: it is often thought that concern with the ordinary use of words is no part of the business of a philosopher. But in so far as philosophy is a conceptual inquiry, such concern is surely essential. For how else could one investigate the concept of knowledge than by studying the various correct uses of the word 'know'? (Which is of course one of the things which Professor J. L. Austin is doing in vol. II, chap. VIII.) Though this is not to say *either* that philosophy is only a conceptual investigation *or* that philosophers should investigate only the ordinary concepts of common sense *or* that they should never try to improve any of the concepts they have investigated (which would necessarily involve changing the present use of the words concerned).[1]

Finally we want to make our acknowledgments to all those without whose co-operation this collection could not have appeared. We thank the contributors for permitting their work to be included: and remind readers that some of the articles were written up to fifteen years ago; so they may often not represent their authors' present views. Nine of the papers have been published before. Chapters IV, V, VIII and X were first printed in the *Proceedings of the Aristotelian Society* for 1938/39 and in the Supplementary Volumes XV, XX and XXI (for 1939, 1946 and 1947); chapter II and chapter IX in *Mind* for 1946 and 1950; chapter III in the *Philosophical Quarterly* for 1951; chapter XI in the *Australasian Journal of Psychology and Philosophy* for 1940; and chapter XII in *Philosophy and Phenomenological Research* for 1951. We thank the editors of these journals for permission to reprint the papers. Also the numerous reviewers of the first volume, especially those who helpfully sent the Editor copies of their comments: all criticisms and suggestions made publicly in reviews or privately in letters have been carefully considered; and the advice given — in so far as he could bring himself to agree with

---

[1] Yet it is surely only prudent to elucidate the current nature of the concept (the current correct usage of the word and its synonyms — and any equivalents in any other language) before rushing forward with suggestions on how to reform it.

it — has been followed in compiling this volume. It would have been concluded with a select bibliography; but the sub-faculty of philosophy at Oxford has been preparing one which will presumably in due course appear to join the similar pamphlet already published[1] under the auspices of the sub-faculty of economics. It would be foolish to duplicate this work; and thus to add unnecessarily to the length, and hence to the expense, of this book. May it be received as kindly and in as many places as the first volume.

King's College
Aberdeen

March 1952

A Bibliography in Economics (Blackwell: frequently revised).

CHAPTER I

LANGUAGE STRATA

By F. Waismann

[This paper has not been published before; but was read in 1946 to the Jowett Society at Oxford. When Dr. Waismann came to revise it for publication here, he found that there was so much that he wished to alter, and so much else that he wished to develop at considerably greater length, that it was clear that the only practicable alternatives were either not to publish it at all or to publish it in its original form. In view of the facts, that it has already had considerable influence in that form, and that it had an important place in the plan of this volume, I tried — successfully — to persuade him to permit its publication here, substantially unchanged: but it is only fair to state these circumstances and to say that the eventual decision to publish was made rather against his better judgment. The morals are obvious. — EDITOR]

I. TYPES OF AMBIGUITY

Both vagueness and 'open texture'[1] must be distinguished from, and likened to, another sort of lack of definition; ambiguity. Of the many types of ambiguity a few examples may be mentioned.

(i) A word may have two altogether different meanings, or better, there may be two words which have the sound in common; thus someone might say, 'How long it is since I have seen the Alps! How I long to see them'. This fact makes possible certain puns — as when a crying child is called the 'Prince of Wails'.

(ii) An extreme case of ambiguity is what is called the *antithetical sense of primal words*. There is evidence that in the oldest languages opposites such as: strong — weak, light — dark, large — small were expressed by the same root word. Thus, in ancient Egyptian *keu* stood for both strong and weak. In Latin *altus* means high and deep, *sacer* both sacred and accursed. Compare further *clamare*, to shout, and *clam*, quietly, secretly, or *siccus*, dry, and *succus*, juice. Nor is it only the ancient languages which have retained as relics words capable of meaning either of two opposites. The same applies to present-day languages. 'To cleave' means to split, but in the phrase 'cleave to' it means to adhere. The word 'without', originally carrying with it both a positive and a negative connotation, is used today in the negative

---

[1] See Vol. I, pp. 119ff.

sense only. That 'with' has not only the sense of 'adding to' but also that of 'depriving of' is clear from the compounds 'withdraw' and 'withhold'.

(iii) It is commonly impossible to distinguish between different senses of a word without considering how it is used in context. When used in different contexts, the same word may assume different senses. Take as an example the transitive and intransitive use of a verb: 'I smell the lilac', 'The lilac smells lovely'. But even when a verb is used transitively, it may take on different meanings when connected with words of different types: 'I caught him', 'I caught measles'. We use the word 'like' often in the sense of 'similar'; we say, for instance, 'That man is like his brother', and in this context we may also say 'very like', 'amazingly like', 'so like that one cannot tell them apart'. On the other hand, it would be amazing to learn of two triangles 'so alike that one cannot tell them apart'. In the one case the word admits of degrees of comparison, in the other it does not. Compare the phrase 'Find the key which — ' with 'Find the number which — '. In spite of the sameness of the construction the difference in meaning is clearly felt. Thus I might have said 'Compute the number which — ', but not 'Compute the key which — ', a sign that the word is used according to different substitution rules. Again, compare 'I am trying to solve this equation', 'I am trying to remember a forgotten name', 'I am trying to fall asleep'.

(iv) A word which is used in a quite definite way and in quite definite contexts may be used in a new sort of context; with this change of use often goes a change in meaning. For instance: 'the fruit of a tree', 'the fruit of his labour', 'the fruit of his meditations'; 'to sow seed', 'to sow distrust'. What we use is a picture. If the image becomes a stereotyped figure of speech, we talk of 'figurative meaning'. (This is one of the means by which language grows. A speaker may, on the spur of the moment, place a word in a new collocation, thus giving rise to a new meaning — a process over which there is little control.) Now the point of this is that it is not always possible to say exactly where the metaphor ends and where the word starts having an independent meaning. The phrase 'to sow distrust' is felt to be a metaphor, perhaps also 'the fruit of his meditations', but not 'a fruitless attempt'. Here the pictorial element has faded. Glance through the following list and consider whether you would venture to draw a sharp line between a figure that is still a live image and one which has become a well-worn metaphor: 'The birth of tragedy', 'Drowned in sorrow', 'An abyss of grief', 'A radiant spirit', 'A flight of phantasy', 'A fiery temper'.

(v) A word may be used in a 'figurative sense'. Remember that almost all terms denoting the mental are derived from words whose primary connotation was sensuous. Thus we speak of an idea 'floating in the mind', we 'call it to mind', we say it is still 'hazy'; an idea is 'engraved upon my memory', it 'makes an impression upon me'; something 'moves us', 'touches us', so that we are 'carried away'; we feel 'stirred', 'beside ourselves'; we talk of a 'brilliant idea', a 'flash of wit'; and so on.

This rising of the meaning of a word from the sphere of the sensuous to that of the mental continues to the present day. Think of expressions such as 'split personality', 'the layers of the subconscious', 'twilight of consciousness', etc. A sensuous element gleams through most of the phrases which denote emotions. We talk of 'shady', 'volcanic', 'unbridled', 'ebullient' characters; 'wooden', 'unpolished', 'crabbed' individuals; of an 'oily', 'smooth' manner, a 'stiff' attitude, a 'lukewarm', 'cool', 'icy' reception; of an 'arid', 'sparkling', 'will-o'-the-wisp' spirit.

The fact that language develops out of the sensuous into the mental produces a peculiar phenomenon: we seem at times to glimpse behind a word another sense, deeper and half hidden, and to hear faintly the entry of another meaning, in and with which others begin to sound, and all accompany the original meaning of the word like the sympathetic chimes of a bell. Hence that deep and sonorous ring in words which is lacking in artificial and invented languages; and hence also the multiplicity of meaning, the indefiniteness, the strange suggestiveness and evasiveness of so much poetry. Hugo von Hofmannsthal once described this phenomenon.

> It leads us into the innermost nature of Oriental poetry, into the very mystery and being of language. For this mysterious-ness is the deepest element in Eastern language and poetry alike, in so far as everything in it is metaphorical, everything remotely descended from ancient roots. The original root is

sensuous, primitive, concise and strong, but the word moves away from it by subtle transitions to new, related meanings, and then to meanings only remotely related: yet in the remotest meaning there is still some echo of the original sound of the word, still some darkly mirrored image of the first sensuous impression . . . In the limitless detail and particularity of description the subject matter itself seems to oppress and overwhelm us: but what would come so close to us as to hurt us, were we limited to immediate meanings, resolves itself by virtue of the multiplicity of meaning in the words into a magic cloud, and so behind the immediate meaning we divine another which is derived from it. Thus it is that we do not lose sight of the proper and original sense: where, however, this sense was commonplace and mean, it loses its implicit commonplaceness, and often, as we contemplate the word, we hesitate in our perceptive awareness between the particular reality which it symbolizes and a higher reality, and this in a flash leads up to the great and the sublime.

(vi) There are other cases in which the meanings cannot be as clearly separated out as, for instance, in the case of the word 'cold' (where I may say of a day or of a reception that it is cold). Consider a word like 'haughty'. That there is a difference in its use is shown in the fact that the word can be combined with words of very different logical types; thus we may speak of a haughty smile, a haughty tone of voice, a haughty face, a haughty look, a haughty bearing, a haughty speech, a haughty person. So there *is* a difference in meaning. Yet all these meanings are connected – in saying of somebody that he is haughty, at least part of what we mean is that he has a haughty face, or a haughty bearing, etc. So the meanings interpenetrate, and unite into a larger whole, a sort of cloud in which the several precise conceits are lost. We may say that they *dissolve into vagueness*. Such an example shows how ambiguity may gradually pass into vagueness.

'But shouldn't we still try to distinguish as clearly as possible all the different shades of meaning the word can assume?' Try, and you'll see how puzzling it is. Paul Valéry put this point very well when he said:

You must . . . at some time or another, have noticed this curious fact — that a given word, which may be perfectly obvious when used in the ordinary course of communication, which presents no difficulties whatever when caught up in the give and take of normal conversation, has a way of becoming almost magically embarrassing, strangely resistant and quite unmanageable in definition, as soon as you withdraw it from circulation with the object of examining it closely and apart from its neighbours, as soon, that is, as you try to establish its meaning in isolation from its momentary function. It is almost comic to note the difficulty with which we are confronted when we try to establish the *precise* meaning of a word which, in the ordinary routine of life, we use daily to our complete satisfaction . . . But isolate it, clip its wings and it turns and rends you. You soon become convinced that the number of its meanings is far in excess of its functions. Formerly it was only a *means*, but now it is an *end*, the object of a terrible philosophical desire. It is something entirely different from what it was, an enigma, an abyss, a source of mental torment.

(vii) Next, consider a number of statements made by psychologists: 'We perceive the surface of the metal, it is true, but its colour seems to lie *behind* this surface'. 'Lustre-light does not lie *in* the plane of the object to which it belongs, but appears rather either *before* the object or *superimposed on* it'. 'When a shadow moves it moves not *in* the surface of the object but *across* it'. 'When a person is speaking with someone in complete darkness, the voice of the one who answers usually sounds distinctly *behind* the darkness, not *in* the darkness'. 'If you look at a colour disk which turns round quickly, it is better to say that there is a flickering *across* the disk or *before* it in space than to say that the disk *itself* is flickering'. Notice that in all these cases the prepositions which symbolize spatial relations take on a somewhat new sense. In the last example, for instance, to say that there is a flickering *before* the disk in space is to use 'before' in a peculiar way, namely so as to make it *meaningless* to ask exactly what distance, precisely how many millimetres before the surface it lies. Here we have a sense of 'before' or 'in front of' which differs from the ordinary sense. The same holds of the 'behind' in our first example. There are intermediate ones: thus a glowing piece of iron is seen as luminous *throughout* its mass; a rainbow, though extended in space before the observer, does not possess a surface. One feels that one can penetrate more or less deeply *into* the spectral colours, whereas when one looks at the colour of a paper the surface presents a sort of barrier beyond which the gaze cannot pass. The words 'throughout' and 'into' come here closer to, though they have not exactly, the ordinary meaning. Many more examples could be collected, but these will do. 'The English prepositions', says Empson, 'from being used in so many ways and in combination with so many verbs, have acquired not so much a number of meanings as a body of meaning continuous in several directions'. Exactly, there are so many senses and they are so firmly interlocked that they seem to form one continuous body. Thus many words which we wouldn't suspect turn out to be ambiguous. One can hardly make too much of this ambiguity of language through which we often seem to see words like shapes in a mist.

(viii) Then there is such a thing as *systematic ambiguity*. This expression was first coined by Bertrand Russell in connection with his Theory of Types. Without entering into it here we can say that his idea, roughly speaking, is that we must distinguish between different *logical types of symbols*. Beginning with names which stand for 'individuals', we come next to predicates which possibly apply to those names, and then to second-order predicates which possibly apply to the first-order predicates, and so on. We are thus led to consider a hierarchy of symbols which, theoretically, goes on without end. This hierarchy corresponds to a similar hierarchy of *statements*. And statements are divided into different types according to whether they are statements about an individual, or statements about a class of individuals, or statements about a class of classes of individuals, and so on. A statement such as 'Socrates is mortal' is true when there is a corresponding fact, and false when there is no corresponding fact. But take now such a statement as 'All men are mortal'. The truth of it can no longer consist in its correspondence to a single fact, for there are indefinitely many facts such as 'Socrates is mortal', 'Plato is mortal', etc. Now Russell's point is that the meaning of 'truth' which is applicable to the latter sort of proposition is *not the same* as the meaning of 'truth' which is applicable to the proposition 'All men are mortal'; i.e. each type of statement has its own sort of truth.

The main ground for accepting that distinction is that it offers an escape from the paradoxes or antinomies which were a threat to logic.

> The imaginary sceptic, who asserts that he knows nothing, and is refuted by being asked if he knows that he knows nothing, has asserted nonsense, and has been fallaciously refuted by an argument which involves a vicious-circle fallacy. In order that the sceptic's assertion may become significant, it is necessary to place some limitation upon the things of which he is asserting his ignorance, because the things of which it is possible to be ignorant form an illegitimate totality. *Principia Mathematica* (Vol. I, Introduction).

Take the case of the Liar, that is of a man who says 'I am lying'; if he is lying he is speaking the truth, and if he is speaking the truth he is lying. We may interpret his statement as saying, 'All propositions which I assert are false'. Is this proposition itself true or false? To clear up the paradox we must distinguish between elementary propositions which do not refer to a totality of propositions, first-order propositions which do refer to a totality of elementary propositions, second-order propositions which do refer to a totality of first-order propositions, and so on. Now if the liar asserts that all propositions which he asserts are false he is making a first-order statement which does not fall within its own scope, and therefore no contradiction emerges. The decisive point to realize is that the phrase 'all propositions' is an illegitimate totality. As soon as a suitable limitation has been put upon the collection of propositions we are considering, as soon as they are broken up into different orders, the contradiction disappears. We may put it like this: if somebody were to tell us that he is a liar, we could ask him, 'Well, a liar of what order?' If he says he is a liar of the first order he is making a statement of the second order, and this statement may be perfectly true. When he says 'I am a liar of the second order' (including the totality of first-order statements) this would be a statement of the third order; and so on. However far he may extend the scope of

c

propositions to which he is referring, his statement about their falsehood will represent a proposition of higher order. Once we reach this stage, there is no contradiction.

Russell's solution is thus based on the ground that 'true' and 'false' are ambiguous, and that, in order to make them unambiguous, we must specify the order of truth or falsehood which we ascribe to a proposition. Similar considerations apply to negation and disjunction, and indeed to any logical particle. It might seem that they were symbols which had throughout the same meaning. But this is due to a systematic ambiguity in the meanings of 'not', 'or', etc., by which they adjust themselves to propositions of any order.

The ambiguity about which I want to speak is not connected with the Theory of Types but with what may be called the 'many-level structure' of language. I shall first of all explain what I understand by *a language stratum*.

II. Language Strata

Let me begin by introducing a distinction between two paths a logical inquiry may follow. It will perhaps be best to illustrate my point with a picture. In studying the geometry of a curve we may wish to find out its behaviour *at some particular point* — for instance, whether it has a tangent there, whether it is continuous there, what its measure of curvature is there, and the like. Then we are studying *local* properties of the curve. Or we may wish to study the behaviour of the curve *as a whole* — for instance, whether it is closed or not, and, if it is closed, whether it is convex, etc. Then we are studying its properties *at large*. This picture suggests two different types of investigation in logic. The one takes its orientation from the logical relations which hold between a number of given propositions; a question of this sort is to ask whether a given proposition follows from another one, or contradicts it, or is independent of it, etc. We are then concerned with the logical nexus *on a small scale*, so to speak with *local* relations between propositions. Suppose, on the other hand, considering a certain deductive theory based upon a number of suitable axioms, say Euclidean Geometry or the Theory of Deduction, we ask whether the system under consideration is *free from contra-*

diction, that is, whether it is ever possible to prove a certain theorem and its contradictory. This is a question of quite a different kind. Suppose we say, 'The theory in question contains no contradiction', then we are making an assertion, not about the relations between two or three or more single propositions, but about the theory *as a whole*. Again, we may inquire whether the deductive theory we are considering is *complete*, i.e. whether any statements that can be constructed in accordance with the given rules (of the theory) can always be decided (in one way or the other) by the means of the theory and decided in a finite number of steps; we may also be investigating whether two given theories are isomorphic (i.e. of the same logical structure so that to each proposition of the one there corresponds precisely one proposition of the other, and vice versa, and that all the logical relations of the propositions in the one are retained in the other). Now in pursuing such questions we are concerned with what may be called the *macrological* features of such theories, in contrast with questions concerning the *micrological* connections of single statements.

A technique has been worked out to deal with problems of that macrological kind. Naturally, these methods — called 'metalogical' and 'metamathematical' — only apply to *deductive systems*. However, it does seem to me that there is also good sense in talking of macro- and micrological features of a *language*. Language, it is true, is not organized in the way a deductive system is; compared with such a system it is of a much more loosely knitted texture. And yet one feels a marked difference when one compares such statements as: a material object statement, a sense-datum[1] statement, a law of nature, a geometrical proposition, a statement describing national characteristics, a statement describing a half-faded memory picture, a statement describing a dream, a proverb, and so forth. It is as if each of these statements was constructed in a different *logical style*. (I will explain presently what I mean by this.) We may set ourselves the task of grouping statements of our language according to the similarity of their usage in distinct domains, in *language-strata* as I shall venture to call them. Thus laws will form one language stratum, material object statements another one, sense datum statements yet another one, and so on. Now the question which I want to consider is

[1]. For an explanation and discussion of this term see Vol. I, ch. vi. — EDITOR.

this: Is it possible to develop out of that vague feeling that 'each of them is built in a different logical style' something more precise? Is it possible, say, by characterizing each stratum on the basis of its intrinsic internal fabric or logical texture? To make this clearer let me return to the picture taken from geometry. It was a memorable achievement of mathematical thought when Gauss succeeded in characterizing a curved surface merely 'from within' without any reference to space outside, which amounted to this that he showed that if two-dimensional beings were living on the surface of a sphere, an egg or a wine-glass, etc., they could, merely through carrying out certain measuring operations within their abode, find out in what sort of surface they were living; in other words, they could learn the 'intrinsic geometry' of their habitation without any reference to three-dimensional space. Now the analogous problem in our case would be this: Can a given language stratum be characterized, not by reference to something outside the subject-matter by dubbing it 'material object', 'memory picture' or the like, but by purely formal motifs? Let us see what means we have at our disposal for such a programme.

We may first investigate the nature of the concepts which a given stratum contains: whether they are absolutely precise and definable with mathematical rigour, or vague, or of an open texture. We may next consider the statements themselves and ask what sort of logic is valid for them. By 'logic' I mean logic in the strict sense, the laws of inference. Aristotelian logic, including the modernized and refined form of its presentation in *Principia Mathematica*, has gone the same way as Euclidean geometry — a number of different 'logics' have grown up alongside it, more or less akin to it, just as Euclidean geometry is now surrounded by a number of similar and cognate systems. One effect of this development is the disappearance of that disturbing air of uniqueness that had puzzled philosophers for so long. Birkhoff and von Neumann, for instance, have indicated a system, different from classical logic, which seems to be in better harmony with the structure of quantum mechanics. On the suggestion of Brouwer a logic has been constructed different from classical logic in which is actually employed mathematical demonstration, a logic in which the law of excluded middle is no longer universally true. And, notice, when we pass from the one logic to the other, we get an altogether different mathematics; which goes to show that the sort of logic we apply is an important characteristic ingrained in a certain field of propositions. Change the logic and then the propositions will take on new meanings. Take another example – the logic of half-faded memory pictures. Here the situation is such that we are often unable to call to mind one or the other point of detail, that is, that we are often unable to decide an alternative. What did that bathroom look like I saw the other day on a visit? Was it ivory, was it cream or pale biscuit or maize? Suppose a pattern-book were shown to me, and I was later asked whether *this* was the colour I had seen, perhaps I would not be able to decide. If I were pressed I might have to say, 'I can't remember so distinctly'; if another different shade of yellow were shown to me then I might give the same reply, finally adding, 'all I know is that it was some light yellowish colour'. Notice that, in this case, it is quite natural to use a *vague* term ('light colour') to express the indeterminacy of the impression. If language was such that each and every word was particular and each colour word had a definite, clearly defined meaning, we should find we could not use it. That is, we should come up against alternatives: 'Was it this colour or not?' – which we could not decide. I cannot get back to the impression I had then, it cannot be pinned down and preserved under glass for inspection like a dead beetle. To insist, in these circumstances, on the law of excluded middle, without any means of deciding the issue, is paying lip service to the laws of logic. There are only two alternatives open to us: We must either be prepared to drop the law of excluded middle when we wish to use a language with precisely defined terms; or we shall have to use a language whose words are in one way or another blurred. But we can't have it both ways. Another way of bringing out this point is to say that, if several colours are shown to me which differ only slightly, they do not necessarily exclude one another. This shows particularly clearly that our attitude towards a half-faded memory image is radically different from that towards a material object. No one would dream of ascribing two different lengths to the table in this room (a *real* table), and saying that both were right. One state- ment, if it proves true, excludes the other. Whereas it is perfectly correct to say of two slightly different colour statements, when applied to an indeterminate memory picture, that both are compatible; which just shows that the logic of colour words, when applied in this language stratum, is different from their usual logic.

Again, the logic of aphorisms seems to be very peculiar. A man who writes aphorisms may say a thing, and, on another occasion, the very opposite of it without being guilty of a contradiction. For each aphorism, as it stands, is quite complete in itself. Two different aphorisms are not parts of one and the same communication. Suppose you go to a museum where several paintings are hung on the wall. Would you complain that they are not correlated and do not fit into one and the same perspective? Well now, each painting has a pictorial space of its own; what is represented in two paintings, though the paintings may be adjacent, is not in the same pictorial space. It is the first aim of Art, it has been said, to set a frame around Nature. Sometimes the frame is large, sometimes small, but always it is there. An aphorism is Literature and done with ink instead of colours. Of two aphorisms each is in a frame of its own; hence no clash. It would be interesting to penetrate the logic of poems, or of mysticism. Here a contradiction may be a perfectly legitimate means to point to what cannot be said in language. No: seeming contradictions are not always absurd.

To return to our subject: I said that the examples given suggest looking upon a logic as a characteristic which sets its stamp upon a particular language stratum. But there are two further characteristics: truth and verifiability.

III. Systematic Ambiguity of Truth and Verifiability

Compare a variety of statements such as: a sense-datum statement, a material object statement, a law of nature, description of something half forgotten, a statement of my own motives, a conjecture as to the motives by which someone else was actuated, quotation of the exact words so-and-so was using, brief summary of the tenor of a political speech, characterization of the *Zeitgeist* of a certain historical period, a proverb, a poetic metaphor, a mathematical proposition, and so on. Now what I want to emphasize is that the idea of truth varies with the kind of statement;

that it has a systematic ambiguity. Take, for instance, a mathematical proposition, say a theorem of geometry. To say that it is true simply means that it can be deduced from such-and-such axioms. As a consequence of this, it may be true in one system of geometry and false in another. And the axioms themselves? They are no concern of the pure mathematician: all he is concerned with is that *if* these and these axioms apply, *then* the theorems apply too. But whether the axioms actually do apply, is not for him to decide. He leaves that to applied mathematics. Hence Russell's definition of mathematics as 'the subject in which we never know what we are talking about, nor whether what we are saying is true'. Here, then, is a very good case for the 'coherence theory of truth'.

Again, a law of nature is never true in the same sense in which, say, 'There is a fire burning in this room' is, nor in the sense in which 'He is an amusing fellow' may be; and the two latter statements are not true in the same sense in which 'I've got a headache' is. Truth, when applied to a physical law, means roughly speaking that it is well established by experimental evidence or other observation, that it brings widely different things into a close connection and makes us 'understand' what seemed a mystery before; that it simplifies our theoretical system, and further, that it is fruitful in leading us to predictions and new discoveries. (That is, incidentally, why the pragmatist identifies truth with usefulness: he has really got hold of one facet, but of one facet only.) Truth, in this case, it may be said, is not *one* idea but a whole bundle of ideas. Nothing of this applies to truth in the case of a simple observation. Suppose you have to make sure that the light is on in your room. Now when you go and look and say 'All right, it's on', your statement is true, *not* because it brings widely different things into connection, *not* because it simplifies I don't know what, *not* because it is fruitful or suggestive – no, nothing of the sort; it is just true because it says so-and-so is as you say it is.

Again, in what sense is one to say of a proverb that it is true? Have you ever tried to put some rare and subtle experience, or some half-forgotten (but strong) impression into words? If you do, you will find that truth, in this case, is inseparably tied up with the literary quality of your writing: it needs no less than a poet to express fully and faithfully such fragile states of mind. How you say it matters even more than what you say.

Similar remarks apply to verification. A law of nature can be verified by experimental evidence, though not conclusively. Whether a material object statement is capable of conclusive verification is a moot point. Take next a case such as 'I've got a terrible toothache'. Suppose I go to the dentist, he examines my teeth and says, 'All right, there's nothing wrong with them'. Would I then reply, 'Oh, I beg your pardon, I *thought* that I've got a toothache, but now I see that I was mistaken'? My toothache cannot be argued away or refuted by examining my teeth, my nerves, etc. If I were asked how I know that I've got a toothache, I might be tempted to reply, 'Because I *feel* it'. What a queer sort of reply! Is there anything else I can do with a toothache but feel it? What my reply aimed at, however, was something different, namely to *shake off* the whole question as improper, beside the point. How do I know? I've simply got toothache, and that's the end of it. I do not grant that I may have fallen victim to a delusion, I do not recognize a medical examination, an observation of my teeth any psychological tests, a court of experts — no dentist in heaven or earth can refute me. In saying 'I just *feel it*' I am expressing the fact that the toothache is something *given in immediate experience*, not a thing *inferred from something else* on the strength of certain evidences. The first person singular has, amongst other uses, the function to indicate the character of *immediacy* of an experience.

Take the statement, 'There are sea serpents'. How would you verify it? Is it enough that some person has seen them? Perhaps for him; for you the situation is different: you have so far only a man who *says* that he has seen them. So you must check up what he says — you may test his eyesight, go into his past and examine his reliability, and so on. The result of this checking will be a number of statements each of which, in its turn, may again be checked: the expert who examined the man's eyesight may himself be examined, the witnesses who testified may in their turn be scrutinized, etc. In following up the threads of verification we nowhere come to an absolute end, that is, we can never say, 'Now it is conclusively proved that the man was right'. What this particular example shows applies in general. At some point we do stop, it is true, for practical reasons, when the evidence seems to be sufficient. But theoretically we may go on checking and re-checking our statements as long as we please. So long as we move amongst statements concerning such evidences as illustrated above, verification has no natural end, but refers continually to ever new statements. In pursuing these fibres, however, we see how secondary lines branch off into other regions: the points where they come to a sudden end represent those immediate experiences which an observer has the moment he experiences them, and which, in this moment, cannot be checked against other evidences. These experiences, expressed in 'I'-sentences, are, so to speak, end points of verification — but of verification in a quite different sense. For if we try to use this verification later, it turns to dust. It lives in the moment, and is gone. Still these experiences are the moments of ultimate fulfilment. It is they from which all light of knowledge flows forth. Or, to change the metaphor, they are the points in which knowledge makes direct contact with reality. Without them all our sentences would float in the air cut off from actual facts. What establishes a con-nection between sentences and reality are these last points of veri-fication, transitory though they may be. Thus a statement may be verified in two quite different senses: either by checking it against other statements, or by appealing to immediate experience. In the case of a material object statement, for instance, some lines refer to other material object statements, i.e. they lead from state-ment to statement within the same language stratum; some others branch off and penetrate into a different stratum, the 'I'-state-ments. Thus verification weaves a complicated net, a ramified pattern of lines.

It is easily seen that the term 'meaningful' displays the same ambiguity: its sense varies with the stratum. For instance, a sen-tence in a novel is meaningful, if (1) it is correct English, i.e. not a broth of words, and (2) it fits in with the other sentences. This meaningfulness has nothing whatever to do with verifiability. (That, by the way, is why Fiction is not false.) This criterion, however, does not apply to experiential statements where verifiability is of some relevance, although it would not be right to equate meaningfulness with verifiability. Again, in which sense is a rule, a definition, a request, a question meaningful?

There may even be a sense in which metaphysical statements have a meaning. The trouble with the Logical Positivists was that they attached too rigid an import to 'meaningfulness' and lost sight of its ambiguity. By virtue of the multiplicity of meaning in this word they lost themselves in a magic cloud out of which they condemned everything that did not conform to their standards. In actual fact they had no machinery, such as they thought they had, by which the senselessness of metaphysics could be *proved*; though it must be admitted that metaphysicians made the greatest efforts to supply them with plausible arguments for such a view. I am afraid what has been said on this subject was of a profound shallowness.

To sum up this point: Statements may be *true* in different senses, *verifiable* in different senses, *meaningful* in different senses. Therefore the attempts at defining 'truth', or at drawing a sharp line between the meaningful and the meaningless, etc., are doomed to fail.

IV. COMPLETENESS

Up till now I have tried to sketch a few leit-motifs which might be used in characterizing a given language stratum. They were: the texture of the concepts together with the sort of logic which obtains and the appropriate senses of 'truth' and 'verifiability' (if the latter applies at all). To these must be added two more factors: the way in which a proposition is integrated into a larger whole; and the relations in which different strata stand to each other.

In order to approach the first point, it will be best to make use again of a geometrical illustration. Suppose you consider a number of statements which are about the same subject *a*. Each of these statements may be represented by a circular area, and the conjunction of two statements by that part of the areas which overlap. The more propositions we take, the smaller will the area become which is common to all the disks; at the same time, the more definite will become the description formed by all these statements. This gives rise to the following problem: Is there anything like a description of *maximum* definiteness, for instance, a description whose geometrical picture is a point? If there was such a thing, this would mean that the description is *complete* in the sense that nothing could be added to it which would make it more definite. Well now, are there language strata in which it is possible to construct something like a 'closed' description? And if so, will such a description contain a finite or an infinite number of single statements?

Geometry provides us with a model in which a complete (closed, perfect) description is attainable and with a finite number of statements. Thus a triangle is determined when its three sides are given: nothing can be added to these data that is not entailed by, or in contradiction with, them. Here, then, is an example of a description which, on logical grounds, cannot be extended.

A quite different situation seems to hold with regard to experiential statements. However many features I may assert of a thing, say of this chair, or however many relations I may state which hold between it and other things, or however many statements I may make about its life-history, I shall never reach a point where my description can be said to be *exhaustive*, that is, such that no further increment in knowledge is possible. Any real thing is inexhaustible. My knowledge of it is always extensible. There is no maximum description. To use the geometrical illustration: Such a description will always be represented by a whole *region*; a point will be a limit toward which the description tends without ever reaching it. Thus the picture which we make of an experiential statement on our map will never shrink to a point.

There are, however, cases where a complete description *is* attainable. Take, for instance, a game of chess played in a tournament: it can be described, completely, move by move, from the beginning to the end, say in the chess notation. Again, a melody is describable completely in the musical notation (disregarding, of course, questions of interpretation). The same is true of a carpet, viewed as a geometrical ornament of shape and colour.

How curious it is when I describe a dream: when I have narrated my dream, told everything that happened, in it, my description is finished. But it comes to an end in a very different way from that in which, e.g., the description of a game of chess comes to an end where there is a natural beginning and a natural end. A dream is fragmentary, enigmatic, and a dream cannot be integrated into a larger whole: you cannot ask, 'What happened before the dream began, or after it was over?' Or rather, *when* you ask such a question, you have already left the dream language and consider the sleeper from outside, from the point of view of a waking man. In this respect a dream has a unity and coherence which makes it nearly akin to a poem, or an aphorism.

The few examples given will suffice to show that statements may be *complete* in very different senses, and that the way they are complete or incomplete is a further important feature of a language stratum.

Finally, we have to investigate in what relations different strata stand to each other. I shall leave this for the moment and confine myself to mentioning one question only: whether the threads of verification, when we follow them up, remain within the given stratum, or lead outside it; in other words, whether a given stratum is *closed* with respect to verification.

V. A New Picture of Language

We are now in a position to sketch a new picture of language which, though still untried, seems to emerge from all these considerations; a picture of language naturally stratified into layers. This new conception contrasts with such a view as that held by Wittgenstein in his *Tractatus Logico-Philosophicus*: according to that view language consists of statements which can, one and all, be derived from atomic propositions by a uniform process. An atomic proposition is one asserting an atomic fact; an atomic fact is a fact which has no parts that are facts; and the uniform method by which any statement can be constructed is that of building up truth-functions of any selection of atomic propositions. This leads to an amazing simplication of the picture we can make for ourselves of the fabric of language. All statements are, so to speak, on a footing, and all are reducible to the same set of atomic propositions. Or better, the totality of propositions is defined by this method of generation. Too good to be true. Apart from the fact that no one has ever succeeded in producing a single atomic proposition, the whole thing is a myth. Moreover, we know for certain that there are many ways of building up statements which have nothing at all to do with truth-functions; such as unfulfilled conditional statements — 'If Hitler had won the war, then . . .' and many others. No: language does not fit this strait-jacket.

There are certain modern trends in Philosophy which seem to

have some such background. Phenomenalism, for instance, seems to presuppose that there is one basic language, the sense-datum language, to which any other statement, or at least any material object statement, can be reduced. According to Pheno-menalism a material object, say a cat, is a bundle of sense-data tied together and with the edges trimmed off; unless it is a bundle of *sensibilia*, that is the sort of thing which you *would* have seen, if you *had* ever looked, in short, a bundle of highly problematical entities. But no: we have simply to recognize that a statement about a cat is a statement about a cat: and not a truth-function of sense-datum statements, or an infinite class of perspectives, or an infinite group of *sensibilia*, or heaven knows what. A thing is, so to speak, a hard core that resists at any attempt at breaking it up and reducing it to the level of other data, whatever they may be. All this talk about material objects and sense-data is a talk about two language strata, about their relation, about the logic of this relationship. The problem arises along the plane where the two strata make contact, so to speak. The difficulty is to under-stand in precisely which way a material object statement is related to a sense-datum statement; that is, what sort of relations hold between members of different strata; and that is a problem of logic.

Similarly, Behaviourism is an attempt to reduce psychological statements, e.g. , 'What a conceited fellow!' to a very, very long list of statements setting out in which way the person in question would behave under such-and-such circumstances; a very success-ful way of describing peculiarities of rats which has been trans-ferred to men. The whole thing rests on a *naïveté* — that there is one basic language (suitable for describing the behaviour of rats) into which everything else must be translated. The motto 'Only rats, no men!' overlooks the fact that psychological statements belong to a stratum of their own; with a logic different from that of the language in which you say how a person looks, how he smiles, in short what he has in common with a rat.

We are now in a position to take a further step. It was hitherto the custom to refer to what I h᷉ᵛe called 'strata' by indicating their subject-matter, using term₃ such as: 'material object state-ments', 'descriptions of vague impressions', 'statements of laws of nature', and the like. What I now suggest we do — and this is a programme for the future – is to reverse the whole situation by saying: 'The formal motifs which we have been considering all combine to impress a certain stamp on a stratum; they give us the means to characterize each stratum "from within" that is with no reference to the subject'. If we carefully study the texture of the concepts which occur in a given stratum, the logic of its propositions, the meaning of truth, the web of verification, the senses in which a description may be complete or incomplete – if we consider all that, we may thereby characterize the subject-matter. We may say, for instance: a material object is something that is describable in a language of such-and-such structure; a sense impression is something which can be described in such-and-such a language; a dream is——, a memory picture is ——, and so on. In this way we shall be able to *formalize* these concepts. The analogy with science is obvious. The questions, 'What is a point?' 'What is a straight line?' have been debated for more than 2000 years until the solution was found in a reversal of the problem situation. All the time it was thought that we must first define the meaning of the primitive symbols in geometry before we can see that the axioms are 'Self-evident truths' given in intuition. In modern times the terms 'point', 'straight line', 'plane', 'between', 'congruent', etc., are defined as those things and relations which satisfy the axioms of geometry. That is, the axioms in their totality *determine* (within pure mathematics) the meaning of the primitive symbols. In like manner we may say that each stratum has a logic of its own and that this logic determines the meaning of certain basic terms. In some respects this is obvious. Whether a melody is a sequence of air-vibrations, or a succession of musical notes, or a message of the composer, depends entirely on the way you describe it. Similarly, you may look at a game of chess, or on the pattern of a carpet from very different aspects and you will then see in them very different things. Notice how all these words – 'melody', 'game of chess', etc. – take on a systematic ambiguity according to the language stratum in which you talk. The same applies to 'doing a sum', 'writing a letter', or to any action indeed. An action may be viewed as a series of movements caused by some physiological stimuli in the 'Only rats, no men' sense; or as something that has a purpose or a meaning irrespective of the way its single links are produced. An action in the first sense is determined by *causes*, an action in the second sense by *motives* or *reasons*. It is generally believed that an action is determined both by causes and by motives. But if the causes determine the action, no room is left for motives, and if the motives determine the action, no room is left for causes. Either the system of causes is complete, then it is not possible to squeeze in a motive; or the system of motives is complete, then it is not possible to squeeze in a cause. 'Well, now, do you believe that if you are writing a letter you are engaged in two different activities?' No; I mean that there are two different ways of looking at the thing; just as there are two different ways of looking at a sentence: as a series of noises produced by a human agent; or as a vehicle of thought. For a series of noises there may be causes but no reasons; for a series of words expressing thought there may be reasons but no causes. What we must understand is that the word 'action' has a systematic ambiguity. And yet we are continually invited to regard motives as a special sort of causes; perhaps because we have only the word 'Why?' to ask both for cause and motive. We do not see the ambiguity of the interrogative.

CHAPTER II

WILL THE FUTURE BE LIKE THE PAST?

By Frederick L. Will

I

In the elaboration of arguments in the last two hundred years for and against scepticism concerning induction, one central point at issue has been that concerning the 'uniformity of nature' and the necessity of assumptions about that uniformity in all inductive reasoning. To this point the sceptics have again and again recurred, following the precedent of Hume, in their arguments to show the overall doubtfulness, the absolutely irremediable lack of cogency of inductive arguments in general; and to this point also have recurred their opponents in their endeavours to refute these same sceptical conclusions. The question which the sceptics have raised concerning the uniformity of nature is expressed partially and in non-technical language in the question of the above title, 'Will the future be like the past?'

There is an advantage of simplicity and clarity in expressing the question thus with reference to the future, as Hume himself did in the *Enquiry*, even though quite clearly the question of the validity of inductive procedures is by no means restricted to conclusions about future things or events. The question about induction which both the sceptics and their opponents have attempted, each in their own way, to answer is a question about all those procedures in which, in science and everyday life, we use the evidence of observed facts or states of affairs to conclude concerning unobserved ones. The unobserved matters about which the conclusion is drawn may be in the past or present as well as in the future. In each case the basic procedure is the same. On the basis of observations now being made or already made which reveal that certain things have a specified characteristic, or set of characteristics, it is concluded that other events or things of the same kind, though unobserved, in the past, present, or future, have these same characteristics. And the question raised about this procedure is likewise the same. By what right do we conclude from the observed to the unobserved? Granted that all the cases which have been tested have shown hydrogen to be inflammable, by what right do we conclude on this evidence that under similar conditions hydrogen has always been, is now, and will continue to be inflammable?

Abstracting from this more general question about induction it is permissible, in the interest of simplicity, to consider the question in but one of its temporal phases, namely that referring to the future. This phase may justly be viewed as a test case of the general question. To the extent that our inductive conclusions about the future can be justified, so can our inductive conclusions be justified generally. If inductive methods can be shown to be all completely without justification when their conclusions refer to the future, this conclusion can be easily generalized to apply to all inductive conclusions whatsoever; and if inductive procedures can be justified in so far as they refer to the future, by exactly the same procedure, and with exactly the same kind of evidence, they can be justified when their conclusions are drawn concerning the present and the past. It may be noted also that even with this restriction of reference solely to the future the question of inductive validity still bears directly upon the question of the validity of scientific laws, which is the aspect of induction which has always appeared to philosophers as most provocative as well as fundamental. For these laws are statements about the course of nature, the connections between things and events, not only as they are in the present, or have been in the past, but also as they will be in the future.

II

The standard argument for complete inductive scepticism, for the belief that inductive procedures have no rational and no empirical justification whatever, is the one stated in a small variety of ways in the writings of Hume. If one consults these writings in search of an answer to the question of inductive validity one finds the same clear answer argued first in technical detail in the *Treatise*, secondly compressed into a few non-technical paragraphs in the *Abstract of a Treatise of Human Nature*, and

D

thirdly, presented again in a non-technical but somewhat fuller version in a chapter in the *Enquiry Concerning Human Understanding*. There is no basis whatever for any conclusion concerning future matters, according to this argument; there is no way whatever in which such conclusions can be established to be certainly true or even probable. For in the first place no such conclusion can be demonstrated by reasoning alone, since they are all conclusions about matters of fact, and since it is the case that the denial of any assertion of a matter of fact is not self-contradictory. But if one gives up the rationalistic aspiration to demonstrate propositions about matters of fact or existence *a priori*, and turns instead to experience, this road, though apparently more promising at first, likewise ends by leading one exactly nowhere. Clearly no statement about future matters of fact can be established by observation. Future things cannot be observed. Any event or state of affairs which can be observed is by definition not in the future. The only recourse which remains therefore is the inductive procedure of employing present or past observations and inferring therefrom the nature of the future. But this procedure to which we are all forced, or rather, to which we all should be forced if we did not, in company with the animals, use it naturally from birth, is in the light of close analysis completely indefensible. For such reasoning assumes, and is quite invalid without the assumption, that the future will be like the past.

> . . . all inferences from experience suppose, as their foundation, that the future will resemble the past, and that similar powers will be conjoined with similar sensible qualities. If there be any suspicion that the course of nature may change, and that the past may be no rule for the future, all experience becomes useless, and can give rise to no inference or conclusion.[1]

Will the future 'resemble the past'? Or be 'conformable to the past'? These are the ways in which in the *Enquiry* Hume expresses the question concerning the uniformity of nature, restricting to its reference towards the future the question which

---

[1] *Enquiry Concerning Human Understanding*, Sect. IV, § 32. The arabic numerals in references to this work indicate the marginal sections in the Selby-Bigge edition of 1902.

already had been asked in broader terms in the *Treatise*. There, without the temporal restriction, it is argued that the principle of inductive conclusions, the principle upon which reason would proceed if reason determined us in these matters, is '*that instances, of which we have had no experience, must resemble those, of which we have had experience, and that the course of nature continues always uniformly the same*'. (Bk. I, Pt. III, Sect. VI).

However the principle is stated, the argument about it remains the same. It is indispensable, if inductive conclusions are to be justified; but just as it is absolutely indispensable, so, and this is the measure of our logical misfortune, it cannot be established as certain or as probable in any way. It cannot be established by any demonstrative argument. For it is clearly an assertion of a matter of fact, and therefore the kind of assertion whose denial is non-contradictory and conceivable.

> That there are no demonstrative arguments in the case seems evident; since it implies no contradiction that the course of nature may change, and that an object, seemingly like those which we have experienced, may be attended with different or contrary effects. May I not clearly and distinctly conceive that a body, falling from the clouds, and which, in all other respects, resembles snow, has yet the taste of salt or the feeling of fire? Is there any more intelligible proposition than to affirm, that all the trees will flourish in December and January, and decay in May and June? Now whatever is intelligible, and can be distinctly conceived, implies no contradiction and can never be proved false by any demonstrative argument or abstract reasoning *à priori*. (*Enquiry*, Sect. IV, § 30. Cf. *Treatise*, loc. cit.)

Any further doubts about the doubtfulness of this principle which is the main-spring of inductive inference are quickly disposed of. No one who understands the principle with its reference to unobserved instances will suggest that it can be simply observed to be true. It is still true that one cannot observe the future, or the unobserved generally. And, finally, no one who has a sound logical conscience and appreciates the indispensability of the principle to induction generally will tolerate the suggestion that the principle may be established by inductions from experience. Such a process would be circular.

> It is impossible, therefore, that any arguments from experience can prove this resemblance of the past to the future; since all these arguments are founded on the supposition of that resemblance.

And again:

> ... all our experimental conclusions proceed upon the supposition that the future will be conformable to the past. To endeavour, therefore, the proof of this last supposition by probable arguments, or arguments regarding existence, must be evidently going in a circle, and taking that for granted, which is the very point in question. (*Enquiry*, Sect. IV, §§ 32, 30.)

On this point the *Treatise* (loc. cit.) and the *Abstract* speak with one voice. One final quotation from the latter may serve to summarize the conclusion.

> 'Tis evident that *Adam* with all his science, would never have been able to *demonstrate*, that the course of nature must continue uniformly the same, and that the future must be conformable to the past. What is possible can never be demonstrated to be false; and 'tis possible the course of nature may change, since we can conceive such a change. Nay, I will go farther, and assert, that he could not so much as prove by any *probable* arguments, that the future must be conformable to the past. All probable arguments are built on the supposition, that there is this conformity betwixt the future and the past, and therefore can never prove it. This conformity is a *matter of fact*, and if it must be proved, will admit of no proof but from experience. But our experience in the past can be a proof of nothing for the future, but upon a supposition, that there is a resemblance betwixt them. This therefore is a point, which can admit of no proof at all, and which we take for granted without any proof. (*Abstract*, 1938 ed., p. 15.)

All inductive inferences about the future depend for their validity upon a fundamental principle which, it now turns out, we have not the slightest reason for believing to be true but which nevertheless we simply take for granted. We have, accordingly, no reason for believing any of these inferences; they are all a matter of custom or habit, or, if one prefers more recent terminology, of 'animal faith'.

III

It would be more promising in respect to logical neatness and precision for one to consider the alleged circularity of all inductive procedure, which is the central point of the above argument, while using as a test case some specific scientific law or principle rather than some affirmation as vague and imprecise as that the future will resemble the past. But, for the purpose of analysing the sceptic's views and meeting the arguments by which these views have been defended, such a procedure would have this deficiency, that no matter what specific scientific generalization were chosen, one reply which would be sure to be made would consist of an appeal beyond this generalization to some general beliefs about uniformity, some general Principle of Uniformity which, it would be urged, is assumed somehow in the inductive establishment of this and other scientific generalizations. Since the sceptical argument has been presented in terms of general Principles of Uniformity, and it is in these terms that it is alleged to demonstrate the logical circularity of all inductive reasoning, it seems worth while to attempt to deal with this argument, if one can, in the same terms – in terms of some alleged Principle of Uniformity for which it has been claimed in recent philosophy that it does serve as a wide and basic inductive assumption.

In his *Treatise on Probability*, J. M. Keynes attempts to formulate a set of principles which, if assumed to be true of a given area of subject-matter, would justify, in accordance with the principles of probability, the employment of inductive methods in that area. One of the principles which he discusses, the simplest and at the same time the one for which it seems, at first view, most plausible to contend that it may serve as a broad inductive assumption, is the one to which he gave the name of the 'Principle of the Uniformity of Nature'. This Principle affirms that nature is uniform in a specific way; and that is in respect to position in space and time. 'It involves', writes Keynes, 'the assertion of a generalized judgment of irrelevance, namely, of the irrelevance of mere position in time and space to generalizations which have no reference to particular positions in time and space' (p. 226. Cf. also pp. 255-6, 263, 276). It is this principle, he argues, which

> ... supplies the answer, if it is correct, to the criticism that the instances, on which generalizations are based, are all alike in being past, and that any generalization, which is applicable to the future, must be based, for this reason, upon imperfect analogy. We judge directly that the resemblance between instances, which consists in their being past, is in itself irrelevant, and does not supply a valid ground for impugning a generalization' (p. 256).

It is, however, difficult to interpret this so-called Principle in such a way that it makes a statement which is both definite and is not at the same time refuted in some areas of experience. Keynes observes that what this Principle affirms is 'that the same total cause always produces the same effect' (p. 248), and this is so; but the difficulty here is that of giving a definite meaning to the important adjective 'same' as it applies to causes and effects. Unless there is a specifiable meaning applicable to causes in all fields, the formula 'same cause — same effect' is not a univocal principle affirming the presence of a specific kind of uniformity in every area of natural phenomena. Yet, when one sets out to specify just what kind of sameness is meant when this formula is employed, one discovers that there is a great variety of interpretations of this word in different fields of inquiry, and that what determines whether a given set of circumstances is regarded as the same cause, for example, varies from field to field, depending upon the nature of the subject-matter as that is revealed in the various generalizations which are regarded as established for that subject-matter. These generalizations exhibit among themselves great differences in scope and precision, as well as in the degree of confidence with which they are accepted. They include, for example, the generalizations about the coherence and constancy of properties which are involved in our belief in and distinctions among various kinds of material objects. And they include the more precise generalizations, frequently expressed in the form of mathematical equations, which would normally be referred to as 'scientific laws', as well as the broader generalizations formulated in various accepted Principles and Theories. When this is understood, when one sees that in the employment of the Principle of Uniformity what determines the kind of sameness to which the Principle affirms that differences in mere position in space and time are irrelevant is the specific generalizations, the laws, principles, and so on, which have been established in that field, one is in a better position to understand this so-called Principle and its alleged employment as a general inductive assumption. In any given field the Principle of Uniformity states that mere differences in space and time are irrelevant in just this sense, that there are certain generalizations, true of this field, which describe the conditions under which certain objects exist and events occur, and in which differences in mere position in space and time make little or no detectable difference. That this is so, accordingly, is not an inductive assumption in that field in the sense that it is specified and made before all inductive inquiry in the field. It is an inductive assumption in the more us al sense that conclusions of previous experience and inquiries are available for employment in any field as bases for further investigation in that field.

The primary purpose here is not to elucidate and specify the variations of meaning which such a Principle or formula must undergo if it is to be understood as applying to the great variety of fields in which inductive inquiry is carried on, to the great variety in the kinds of uniformity which the generalizations in these fields describe. The primary purpose is to inquire whether the sceptics are right in insisting that it is impossible to provide genuine evidence for beliefs about uniformity, or whether, on the contrary, it is possible to furnish empirical evidence for these beliefs, which, in its employment, does not involve circular reasoning. It is granted that what the Principle of Uniformity affirms in any field, if 'Principle' it may be called, is that there is uniformity in that field in this sense and no other; that there are certain specific generalizations which apply to that field and

in which mere differences of position in time and space are regarded as irrelevant. In the light of this interpretation of uniformity the question briefly is, how can such a broad affirmation
be confirmed or verified by induction without circularity?

IV

For purposes of simplicity, in order to secure the clearest
statement of the argument in the fewest words, it will be useful
in what follows to abbreviate the statement of this Principle of
Uniformity and also to consider it only in reference to time. If
it can be shown that what the Principle affirms concerning the
irrelevance of time in specific generalizations can be confirmed
inductively, it can also be shown in exactly the same way that
it is possible to confirm the Principle in its spatial reference also.
So abbreviated and restricted, the Principle asserts that, in the
specific way just defined, differences in time make no difference.
Can this interpretation of the assertion that the future will
resemble the past be confirmed? What, if any, is the evidence
for it?

It follows directly from the interpretation which has just been
given of this principle what the evidence for it must be. If the
Principle affirms no more for any given area of fact than the
validity in that area of certain generalizations which are uniform
with respect to space and time, then the evidence for the Principle
must be whatever evidence there is for these particular generalizations. This includes all the observations in the past and present
which confirm the presence in that area of the uniformities of
which these general statements speak. Belief in the uniformity
in a given area is not something which is specifiable apart from
the laws, principles, and other generalizations regarded as established in that area, but is itself belief in just the kind of uniformities which these generalizations describe and define. If it is
correct, then, to say of any generalization, e.g. of any scientific
law, that it is confirmed or verified by empirical evidence, is it
not correct to say that, to that extent, there is evidence for belief
in the uniformity of nature?

The sceptic's answer to this question repeats that final rejoinder of Hume. Granted that there is empirical evidence which

has been used to establish various scientific laws, all that it is evidence for, he insists, is the assertion that *in the past* these laws were true, that in the past differences in time have made no difference. This evidence is absolutely worthless for inferences which speak about the future unless it is possible to assume that the future will be like the past. But stop! That is part of what one is trying to show, that is, that mere differences in temporal position, whether past or future, make no difference in these laws of nature. That the future will be like the past means, among other things, that in the future these laws will hold, that in this specific respect differences in time will make no difference. This cannot be inductively confirmed, the sceptic is saying, because any inductive argument for it assumes it and is therefore, as evidence, completely valueless.

One major source of the plausibility of the sceptic's reasoning lies in the analogies which knowing the future easily suggests and in terms of which one is apt to think and be misled. Is this not, one may ask, like any case of sampling? And must one not take care, when reasoning inductively from samples, that one's samples are fair? If a scientist reasons concerning the behaviour of oxygen, nitrogen or hydrogen on Mars, if such elements there be on Mars, on the basis of the known behaviour of these elements on the earth, he is assuming that in some respects the samples of the elements on the other planet are like those we have here. Similarly in reasoning about the future behaviour of these elements on the basis of present and past behaviour one must assume that future samples of these elements will be like present and past ones. Now if it is the case that past samples may be regarded as evidence about future ones only upon such an assumption, then no examination of past samples, however extensive, can be regarded as yielding evidence for the assumption itself. Any reasoning which did attempt to employ such samples as evidence for the assumption would be forced to use the assumption as a principle in the reasoning and would therefore beg the whole question at issue.

A physical representation of the kind of analogy presented here might be as follows: Suppose that there was somewhere in the world an enclosure beyond which it was impossible for anyone ever to go or to make any observations. Nothing could be seen, heard, or in any other way perceived beyond the border. The territory beyond the enclosure, for ever barred from human perception, is the land of Future. The territory within the enclosure is the land of Present and Past, but since it is over-whelmingly the latter, it all goes under the name of Past. Now suppose that someone within the enclosure is interested in some proposition about the way things behave beyond the enclosure, say, a simple and homely proposition about chickens, to the effect that beyond the enclosure roosters fight more than hens. And he wonders what evidence, if any, there is for this proposi-tion. Of course he cannot observe this to be true. He must base it upon his observation in the land of Past; and if he does base it upon the observed fact that roosters in the land of Past fight more than hens, he must assume that in this respect chickens beyond the enclosure behave like chickens within it, so that, knowing that in the latter area roosters are the more pugnacious, he may employ this knowledge as evidence that things are this way also in the former area. This is an assumption which no empirical evidence, confined as it must be to evidence in Past, can be employed to support. Any attempt to support it with such evidence must itself assume that in respect to the phenomena involved differences between Past and Future are negligible; and since that is exactly what the reasoning is attempting to establish, the process is patently circular.

This is the kind of metaphor which makes friends, and in-fluences people, in this case, to draw the wrong conclusions. There are several faults in the analogy. The chief one is that, as represented, the border between Past and Future is stationary, while in the temporal situation it is not. To duplicate the temporal situation in this respect the analogy should represent the border as constantly moving, revealing as it does constantly, in territory which has hitherto been Future, hens and roosters similar as regards difference in disposition to those already observed in Past. The matter of evidence for the proposition about hens and roosters is then also different. If this proposition is in a position analogous to the beliefs about uniformity which are represented in modern scientific laws, the situation is something like this. Previously inhabitants in Past had drawn more sweep-ing conclusions concerning the difference between the disposition to fight of male and female chickens. They have discovered recently that in respect to young chicks and pullets this generalization did not hold. They have therefore revised the proposition to exclude all the known negative instances and speak only and more surely of the behaviour of hens and roosters, meaning by these latter terms just fully grown and developed female and male chickens.

So far as there is any record, chickens in Past have verified this rule; so far as there is any record, every chicken revealed by the ever-receding border has likewise verified it; so far as there is any record there has not been one negative instance. Is it not the case that the inhabitants of Past do have evidence for the proposition that all chickens obey this rule, those already in Past, which they call 'Past-chickens', and those also which are not yet in Past but which will be subsequently revealed by the moving border, and which they call not unnaturally 'Future-chickens'? They have a vast number of positive instances of the rule, and no negative instances, except those in respect to which the rule has already been revised. In view of the present evidence that in all cases, year after year and century after century, the progressively revealed chickens have verified and do verify this rule, must one not conclude that the inhabitants of Past do have evidence for this proposition, and that anyone is wrong who says that they have actually no evidence one way or other?

The sceptic, however, is still prepared to argue his case, and his argument, in terms of the present analogy, has a now familiar ring. That the inhabitants of Past have no evidence whatsoever about the behaviour of Future-chickens, he will insist; and as grounds he will point out that although the border does progressively recede and reveal chickens like those previously observed in Past, these are really not Future-chickens. By the very fact that they have been revealed they are no longer Future-chickens, but are now Past-chickens. Observation of them is not observation of Future-chickens, and any attempt to reason from such observation to conclusions about Future-chickens must therefore assume that Future-chickens are like Past-chickens. For the inhabitants of Past, in these efforts to know the land beyond the border, this is both an inescapable and unknowable presumption.

What should one say of an argument of this kind? Only
through some logical slip, one feels strongly, would it be possible
to arrive at such a conclusion. One would have thought that
the receding border was a matter upon which the inhabitants
of Past may legitimately congratulate themselves in the light of
their interest in learning what Future-chickens, when they become
Past, are going to be like. If the border had not yet begun to
recede they would indeed be in an unfortunate position for
securing such knowledge. But happily this is not the case. The
border is constantly receding. And granting that it will constantly recede, revealing always more of the land of Future, and
even granting also that this means that there is an inexhaustible
area to be revealed, the inhabitants of Past are in the fortunate
position that with the progressive recession they may learn
more and more about chickens, Past and Future. They may
derive hypotheses from their experience of what has already been
revealed and proceed further to test these by the progressive
revelations of Future, in the light of which they may be confirmed,
refuted, or revised. The sceptic's argument amounts to the
assertion that all this apparent good fortune is really illusory
and that the sorry Pastians are actually in no better position
with respect to knowing about Future-chickens and Future-
things generally than they would be if the border never moved at
all. For the movement of the border does not reveal Future-
chickens, since Future is by definition the land beyond the border.
No matter how much or how little is revealed, by the very fact
that it is revealed and on this side of the border it is not Future
but Past, and therefore, since the land of Future always is beyond
observation, no empirical method can produce any evidence that
what is in that land is in any way similar to what is not. That this
rendering of the sceptic's position, though in the language of the
above metaphor, is undistorted and fair may be seen by consulting
the words of an illustrious modern sceptic and follower of Hume,
Bertrand Russell. In his chapter, 'On Induction', in *The Problems
of Philosophy*, Russell expressed the matter in this fashion:

> It has been argued that we have reason to know that the
> future will resemble the past, because what was the future has
> constantly become the past, and has always been found to

resemble the past, so that we really have experience of the future, namely of times which were formerly future, which we may call past futures. But such an argument really begs the very question at issue. We have experience of past futures, but not of future futures, and the question is: Will future futures resemble past futures? This question is not to be answered by an argument which starts from past futures alone. We have therefore still to seek for some principle which shall enable us to know that the future will follow the same laws as the past (pp. 100-1).

This is the central difficulty urged by Hume, Russell and others in arguing that there can never be any empirical evidence that the future will be like the past. Empirically, in Russell's language, it is possible to have evidence only that this has been true of past and possibly present futures, not that it will be true of future futures. It is the situation in the land of Past all over again. There are generalizations which are constantly being confirmed by experience. But every time a confirming instance occurs it is nullified as evidence by the argument that it is not really a confirming instance at all. For by the fact that it has occurred it is an instance of a past future, and therefore it tells nothing whatever about future futures. In treating of the land of Past it was suggested that there is involved in arguing in this manner a logical slip or error. It remains to investigate how this is the case.

V

Suppose that in 1936, to take but a short span of time, a man says that in the above-defined sense the future will be like the past. In 1936, if he could somehow have shown that 1937 would be like 1936, this would have been evidence for his statement, as even a sceptic would admit. But in 1937, when he does establish that 1937 is like 1936, it has somehow ceased to be evidence. So long as he did not have it, it was evidence; as soon as he gets it it ceases to be. The constant neutralization of the evidence which is effected in this argument is effected by the same kind of verbal trick which children play upon one another in fun. Child A asks child B what he is going to do tomorrow. B replies that he is going to play ball, go swimming, or what not. Thereupon A says, 'You can't do that'.

B: Why not?

A: Because tomorrow never comes. When tomorrow comes it won't be tomorrow; it will be today. You can never play tomorrow; you can only play today.

Again, if a prophet announces that next year will bring a utopia, and if each succeeding year, when the predicted utopia does not come, he defends himself by pointing out that he said 'next year' and that obviously this is not next year, no reasonable person would pay much attention to him. Such a person would realize, on a moment's reflection, that the prophet is being deceptive with the word 'next'. In 1936, 'next year' means '1937'; in 1937 it means '1938'. Since every year 'next year' means a different year, a year yet to come, what the prophet says can never be verified or disproved. If in 1936 he meant by this phrase 1937, as he sensibly should, then this statement can be verified or refuted in 1937. But if, when 1937 comes, he insists that he did not mean 1937, but 'next year', and if in 1938 he again insists that he did not mean that year, and so on, then what he seems to be meaning by 'next year' is the $n + 1$th year where n is the ever progressing number of the present year. No one should alter his present activities or his plans for the future on the basis of such a prediction, for, of course, it really is not a prediction. While in the form of a statement about the future it does not say anything about the future, anything which could possibly be true or false in the infinity of time, if infinity it is, which yet remains to transpire. For what the prophet is saying is that utopia will come next year, and by his own interpretation of the words 'next year' he is affirming that next year will never come. In other words, at the time which never comes, and hence when nothing occurs, a utopia will occur. This is not even sensible speech; it is a contradiction.

In a similar though less simple way those who employ the sceptical argument about uniformity to show that there is no evidence whatever for any statement about the future are being themselves deceived and are deceiving others by their use of expressions like 'next', 'future', 'future future', and 'past future'. The man who said in 1936 that the future would be like the past, that mere differences in temporal position make no difference in the behaviour of nature which is described in scientific laws, meant, as he sensibly should, that this was true of the years 1937, 1938, and so on. He said something of the form 'all A's are B's' and it has been possible since 1936 to examine the A's of 1937 to 1952 and to see whether what he said is confirmed or disproved by the available evidence. If, however, now that it is 1952, and all this evidence is in, he should remark that since it is 1952 the years 1937-52 are no longer future and therefore have ceased to be evidence for the proposition, then he is guilty of using, or rather abusing, the word 'future' in the way in which the prophet in the previous example was abusing the word 'next'. For the only basis for his contention that the observed A's are not confirming evidence, or what is the same thing, that they are confirming instances only if one assumes quite circularly that the future is like the past, is in his illusive use of the word 'future'. Time does pass, and, because it does, the present is a constantly changing one; and the point of reference for the use of words like 'future' and 'past' is accordingly different. The correct conclusion to be drawn from the fact that time passes is that the future is constantly being revealed and that, in consequence, we have had and shall have the opportunity to learn more and more accurately what the laws of nature's behaviour are and how therefore the future will be like the past. But this sceptical man has his eyes fixed in fatal fascination upon the movement of time, the constantly changing present. And seeing that, as the present changes, what was once future is not now future, but present, and will shortly be past, he is led to draw the conclusion that after all, for any present whatever, the future is forever hidden behind a veil.

Now in a sense this is true, and in a sense it is not. And it is the confusion of the two senses which makes the trouble. The one sense, the kind of future which is forever hidden behind the veil of the ever-moving present, is not the kind of future of which this man began to speak. The kind of future of which he began to speak was the future of 1937, 1938 and so on; the kind of future years or futures which do become present and then past. This kind of future is constantly being revealed; in this sense of 'future' the A's of 1937 to 1952 are positive instances confirming our beliefs about scientific uniformity. But the sceptical man, although under the impression that he is still talking about the future in this sense, the sense of things which have not yet happened but which may happen, is actually talking about the future in the other sense; at least he is saying things which are true only if the word is interpreted in this other way. That is why he is deceived. He is unaware that the meaning of the word has changed. He thinks when he asserts that there is no evidence that the future will be like the past, and that all one has evidence for is that past futures have resembled their pasts, that he is using this crucial word in the way in which he began, in the way people are constantly using it to make sensible observations about the next and future months, years, and so on. But he is not using it in this way, and the key to this particular puzzle about knowledge of the future lies finally in realizing that he is not. Like a prophet who says that a utopia lies around the next corner, a corner which, no matter how many corners we turn, and no matter how many utopias or hells on earth we find in turning, is still the next corner, like him the sceptical man is talking about a future which by definition will never come. In this sense of the word the statement that the future will be like the past no longer means, as it originally did, that the years, or rather events in the years 1937, 1938, and so on, have a certain characteristic. It means instead that in a future which is always future, in years which never come, events will have this characteristic. In short, he is now saying that at a time which never comes differences in time will make no difference, that at a time when no events occur (for if they did it would be present and not future) certain types of events will obey certain fairly uniform laws.

There are then, two senses of the word 'future' to be carefully discriminated. They may be designated future-1 and future-2. In the sense of future-1, when one speaks about the future he is speaking of events which have not occurred, of things which do not exist, but of events and things which, with the constant movement of the line of the present, may sometime occur or exist. In the sense of future-2, when one speaks about the future he is speaking of the time which is always beyond the line of the moving present, of a time which never comes, which by definition can never come, no matter how far the line of the present moves.

Interpreted in the sense of future-1 there are beliefs about the way the future will be like the past, which have been and are being confirmed constantly by the uniform experience of countless positive instances in everyday life and in vast areas of science. Because they have been thus confirmed they constitute a vast set of assumptions with which scientists and laymen approach their problems in the various areas to which the confirmation applies. It is when these beliefs are interpreted in the sense of future-2 that the sceptics are able to produce a plausible argument to show that these beliefs are not empirically confirmable and are hence unknowable. But, when these are so interpreted, the argument has no bearing whatever, favourable or unfavourable, upon the soundness or success of any inductive inquiry. It asserts that specific types of events occur in specific ways, not in 1945, 1955, or any other year which will ever come, but in a year and a time which will never come. That one cannot produce empirical evidence for the statement that at a time which never comes and when no events occur, events will occur in these rather than other ways, may be readily admitted. But this is no good reason for scepticism. No scepticism is entailed by this admission so long as it is made with the understanding that there is evidence about the other kind of future, the kind which will come and in which events do occur. And it is this latter kind of future only, of these two kinds, with which our inductions are concerned. It is this kind of future alone about which our inductions predict, and this kind alone which will ever confirm or refute our assertions. It is, therefore, not sensible for anyone to worry, in his inductive reasoning, about the character of a future which by definition can never come, about his incapacity to prove that if this future did come, which is itself a contradictory condition, it would have this or that character. And no one would worry about such a thing for an instant unless misled by fallacious reasoning such as that which has just been exposed. No one, for example, in the present international puzzlement or uncertainty, wastes a moment worrying about the kind of future wars, future-2 wars, which by definition cannot happen. The kind of future wars which one does worry about and is concerned to prevent is the kind which may come, which can occur in some present. And just as a future war which by definition cannot occur is not

B

a future war in any sense which is pertinent to our present international deliberations, so generally a future event which by definition can occur in no present is not a future event in any sense which is pertinent to the validity of our inductive reasoning beyond the present and past, either in science or in everyday life.

CHAPTER III

UNIVERSALS

By D. F. Pears

'Do universals exist?' This question was debated so long and vehemently because it was mistaken for a factual question about some airy realm of being. But why was this mistake made? One diagnosis is that general words were tacitly assimilated to proper names,[1] and that, when this practice is exposed, it becomes harmless but pointless.[2] But this is a description of what happened rather than an explanation; it gives something more like a symptom than a cause. Could so many philosophers have been so silly in such a simple way? Even moderate scepticism on this point would lead to an attempt to supplement this suggestion. This article is such an attempt.

'Universals exist' has a deceptive logic. Realists offer it as the conclusion of many arguments: but unlike the premisses of these arguments, it cannot be understood as a verifiable statement of fact. On the other hand, if it is taken merely as an esoteric way of stating those premisses over again, the vehemence of the controversy becomes inexplicable. Faced with this difficulty of interpretation, some modern philosophers suggest that it is no good puzzling about its literal meaning, just as it is no good puzzling about the literal meaning of dreams. For traditional philosophy provided a small set of possible conclusions to arguments about the generality of thought and language, and tradition was strong. If a tribe educated its children to dream according to a tradition which restricted their manifest dream contents within narrow limits, it would be difficult to discover their much more varied latent dream contents.[3] Similarly, although realists are argumentative, it is difficult to answer the question why they

---

[1] Cf. J. S. Mill, *Examination of Sir William Hamilton's Philosophy* (5th edn., London, 1878) chap. XVII, p. 381, and Berkeley, *Principles of Human Knowledge*, Introduction §18.
[2] Cf. M. Lazerowitz, 'The Existence of Universals' (*Mind*, 1946, pp. 1ff.).
[3] Cf. Freud, *The Interpretation of Dreams*, tr. A. A. Brill (London, 1913), p. 166.

maintain that universals exist. Any answer must be based on a selection from among the many reasons which they themselves proffer: and a good selection will be diagnostic; it will successfully explain the doctrine. There is no sharp boundary here between descriptions of the premisses of philosophical arguments and diagnoses of their conclusions: because success in explaining, which is the criterion of a diagnosis, is a matter of degree, and because the reasons which philosophers themselves give for their doctrines sometimes completely explain why they held them. Quine's remark, that realists find a universal for every property which can be existentially generalized,[1] is an extremely brief description. The thesis of Berkeley and Mill was more than this: it was a diagnosis, but an inadequate one. I shall try to provide a less inadequate diagnosis.

'Because universals exist' is the answer to at least two general questions: 'Why are things what they are'?[2] and 'Why are we able to name things as we do'? Though Plato and Aristotle sometimes distinguished these two questions, it was characteristic of Greek thought to confuse them. Yet they can be clearly distinguished, the first requiring a dynamic answer from scientists, and the second a static answer from logicians. Now philosophy has often staked premature claims in the territory of science by giving quick comprehensive answers to questions which really required laborious detailed answers. And clearly this is what happened to the first of the two questions. When detailed causal answers were provided to it, the comprehensive answer 'Because universals exist' was no longer acceptable or necessary.[3] But what would detailed answers to the second question be like? Presumably they would be explanations of the meanings of words. But philosophers are easily led to neglect such detailed progressive answers to the second question, and to seek instead a comprehensive and ultimate explanation of naming. For, though comprehensive answers to the first question are clearly futile, there are no obvious penalties attached to answering the second question

---

[1] Cf. 'Designation and Existence' in Feigl and Sellars, *Readings in Philosophical Analysis* (New York, 1949), p. 48.

[2] Aristotle criticized Plato's theory largely as an inadequate answer to this question.

[3] Socrates in the *Phaedo* (100d) says that it is the only acceptable answer to the first question. But the advance of science has undermined this thesis more thoroughly than the advance of logic has undermined the thesis that it is an acceptable answer to the second question.

in a comprehensive way. Yet, I shall argue — and this will be my first thesis — that any comprehensive explanation of naming is necessarily circular: and that philosophers think that, in spite of this disadvantage, such explanations have some point largely because they wrongly assimilate naming to natural processes. Yet surely naming cannot be utterly artificial? My second thesis will be that the desire to understand naming leads to a hunt for a completely satisfactory analogy: but that all other processes either already contain the very feature of naming which was puzzling, or else are too natural or too artificial to be really analogous; and that it was the inevitable oscillation between these three points which prolonged the controversy about universals.

It is unnecessary to produce evidence that philosophers who proposed the existence of universals thought that they were explaining the unity of classes and hence the possibility of naming. What is debatable is whether this was an important motive, and this can be decided only in the sequel. My first thesis, which I must now try to establish, is that realism is necessarily a circular explanation of naming. Now the answer to the question 'Why are we able to name things as we do?' is 'The reason varies'. For it is always possible with more or less ingenuity, depending on the degree of atomicity of the name, to give a detailed informative reason; and this reason will vary with the name. But ultimately there must be some exit from the maze of words, and, wherever this exit is made, it will be impossible to give an informative reason except by pointing. For the only other way of giving an informative reason is to give a new word, and this would prevent the exit from the maze of words from being made at this place.[1] Still at the place where the exit is made it is always possible to give a detailed reason like 'We are able to call things red because they are red', which is too obviously circular even to look informative. Or alternatively it is possible to say 'We are able to call things φ because they are φ', and this is a general reason which is almost as obviously circular and uninformative. What philosophers who propose the existence of universals do is

---

[1] Cf. the view sketched by Socrates in the *Theaetetus* 201e-202c, and Antisthenes' view given by Aristotle in *Met.* H, 1043 b 23-32; also L. Wittgenstein, *Tractatus* 5; M. Schlick, *Grundzüge der Naturphilosophie* (Vienna, 1948), p. 21; and A. J. Ayer, *Thinking and Meaning* (London, 1947), p. 28.

to propose a general reason which looks informative because it shifts to another level, but unfortunately is not. It merely marks time: but marking time can look very like marching if only the movements of the performers are watched, and not the ground which they profess to be covering. Yet this ground could not be covered. For the reason could not be informative even if it were detailed; since there could be a non-circular answer to the question 'What universal?' only if the exit from the maze of words were made at some different point, which would merely put off the moment of embarrassment from which in the end neither speech nor thought can be saved. Thus realism fails to escape the limitations of all explanations of naming; that they can be informative only if they are not general but detailed, and then only if they are not given at the point where an exit is made from the maze of words.

Uninformative answers have their point. They are silencing. What is wrong with realism is not this, but that it masquerades as an answer which advances knowledge one step further. The analytic machine acquires a momentum which carries it beyond the point where it ought to stop. And there is an inveterate philosophical habit which strengthens the tendency to go beyond this point, or rather to think that one has gone beyond it. 'A thing is called by a certain name because it instantiates a certain universal' is obviously circular when particularized, but it looks imposing when it is left in this general form. And it looks imposing in this general form largely because of the inveterate philosophical habit of treating the shadows cast by words and sentences as if they were separately identifiable. Universals, like facts and propositions, are such shadows; and too often philosophers by appealing to them in general terms have produced in their readers a feeling of satisfaction which ought to have been produced only by specifying them.[1] But universals are specifiable only by reference to words. Similarly facts may be brute and propositions may be definite, but what exactly it is about them which is brute or

---

[1] The same trick is played by those who say that laws of nature exhibit connections between universals. This gives the impression that we could independently know the eternal framework in which temporal things move and change, rather as we independently know how a piston must move by looking at a cylinder: cf. what Köhler says about Aristotle's astronomy and Descartes' neurology (*Gestalt Psychology*, London, 1930, pp. 82-6).

definite can be specified only by reference to the sentences which were the unacknowledged starting-points. In all these cases it is tacit re-duplication which makes philosophers think that they can enjoy the benefits of specifying without actually specifying. Yet the explanation of naming is incomplete until a particular universal is specified, and, when it is specified, the explanation immediately fails through circularity. Naming is hazardous,[1] and any attempt to make it foolproof by basing it on an independent foundation must fail in this way. It is impossible to cross the gap between language and things without really crossing it.[2]

Since the failure of realism to perform this feat is inevitable, its rivals fail too. Nominalism, conceptualism and imagism,[3] in so far as they are rivals of realism, are attempts to provide a unity which will explain naming. Nominalism says that a name is merely connected with a multitude of things, sometimes adding that these things are similar. Conceptualism says that the name is not directly connected with the things but only via a concept, thus changing the nodal point. Imagism says that the nodal point is an image. And realism says that there is really no nodal point, since a name, though it appears to be connected with a multitude of things is all the time connected with only one thing, a universal. This is an over-simplification of what these theories say about the One and the Many; but it is enough for my next purpose, which is to show that these rivals of realism cannot produce a non-circular explanation of naming at those points where an exit is made from the maze of words.

The two psychological theories say that one word can apply to many things only because of the mediation of a concept or of an image. Locke's abstract general idea is 'the workmanship of the understanding, but has its foundation in the similitudes of things'.[4] And Berkeley replaces it by an idea which 'considered in itself is particular but becomes general by being made to represent or stand for all other particular ideas of the same sort'.[5] But what

[1] Cf. Bradley, *Appearance and Reality*, p. 22 and p. 533; and C. S. Peirce, *Collected Papers* (vol. I, para. 145): 'Direct experience is neither certain nor uncertain, because it affirms nothing — it just is.'
[2] Cf. Stuart Hampshire, 'Scepticism and Meaning' (*Philosophy*, July 1950, p. 245).
[3] Cf. H. H. Price, *Thinking and Representation* (British Academy Lecture, 1946).
[4] Locke, *Essay concerning Human Understanding*, Bk. III, chap. III, § xiii.
[5] Berkeley, *Principles of Human Knowledge*, Introduction, § 12.

similitudes, and what representation? In the end both Locke's concept and Berkeley's image are completely identifiable only by their use.[1] Of course we can partly identify images by describing their features: and in this way we may even almost completely identify them, since certain images most naturally stand for certain things. And the same could be said of concepts, if they were not merely philosophers' reifications of mental processes. But this will not completely identify either of them, since thought may not follow the most natural course; nor is it always clear which is the most natural course. It is not so much that thinking is speaking as that thinking is like speaking in the only way that matters: it uses one thing as a symbol to stand for many things. And the only tool which could not be used differently is the use. Even something which had its use written on it could be used differently.[2] And, if the psychological tool, whether concept or image, can be completely identified only by the things on which it is used, it cannot explain naming without circularity. For, unless we point, the use can be specified only by backward reference to the name. Nor is this circularity surprising. For psychological tools have no advantage over words: they are like them in being symbols, and unlike them only in being shadowy symbols.

The type of nominalism which says that a name is applied to a number of things which are similar immediately falls into the same circularity. For 'similar' is an incomplete predicate, anything being similar to anything in some way, perhaps a negative way.[3] And in the end the kind of similarity which is meant can

---

[1] This is due to Wittgenstein: cf. e.g. *Tractatus*, 3.326, 'In order to recognize the symbol in the sign we must consider the significant use'.

[2] W. T. Stace in 'Russell's Neutral Monism' in *The Philosophy of Bertrand Russell*, pp. 381-3, complains that neither Berkeley's precise image nor Russell's vague image (in *An Inquiry into Meaning and Truth*) succeeds in explaining the generality of thought. But no description of any item of mental furniture which included only its momentary properties and not its habitual use could possibly explain the generality of thought.

[3] Hence the point of many riddles. Cf. Stuart Hampshire, 'Scepticism and Meaning' (*Philosophy*, July 1950, p. 238). Also Plato, *Protagoras* 331 d. The Platonic theory avoids the 'similarity' difficulty, but not of course the general difficulty of which this is only one form. Speusippus, who abandoned the Platonic theory, seems to have held that, since every species is like every other species in some way, it is impossible to define one species without defining every other species. Cf. Aristotle, *Post. An.* 97 a 6-11. Cf. H. Cherniss, *Aristotle's criticism of Plato and the Academy* (I. 60), quoted by W. D. Ross in his note on this passage. J. Stenzel, in Pauly-Wissowa Real-Encyclopädie, *s.v.* Speusippus, pp. 1650 and 1655, brings out the affinity between Speusippus' view and Post-Kantian Idealism. Cf. Brand Blanshard on individuals (not species). 'One never gets what is fully particular until one has specified its relations of every kind with everything else in the universe', *The Nature of Thought* (London, 1939), vol. I, p. 639. Curiously enough N. R. Campbell

be specified only by a backward reference to the name. Equally the type of nominalism which merely says that a name is applied to a class of things cannot say which class without a backward reference to the name. Here the circularity is so obvious and there is so little to cushion the shock of the realization that naming is naming that this type of nominalism seems hardly tenable. For, however strongly nominalists react against realism, they can never quite escape its influence: once somebody had said that universals exist it could never be quite the same again. Surely, one wants to protest, there must be some way of giving the class besides reference to the name? Well there is, of course, enumeration. But this answer seems to fail to allow for the possibility of ever using the name correctly in any synthetic sentence. For, if the class is given by enumeration, surely every use of the name must be either incorrect or analytic? Since, if to call a thing 'φ' is to include it in the class of things called 'φ', then surely either it is incorrect to call it 'φ' or else the class cannot be given without reference to it? It is the example of realism which encourages these protests. But it is a bad example. Such neatness is not to be had. For, first of all, these classes cannot be given by enumeration of all their members, since, except for words belonging to dead languages, they are never complete. Nor is it true even that each member must either contribute or not contribute towards giving a class; since a name may be applied to the same thing twice, once analytically and once synthetically, and even a single use of a name may be synthetic for the speaker and analytic for the hearer. In fact the disjunction 'Analytic or Synthetic' cannot be applied simply to the addition of a member to a class without further caveats. But this in itself is not enough to remove the difficulty; it only makes it reappear in a new form. For if the addition of a member to a class can be synthetic for the speaker and analytic for a subsequent lexicographer, then to what class was the member added? Surely we now have two classes on our hands instead of one? An analogy will help us to deal with this new form of the difficulty. Naming is like electing the sort of member who makes

arrives independently at a similar conclusion about species, when he is discussing the definition of such substances as silver, mercury or lead (*Physics. The Elements*, Cambridge, 1920, p. 50). All attempts to explain the unity of a species by similarity — whether by similarity of the individuals to one another, or by similarities and differences between the species and other species — suffer from the same incompleteness.

a difference to a club. Strictly we cannot say without qualification to what club he was elected, since it was one club before he was elected and another club after he was elected. The club building might be pointed out, and of course there is no parallel move in the case of naming, although realism pretends that there is. But, even if there were no building or anything else of that kind, the puzzle about the two clubs would not be very perplexing. Similarly, when we reject the simple application of the dichotomy 'Analytic or Synthetic' the resulting puzzle about two classes is not very perplexing. All that is necessary is to point out that a class is incompletely given by a changing quorum. This may be untidy, but why not? There is something radically wrong with a request to be given a class which is not satisfied either with a reference to the name or with progressive enumeration. It is a request to be given something without being given it; as if somewhere, if only philosophers searched long enough, there could be found something which possessed all the advantages of a word and none of its disadvantages, an epistemological vehicle which carried all its destinations.

I now turn to my second thesis, that nothing is sufficiently like naming without being too like naming. Defenders of realism, like defenders of the other theories of naming, might object that the criticism contained in my first thesis is obvious, superficial and directed against a man of straw. For realism does not offer a non-circular detailed explanation of naming – how could it? – but simply gives a general characterization of the sort of unity which makes naming possible. But notice how very like a dream realism is. Taken literally it seems to be of little importance. But, if it is taken as the expression of a doctrine which, if *per impossibile* it were true, would give it great importance, the suggestion is immediately repudiated. Yet it does express such a doctrine, even if its exponents intermittently deny that it does; and it is to the devious expression of this doctrine that it owes most of its attractiveness. Its manifest content is little more than a harmless caprice, but its latent content is a serious error.

But has realism no point when it is taken simply as a general characterization of the sort of unity which makes naming impossible? One might answer that it has no point, and that it succeeds in appearing to have some point only by the device of inventing a new comprehensive term: and that this device is considered effective only in philosophy, since outside philosophy it is too obviously like making an impressive gesture in the direction of the interesting object, opening one's mouth and saying absolutely nothing. But such a denial would be tantamount to a denial that any general characterization of the sort of unity which makes naming possible could have a point. And surely such a denial would be wrong, since something can be done towards explaining the general possibility of naming by finding analogous processes? For instance, what makes naming possible is one thing which is in many things as an ingredient.[1] But does this analogy throw much light on naming? Any feature of logical mixing which is at all interesting seems to distinguish it from all other sorts of mixing. The values of an unrestricted variable are strange receptacles. What prevents contrary ingredients from being put in together, or an implicans from appearing without its implicate, is never the causal consequences. And anyway the whole notion of mixing ingredients which were not there before the mixing is peculiar. Could there be a logical conjuring trick?

Here defenders of realism might object that a new misunderstanding had replaced the old one. For, if realism is to be understood, not only must a general characterization of naming be allowed, but also the verification principle must not be applied too crudely. And anyway, if mixing is not a good analogy, this only means that some better analogy must be sought. This objection might lead to a tolerant examination of other analogies.[2] But fortunately it also opens up a short cut to the heart of the matter, which I shall soon take. Now it would be taking too short a cut to repeat the platitude that naming is *sui generis*. For it is natural to seek an analogy even if the search can never be completely successful. And anyway Butler's truism applies to everything. What is needed in order to explain the peculiar persistence of the debate about universals is something slightly longer, a demonstration that no analogy can be sufficiently close to satisfy philosophers without being too close.

It is most natural to seek a visible process as an analogy to

[1] Cf. A. N. Whitehead, *Science and the Modern World* (Cambridge, 1928), pp. 197ff. For a criticism of this analogy, cf. Bentham, *Works*, vol. VIII, p. 335.

[2] Metaphors must not be dismissed just because they are metaphors, as, e.g. 'copying' and 'participation' are by Aristotle, *Met.* 991 a 20.

naming, particularly for the Greeks who began this controversy.[1]
Now previously I insisted that it is impossible in the end to give a
detailed non-circular description of what makes it possible to
name anything. Here, however, it would be unfair to object
that, if naming in general is compared to a visible process, still
that process itself must be named. For this sort of circularity is
the inevitable result of the philosopher's predicament. However, it is dangerous to begin speaking at all where so little can
be said. For it is fatally easy to think that one has separate access
to what makes a name applicable just because one has separate
access to whatever stands for this in the analogy. But, waiving
this, let us now take the short cut and ask what sort of visible
process could be analogous to naming. Let us try a rough analogy
and say that one word is connected with many objects in the same
way that the estuary of a river is connected with its many sources.
But this analogy fails because this connection just happens
naturally. We might then try to mend the analogy by saying
that water follows the easiest course. But this could be called
choice only anthropomorphically, in an extended and weak sense
of 'choice'. In order to introduce choice in a restricted, strong
sense, it is necessary to alter the analogy and say that people by
directing the streams choose which sources shall feed the river.
But, if the first process was too natural to be like naming, the second
is too artificial, since, for the analogy to work, the sources ought
to have something in common besides the fact that the river is
fed from them. And it is difficult to find an analogy which is
neither too natural nor too artificial. The characteristic of naming
which is difficult to match is that the objects have something in
common besides being called by one name, but nothing in
common which counts except that in virtue of which they are
called by one name. And this characteristic can be matched only
by allowing that something makes it convenient but not absolutely
necessary for people to canalize streams into the river in the way
they do, and that whatever it is which makes this choice convenient is the only thing common to the sources which counts.
But this compromise between the two extremes introduces into
the analogy the very feature which it was intended to explain. For
just how something works in influencing usage was what was to be

[1] Cf. J. Stenzel, *Plato's Method of Dialectic* (Oxford, 1940), p. 37.

explained. Nor is there a fourth alternative. So after all even general analogical characterizations of naming do fall into a circularity which is closely related to the type of circularity which my first thesis exposed. Neither in detail nor in general is it possible to step outside language.

This short way with analogies looks too superficial. For suppose that it is granted that one of the things that metaphysicians do is to seek the unattainable: that they hunt for definitions which would in no way involve their definienda,[1] and for analogies which would in no way involve what they were intended to explain. Yet even so metaphysics is a natural and inevitable pursuit, since the easiest way to discover how far one can go is to try to go one stage farther. And anyway there is a difference between complete failure and partial success; since, so long as analogies do not reach the point of self-frustration they get better and better as they approach it. These two qualifications are just but they only serve to strengthen my thesis that it was oscillation between the three points which prolonged the controversy about universals. For unless the possible analogies are mapped out in this simple way, it seems always conceivable that some altogether better analogy might lurk in an unexplored corner.

And what more are the rival theories of naming doing than seeking a completely satisfactory analogy? It is only jargon which makes them appear to be doing something more. The type of nominalism which suggests that things which are called by one name have only their name in common represents the extreme of artificiality.[2] It suggests that there are never any ways of telling even approximately whether a word is used in one sense or two senses. At the other extreme stands the type of realism which suggests that there is always one method of getting a precise answer to this question. In between are all the other theories of naming, which allow that it is neither impossible for the lexicographer to succeed in answering this question nor impossible for him to fail. None of these middle theories is really wrong, since of course we do bestow common names on certain chosen groups

---

[1] Cf. J. Wisdom, 'Metaphysics and Verification' (*Mind*, 1938, pp. 465ff.)
[2] There are traces of such an extreme form of nominalism in Hobbes. Cf. *Leviathan*, Pt. I, chap. IV, p. 13 (Everyman edition).

of things which exhibit certain similarities (else why should we do it?) or instantiate certain universals (why else were they invented?). But on the other hand none of them goes deep enough to satisfy the true metaphysician who is in all of us; since though they take us to the bottom of naming, we were in a simpler way already there, and they do not succeed in showing us how naming is founded on something else which lies even deeper. Hence each of these middle theories (except imagism, which says something empirical which seems to be false) develops its own thesis with embarrassing success up to a point, and can discredit its rivals only by accusing them of not going beyond that point. But, since naming cannot be explained by anything which really goes beyond a reasoned choice of usage, this is an unfair accusation. And its unfairness is concealed from those who make it only because each tacitly and wrongly assumes that his own theory alone does go beyond this point. Thus moderate nominalists maintain that similarity is a better explanation of the unity of a class than the presence of a universal. (But why should people not *just* recognize the presence of universals?) And moderate realists retort that this admits the existence of at least one universal, similarity. (But why should the presence of a universal explain the recognition of similarity if it cannot explain the recognition of anything else? Why should people not *just* recognize similarity?) Really these are not two arguments but two bare assertions of superiority. They are manœuvres which are carried out in a way which suggests that they are difficult and that they must be advances: but both these suggestions are false. Yet these theories do seem to be striving towards something. And they are. Their goal is the unattainable completely satisfactory explanation of naming. And, as so often happens in metaphysics, progress is measured by distance from the starting-point and not by proximity to the goal whose unattainability each uses against its rivals without allowing it to deter itself.

Thus theories of naming, which seem to flout the verification principle without therefore saying nothing, can be interpreted as disguised analogies. And, though there is a common limit beyond which they cannot go, the success with which they stealthily approach this limit, camouflaged in the technical terms of epistemology, varies. But if this almost mechanical oscillation is avoided what else can be said about naming? Certainly as the first part of this article showed, detailed answers to the question why we name things as we do will in the end be circular. Only the trick of giving a general answer as if it were a detailed one cloaks their failure. If a word is explained ostensively, then however difficult this process may be it really is explained ostensively. It is no good trying to combine the concreteness of ostensive definition with the clarity of verbal definition. Verbal definitions have such an easy task just because ostensive definitions have such a difficult task. Surveyors find it easier to fix the positions of points which they can visit than to fix the positions of points which they cannot visit. Similarly it is easy to fix the relative positions of words: but the points in things to which words are related are in the end inaccessible to logicians.

Then what else can be said about naming? How *does* the lexicographer tell when a word is used in two senses rather than in one sense? Surely there must be something in common to all well constructed series of things? Yes, just that they *are* well constructed. For this question already contains the equivalent of any possible comprehensive answer which could be given to it. And, though in one way it is hard to see what detailed answers could be given to it, in another way it is only too easy to see. For we never reach a point where an exit *must* be made from the maze of words. Admittedly, if a verbal explanation is given at one point, it is only successful if at some other point a connection with things is already understood; and at some points it is more natural not to offer more words. But at no point is an exit obligatory. So, if detailed reasons why we call a thing what we do are required, it is easy to give them; but never ultimately or in the end, since here *ex vi termini* it is impossible to give them. But philosophers tend to ignore this kind of detailed answer and press on. But where to? Perhaps to experimental psychology, in order to discover how changes in the sense organs, in training and in interests alter the ways in which people group things. But this sort of investigation only gives the varying tests of the good construction of a series, and not its essence. But what could its essence be? When general analogical characterizations of naming have been mentioned, and detailed reasons why we call particular things by particular names, and the psychological background of all this, what is left? The desire to go on explaining naming is to some extent the result of the way these three fields have been confused, and to some extent the result of a natural feeling that in such a vast territory there might be something which lies outside these three fields. But above all it is the result of the Protean metaphysical urge to transcend language.

CHAPTER IV

CATEGORIES

By G. Ryle

DOCTRINES of categories and theories of types are explorations in the same field. And the field is still largely unexplored. Moreover the exploration of it is at present handicapped by certain vocabulary-differences between philosophers, which hinder them from reading one another's maps. My object in this paper is rather to remove certain obstacles to the exploration than to proffer surveys of my own.

The matter is of some importance, for not only is it the case that category-propositions (namely assertions that terms belong to certain categories or types) are always philosopher's propositions, but, I believe, the converse is also true. So we are in the dark about the nature of philosophical problems and methods if we are in the dark about types or categories.

I begin with some historical remarks, not in order to exhibit adeptness in philosophical palaeontology or even to make upstart doctrines respectable by discerning Norman blood in them, but as a convenient way of jointly opening up the philosophical questions and explaining some traditional terminologies of the topic.

ARISTOTLE'S CATEGORIES

What did Aristotle think that his list of Categories was a list of? The word 'category' meant what our word 'predicate' means and shared all the vagueness and ambiguity of this English substantive. But Aristotle's list of categories was not a glossary of all the predicates that there are. On at least a plausible interpretation of the doctrine, Aristotle's list is intended to be a list of the ultimate types of predicates. But what does this mean?

There are simple propositions, namely those which do not consist of more elementary propositions in conjunction with each other, that is to say there are propositions into the expression of

F

which there cannot enter such conjunctions as 'and', 'or', 'if', 'although', 'because', etc. Of these simple propositions some are singular propositions, namely those each of which is about at least one named or directly indicated particular.

Collect a range of simple, singular propositions, all similar in being about the same particular or particulars, then the respects in which these propositions differ from one another will be their predicates. And these predicates are classified into a finite number of families or types, the differences between which types can be indicated, though not defined, in the following way.

Any simple proposition about Socrates, say, is an answer, probably a false one, to some question about Socrates. Any given question about Socrates will generate a range of possible answers, but not any proposition about Socrates will be an answer to this question about him. There are as many different types of predicates of Socrates as there are irreducibly different sorts of questions about him. Thus 'How big?' collects 'Six foot tall', 'five foot tall', 'ten stone', 'eleven stone', etc., and does not collect 'fair haired', 'in the garden', or 'a stonemason'. 'Where?' collects predicates of location, 'What sort?' collects predicates of kind, 'What like?' collects qualities, and so on.

Any two predicates which satisfy the same interrogative are of the same category, and any two which do not satisfy the same interrogative are of different categories. In the main Aristotle seems to content himself with taking ordinary language as his clue to the list of heads of questions, and so of types of predicates.

This programme of cataloguing types was then expanded, either by Aristotle or by his followers. We can not only ask about a particular a series of questions, each of which will yield in its answers a range of possible predicates of that particular; we can also ask with reference to any such predicate 'Who has it?' or 'What (in the sense of "which") has it?' The answers to these questions will name or indicate particulars, like 'Socrates', 'Fido', 'I' and 'the Queen'. Obviously these questions do not generate ranges of predicates, but ranges of subjects or possessors of predicates, that is, particular substances. So *Socrates* is in the category of Substance, whereas *snub-nosed* is in the category of Quality and *husband* in that of Relation. As a result of this expansion, 'category' no longer means 'type of predicate' merely, but 'type of term' where 'term' means 'abstractible factor in a range of simple, singular propositions'.

Aristotle's actual list of ten (or sometimes eight) types of terms is doubtless unsatisfactory. Certain of the alleged ultimate types are patently only subordinate branches of others, and the criteria used by Aristotle for determining whether a term is of this or that category are fairly loose, where they occur at all. But for his purposes this does not matter much. He chiefly required to be able to demarcate (*a*) qualities from relations, (*b*) both from substances, and (*c*) all three from sorts or kinds. And this he was now able in a rough and unprecise way to do. But we have other fish to fry, so we have to notice other defects in his scheme.

1. It is not an easy matter to decide when a sentence expresses a simple proposition. For the fact that a sentence contains only one verb and no conjunctions does not prove that the proposition expressed by it is simple, i.e. that the sentence *could* not be paraphrased by a sentence containing conjunctions and a plurality of verbs. And in fact any sentence containing a description, or any sentence containing a dispositional adjective like 'brittle', or, again, any sentence containing a kind-name is thus paraphrasable or 'exponible'. Most grammatically simple sentences express non-simple propositions and so are exponible. (Modern logic largely consists in taking exponibility seriously.) And this involves that the isolation of terms is no simple matter either. Grammatically simple nominative-expressions and predicative-expressions do not necessarily or often stand for logically simple constituents or components of propositions. The classification of types of abstractible factors in simple propositions must be postponed to the classification of the varieties of propositional forms. We require first a docketing of what are expressed by form-words, namely 'syncategorematic' words like *all, some, a, the, any, not, if, or, and, than,* etc., together with what are expressed by grammatical constructions, before we can hope to pin down for indexing any irreducible 'categorematic' words.

2. Moreover we need a method for exhibiting and, what is quite different, a method for establishing type-homogeneities and type-heterogeneities. Aristotle's method, so far as he had one, seems to have consisted in collecting the ordinary interrogatives of everyday speech. He then labels his more important

types with nouns formed from these interrogative words. But no reason is given for supposing that the Greek stock of interrogative words is either as economical as possible or as rich as might be desired. However his clue, such as it was, was not a completely silly one. For after all 'propositional function' is only 'question' writ sophisticatedly. The propositional function 'x is snub-nosed' differs only in practical associations from 'Who is snub-nosed?'; and 'Socrates is φ' exhibits no more or less than 'Where is Socrates?' or 'What-like (qualis) is Socrates?' or 'How big is Socrates?' according to the *genre* selected for φ. (Cf. Lewis and Langford, *Symbolic Logic*, pp. 332-4; and Carnap on 'W . . . questions' in *Logical Syntax of Language*, p. 296.)

In order to state more precisely where Aristotle was on the right track and where his enterprise is unsuccessful, and also because I shall need them later on in the course of this paper, I want here to introduce some technical idioms. It is patent that in a certain sense, sentences contain parts; for two sentences can be partially similar and partially dissimilar. Let us call any partial expression which can enter into sentences otherwise dissimilar a 'sentence-factor'. Thus single words will be sentence-factors, but so will phrases of any degree of complexity as well as entire clauses. Thus in the sentence 'I am the man who wrote this paper', 'I', 'the man who', 'who wrote this paper', 'wrote this paper' are all sentence-factors.

I call them 'factors' rather than 'parts', since 'parts' would suggest, what is false, that the elements so abstracted can exist outside any such combinations as constitute sentences and, what is worse, that they can occur indifferently anywhere in any such combination, i.e. that they are both independent and freely shuffleable counters. The word 'factor' is intended to suggest, what is true, that they can only occur as factors in complexes of certain sorts, and can only occur in them in certain determinate ways.

Now though sentence-factors cannot be extracted from all combinations, they can be abstracted from any specified combination. If we take any sentence and substitute for any fragment of it a dotted line, or the phrase 'so and so', what is left is a sentence-factor with a signal (namely 'so and so' or the dotted line), to show that and how the sentence-factor requires completion. But the dotted line, though it requires some complement or other, would tolerate as its complements any out of an indefinite range of factors. Thus 'Socrates is . . .' or 'I am the man who so and so', or 'Such and such implies that tomorrow is Saturday', are not sentences but sentence-frames only, the gaps in which require to be completed by further sentence-factors. The required complements would, of course, have to be of different sorts in the three different frames. '. . . ugly' would complete one, '. . . visited Edinburgh yesterday' would complete the second, and 'today's being Tuesday . . .' would complete the third, and none would complete either of the others.

But though not any factor is fit to be the complement of any gap, there is an indefinite range of possible factors of the same pattern which would complete any given gap. So we abstract a factor from the other factor or factors in any concrete sentence by putting dotted lines or 'gap-signs' (like 'so and so' or 'x' or 'φ' or 'p') in the place or places of the other factor or factors. A gap-sign is not itself a word, or a phrase or a clause, nor is it the name or description of one; it is the name or index of a place for one or for any of a range of appropriate sentence-factors.

Now sentences and sentence-factors are English or German, pencilled or whispered or shouted, slangy or pedantic, and so on. What logic is concerned with is something which is indifferent to these differences — namely (it is convenient though often misleading to say), propositions and the parts or factors of propositions. When two sentences of different languages, idioms, authors or dates say the same thing, what they say can be considered in abstraction from the several sayings of it, which does not require us to suppose that it stands to them as a town stands to the several signposts which point to it. And, just as we distinguish propositions from the sentences which propound them, so we must distinguish proposition-factors from the sentence-factors which express them. But again we must not suppose that this means that the world contains cows and earthquakes *and* proposition-factors, any more than we are entitled by the fact that we can distinguish the two faces of a coin to infer that when I have a coin in my hand I have three things in my hand, the coin and its two faces.

Next, we have seen that the gap in a given sentence-frame can be completed by *some* but not by *any* alternative complements. But there are two sorts of 'can' here. 'So and so is in bed' grammatically requires for complements to the gap indicated by 'so and so' nouns, pronouns or substantival phrases such as descriptive phrases. So 'Saturday is in bed' breaks no rule of grammar. Yet the sentence is absurd. Consequently the possible complements must be not only of certain grammatical types, they must also express proposition-factors of certain logical types. The several factors in a non-absurd sentence are typically suited to each other; those in an absurd sentence, or some of them, are typically unsuitable to each other. To say that a given proposition-factor is of a certain category or type, is to say that its expression could complete certain sentence-frames without absurdity.

If the interpretation that I have given of Aristotle's doctrine of categories is correct, we can say that in one important respect it was on the right track. For interrogative sentences, when considered in abstraction from their practical role as petitions or commands, are sentence-frames, and the interrogative words in them are gap-signs. And by distinguishing varieties of sorts of questions, Aristotle is using a general method for exhibiting varieties of type of the factors which would be answers to those questions or complements to those gap-signs.

On the other hand his procedure is defective in the following ways. He only attempts to classify the types of a small sub-class of proposition-factors, namely the constituents and components of simple, singular propositions. Let us call these by their traditional (and typically ambiguous) title of 'terms'. All terms are factors but most factors are not terms. He proffers no test of when a sentence-factor does and when it does not stand for a term, and seems to assume that a grammatically simple word always stands for a constituent or component of a simple proposition. He relies, apparently, solely upon common sense and common parlance for evidence that a given factor is suited to fill a given gap. But worse than this, he does not recognize that the types of factors control and are controlled by the logical form of the propositions into which they can enter, except in the solitary case of particular substances which, he recognizes, cannot occupy the berths of qualities, relations, magnitudes, positions, kinds, etc., in what he takes to be simple propositions.

He, with the logicians of later ages, seems to have thought that while terms are coupled in propositions and while there are various types of terms, yet there is only one sort of coupling. For the very same term which occurs in one proposition as 'subject' can occur in another as 'predicate'.

As any letter of the alphabet may be juxtaposed with any other letter, without modifying the designs of those letters, so it seems to have been thought that there is no interaction between the form of a proposition and the types of the factors composing it. So no connection was established between the formal properties of propositions which render inferences embodying them possible or impossible, and the formal properties or types of the terms or other factors in them. The syllogistic rules which Aristotle discovered turn on the concepts expressed by such form-words as *all*, *some*, *this*, *not*, *and* and *implies*, but his treatment of them neither infects nor is infected by his classification of types of terms.

It is as though a grammarian were in his first chapter to give definitions of the types of parts of speech, such as nouns, prepositions, verbs, conjunctions, etc., and in a later chapter to give a quite independent discussion to the rules of syntax, when in truth just these rules must already be latent in the notions of noun, verb, conjunction, etc. It is to treat as freely shuffleable counters factors the determinate roles of which in the combination into which they can enter are just what constitute their types.

To know all about the logical form of a proposition and to know all about the logical types of its factors are to know one and the same thing. (I apologize, not very humbly, for terminology which, here and elsewhere in this paper I substitute for the terminology of 'propositional functions', 'variables,' values and the rest. I do so for the simple reason that this terminology has led to many confusions. Especially it failed to make obvious whether in talking of functions, variables, values, etc., we were talking of certain sorts of expressions or talking *with* certain expressions *of* certain sorts of things. Should we say that Socrates or 'Socrates' is a value of the variable in 'x' is snub-nosed'? The terminology which I use is meant to be overtly semantic. Its items, too, are meant to be reasonable self-explanatory.)

KANT'S JUDGMENT-FORMS AND CATEGORIES
Kant's doctrine of categories starts from quite a different quarter from that of Aristotle, and what he lists as categories are quite other than what Aristotle puts into his index. Kant quaintly avers that his purpose is the same as that of Aristotle, but in this he is, save in a very broad and vague sense, mistaken. Unfortunately Kant borrows for three out of his four heads of categories the same labels as Aristotle had used for three of his ten. As we shall see 'Quantity', 'Quality' and 'Relation' mean completely different sorts of things for the two philosophers.

Kant begins by giving a catalogue of judgment-forms, a catalogue, that is to say, of the several ways in which one proposition may resemble or differ from another not in topic but in form. He makes no attempt to define the notion of form, or even to justify his catalogue, save by declaring, what is false, that it derived from the findings of traditional logic, which he assumes to be a completed body of ascertained truth. (1) All propositions are determined in respect of 'Quantity', that is in respect of the extension of their subjects, and so must be either universal, particular or singular, i.e. of the 'all', 'some' or 'this' form; (2) all propositions are either affirmative, negative or infinite, which are the three 'Qualities' of propositions; (3) all propositions are of one of the three 'Relation' patterns, 's is P', 'if p then q', and 'p or q'; and (4) all propositions are of one of the three varieties of 'Modality', i.e. of the 'is' form, the 'may be' form or the 'must be' form. These judgment-forms are not yet Kant's categories, but they are the source from which he, somewhat mysteriously, proposes to derive or deduce them.

Kant's line of approach was, in principle, much more enlightened than Aristotle's had been. Unfortunately his execution was hopelessly misguided. His sub-variety of 'infinite' judgments is a fraud; there are several sorts of 'universal' judgment, but the sort which he was considering should come under the heading of hypothetical judgments; the division into assertoric, problematic and apodeictic is wrong-headed, the two last being special cases of hypotheticals; the division into categorical, hypothetical and disjunctive embodies a cross-division and contains one glaring omission, for (a) what he had in mind was the distinction between simple and compound propositions and (b) he omitted from this latter class conjunc-

tive propositions of the 'p and q' form. Only of simple propositions
is it true that they must be either affirmative or negative and either
universal or particular or singular, since in a two-limbed con-
junctive, disjunctive or hypothetical proposition, for instance,
one of the conjoined propositions may be one while the second
is one of the others. The distinction between the disjunctive and
the hypothetical forms is false. No overt distinction is drawn
between general and non-general propositions; no place is found
for such propositions as 'seven cows are in the field', 'most men
wear coats', 'John is probably dead'. And lastly, in simple singular
propositions no distinction is drawn between attributive and
relational propositions; Aristotle's category of relational predicates is completely ignored. Indeed Kant fails to follow Aristotle's
doctrine of categories at all, for he notices no type-differences
inside subject-predicate propositions, and purloins the titles
'Quality', 'Quantity' and 'Relation' for his own quite different
purposes. Namely, in Aristotle's use 'green', sweet' and 'honest'
signify qualities, but in Kant's use, 'Quality' signifies a proposition's being affirmative or negative. 'Quantity' is, for Aristotle,
the name of the family of predicates of magnitude or size; for
Kant it is the name of the respect in which propositions are of the
'all . . .' or the 'some . . .' or the 'this . . .' form. Relations,
lastly, are in Aristotle's use such predicates as 'cousin of', 'above',
'bigger than', but in Kant's they are what are expressed by such
conjunctions as 'if', 'or' and (he should have added) 'and'.

But when all this is said, it has to be acknowledged that Kant
was recognizing as cardinal in the search for categories or types
facts which Aristotle had not noticed at all in this connection.
Kant saw that there is a variety of respects in which propositions
may be formally similar and dissimilar. As we saw, in Aristotle's
doctrine of categories, the roles of 'form-words' like *all, some, the,
a, any, if, or, and, not* are unnoticed, and medieval followers
relegated these words to limbo under the grudging appellation
of 'syncategorematic'. Kant's doctrine (though he does not
notice the point) restores them from the limbo of logic to its
workshop.

Aristotle seems generally to suppose that while there is a
moderate variety of types of factors, yet there is only one sort of
coupling to which they are subject. (In his doctrine of Predicables

he half sees that in general propositions there are different sorts of coupling, but this is not allowed to modify his theory of terms.) Kant sees that there is a galaxy of sorts of coupling and that these determine or are determined by the sorts of factors that can be coupled. Aristotle's is an 'alphabetic' theory of factors and a simple 'juxtaposition' theory of their combinations; Kant's is a 'syntactical' theory about the combinations of factors, and consequently a 'syntactical' theory about the types of those factors — or so I interpret his cryptic utterances about 'functions of unity'.

However, Kant's categories are not identical with his forms of judgment. They are, in some obscure way, the projections of these logical forms upon the fields of natural things and events. Natural facts, facts that is that are establishable by observation or by memory of or induction from or causal inference from observations, all embody certain principles of structure, which somehow derive from the items in the table of judgment-forms. Nature consists of things possessing extensive and intensive magnitudes, being in states at particular moments of time and undergoing mutations or perpetuations of state according to causal laws. Everything empirical must and nothing non-empirical can embody these categories. So metaphysical propositions trespass against category-rules.

The mysterious Metapsychology, by means of which Kant tries to prove both that Nature must be so constituted and that we can know that it must be so constituted, need not be considered here. What would be relevant would be an exposition of the differences that Kant professes to find between his logical types and his categories or natural types. It looks as though he confusedly believed that there exist two sorts of facts or propositions, logicians' facts or propositions and scientists' facts or propositions, and that the forms of the latter are step-children of those of the former. But this would be an absurd view, for in fact the logicians' forms are simply what they abstract from ranges of partially similar and partially dissimilar propositions which hail, very likely, directly from the text books of scientists, historians, explorers, mathematicians or theologians. So the alleged distinction is, I think, a bogus one.

Kant contributes nothing to the technical problem how to

exhibit or symbolize type-homogeneities and heterogeneities in abstraction from the concrete factors which exemplify them. Nor does he explain how they are established, save by recommending us to read traditional logic.

Before leaving the history of the topic, we should notice one presupposition which Aristotle and Kant share, which is, I believe, unreflectively shared by a number of contemporary philosophers. Namely, it was supposed that there exists a finite catalogue of categories or types; for instance, that there exist just ten (or eight) types of terms, or that there exist just twelve judgment patterns, just as there exist just twenty-six letters in the English alphabet, just sixty-four squares on the chess-board and just six species of chessmen. This seems to be pure myth. There are various gambits at chess, but there is no finite roster of them; and there are various grammatical constructions of English sentences, but there can be no complete table of those varieties.

Scholasticism is the belief in some decalogue of categories, but I know of no grounds for this belief.

It follows that I do not think that we can ever say of a given code-symbolism in formal logic that its symbols are now adequate for the symbolization of all possible differences of type or form. It may, of course, be adequate for the exhibition of all the type-differences that concern us in the course of some particular inquiry.

GENERALIZATION OF THE TOPIC

When a sentence is (not true or false but) nonsensical or absurd, although its vocabulary is conventional and its grammatical construction is regular, we say that it is absurd because at least one ingredient expression in it is not of the right type to be coupled or to be coupled in that way with the other ingredient expression or expressions in it. Such sentences, we may say, commit type-trespasses or break type-rules. Latterly the attention of logicians has been focused on certain sorts of type-trespasses, like those which are committed by 'I am now lying' and ' "Heterological" is heterological'. These sorts are interesting, because their absurdities are not obvious but manifest themselves in the generation of contradictions or vicious circles, whereas 'Saturday is in bed' is obviously absurd before any contradictions are seen to result from the hypothesis that it is true.

Moreover we can be actually led by seemingly valid arguments to propounding propositions of the former sorts, whereas only the deliberate intention to produce balderdash would get us to formulate sentences of the latter sort. That is, some type-trespasses are insidious and others are not. It is the insidious ones which force us to consider type-rules; the others we only attend to because we are already considering type-rules. But it would be a mistake to restrict the theory of types to the theory of certain special type-rules.

To ask the question To what type or category does so and so belong? is to ask In what sorts of true or false propositions and in what positions in them can so and so enter? Or, to put it semantically, it is to ask In what sorts of non-absurd sentences and in what positions in them can the expression 'so and so' enter? and, conversely, What sorts of sentences would be rendered absurd by the substitution for one of their sentence-factors of the expression 'so and so'? I adopt the word 'absurd' in preference to 'nonsensical' or 'meaningless' for the reason that both the two last words are sometimes used for noises like 'brillig' and 'abracadabra', and sometimes for collocations of words having no regular grammatical construction. Moreover, both have recently been adopted for polemical purposes in aid of a special theory. 'Absurd' has helpful associations with the *reductio ad absurdum*, and even its nuance of ridiculousness is useful rather than the reverse, for so many jokes are in fact type-pranks.

What are Types Types of?

Only expressions can be affirmed or denied to be absurd. Nature provides no absurdities; nor can we even say that thoughts such as beliefs or supposals or conceptions are or are not absurd. For what is absurd is unthinkable.

So it is, on the whole, prudent to talk logic in the semantic idiom and to formulate our theories and inquiries in such a way as to advertise all the time that we are considering whether such and such expressions may or may not be coupled in such and such ways with other expressions.

The danger is, of course, that we shall be taken and shall unwittingly take ourselves to be talking grammar, as if it was all part of one topic to say 'Plural nouns cannot have singular verbs' and 'The dotted line in " . . . is false" can be completed with "What you are now saying . . ." and cannot be completed with "What I am now saying. . . ." '

We try, then, to say that absurdities result from the improper coupling not of expressions but of what the expressions signify, though the coupling and mis-coupling of them is effected by operating upon their expressions.

But there is not and cannot be any univocal title for all the *significata* of expressions, since if there was such a title, all these *significata* would be of one and the same type. And just this is what was at bottom wrong with the Lockean terminology of 'ideas' and the Meinongian terminology of 'objects', words which were employed to perform exactly this impossible task.

Other commonly used titles have extra nuisances as well. 'Terms' retains some of its traditional associations and should be used, if at all, for particulars-or-qualities-or-relations, etc. 'Concepts' does not cover either particulars or entire propositions or even complexes of concepts. So I use 'proposition-factor' (intending it to have all possible type-ambiguities), to collect whatever is signified by any expression, simple or complex, which can be a complement to a gap-sign in some sentence-frame or other (or which can be a value of a variable in some propositional function or other). And, if asked such questions as Do proposition-factors exist? How many of them are there? Are they mental? What are they like? my answer is 'All such questions are ridiculous, since "factor" is and is meant to be the meeting-place of all type-ambiguities'.

Of course we could dispense with any such word. Its functions are purely stenographic. Questions about the types of factors are, in a way, just questions about the possibilities of co-significance of certain classes of expressions. But just as the 'factor' idiom (like the 'idea' idiom) is liable to entrap us in myth, so the semantic idiom is liable to entrap us in a confusion between logical and grammatical questions.

Two proposition-factors are of different categories or types, if there are sentence-frames such that when the expressions for those factors are imported as alternative complements to the same gap-signs, the resultant sentences are significant in the one case and absurd in the other. It is tempting but not quite correct to say, as the converse of this, that two factors are of the same type if there is any case where both can fill the same gap. For 'I' and 'the writer of this paper' can be alternative nominatives to hosts of significant sentences but both cannot fill the gap in '. . . never wrote a paper'. It follows that though nearly, it is not quite true to say that every gap-sign in its context in a determinate sentence-frame indicates the category of all its possible complements. But wherever a particular gap-sign is thus tolerant of typically dissimilar complements, that gap-sign has typical ambiguity which a better symbolism would escape. For the fact that a given gap in a sentence-frame *can* be filled by complements between which there are certain differences of form is itself a fact about the types of those different complements.

THE GENESIS OF TYPE-RIDDLES

How do we come to be exercised about the forms of propositions or the types of proposition-factors? Or, to put it in a less new-fangled way, what makes it urgent for us to find definitions or analyses of concepts? For we do not gratuitously rummage in dictionaries or encyclopaedias after notions on which to perform elucidations. Type-problems seem to be forced upon us in two main ways.

(1) There are concepts with which we are perfectly familiar and which we are perfectly competent to employ — incessantly occurring, for instance, in questions which we know quite well how to solve. Yet whole classes of ordinary propositions embodying one or more of such concepts, some of which propositions we have perfectly good reasons for accepting as true, are ruled out as false by other propositions, no less well authenticated, embodying other equally familiar concepts. In a word, we are confronted by antinomies. We are sure that some out of one family of propositions are true and that some out of another family are true, yet the truth of any from the one family seems flatly to contradict all out of the other. I see a bent stick and the stick is straight; I am to blame for an action, and the action

issued from a character which my forebears bequeathed and my school moulded, and so on.

Now if the apparent contradiction or, rather, class of contradictions is resoluble, it can only be because the logical forms of the conflicting propositions are not what we had supposed, since it is only in virtue of the forms of propositions or the types of their factors that they do (or do not) imply (or imply the negatives of) one another.

(2) Then, when we have begun to explore the mechanics of some of our concepts and propositions, we find ourselves embarrassed by some purely technical perplexities. We are not quite sure how to use our own professional implements. But we only want to be sure of the designs of our trade-keys because we want to use them upon locks which were recalcitrant before we started our operations — unless we are carried away by virtuosity. Inquiries such as this one, into the nature of categories, or into the species of relations are in fact such technical questions. But *any* uncharted concept is liable to generate antinomies, for ignorance of its chart is ignorance of some of the implications and compatibilities of the propositions containing it. Concepts of common sense, of the sciences and of philosophy itself can and do all generate antinomies. The problem of the internality of relations arose out of antinomies resulting from the philosophers' technical concept of *relation*.

HOW ARE TYPES DETERMINED?

It has long been known that what a proposition implies, it implies in virtue of its form. The same is true of what it is compatible and incompatible with. Let us give the label 'liaisons' to all the logical relations of a proposition, namely what it implies, what it is implied by, what it is compatible with, and what it is incompatible with. Now, any respect in which two propositions differ in form will be reflected in differences in their liaisons. So two propositions which are formally similar in all respects save that one factor in one is different in type from a partially corresponding factor in the other, will have liaisons which are correspondingly dissimilar. Indeed the liaisons of a proposition do not merely *reflect* the formal properties of the proposition and, what

this involves, those of all its factors. In a certain sense, they are
the same thing. To know all about its liaisons is to know all
about the formal structure of the proposition, and vice versa.
Though I can obviously entertain or believe a proposition without
having yet noticed all its liaisons. Indeed I must grasp it before I
can consider them, otherwise I could not be the victim of antinomies.

The operation of extracting the type of a factor cannot exclude
the operation of revealing the liaisons of propositions embodying
it. In essence they are one operation. Of course, with the familiar
sorts of propositions upon which logicians have worked for
centuries or decades, we short-circuit the inquiry, by subsuming
them direct under the appropriate formulae. But to be told that
a proposition is of the form 'S a P' or of the form 'Ex. φx. ∼ ψχ'
is to be told nothing unless we are able to work with the code-
symbols according to the rules of their use, which means unless
we know how to read off the liaisons, the patterns of which are
what these symbols prescribe.

Now the operation of formulating the liaisons of a proposition
just is the activity of ratiocination or argumentation (in which of
course there need not be, though there may be, a polemical
purpose). And this is why philosophizing is arguing, and it is
just this element of ratiocination which, as a rule, is left out of
the latter-day definitions of philosophy as 'analysis'. For these
generally suggest that analysing is some sort of paraphrasing.
But some sorts of paraphrase throw no philosophical light, for
they fail to exhibit just those features of propositions and their
factors, obscurity about which involves us in antinomies, namely
their liaisons which flow from or constitute their logical types
and forms. Mere increase of prolixity is not enough. When an
argument is a philosophical one and when not, are further questions the discussion of which would not here be in place.

THE TYPE OF CATEGORY-PROPOSITIONS

I call a proposition a 'category-proposition' which asserts
something about the logical type of a factor or set of factors.
Some types have been officially recognized and endowed with
trade-names, like 'quality', 'state', 'substance', 'number', 'logical

construction', 'category', etc. We could call these 'category-words'. Carnap misleadingly calls them 'universal words'. But propositions asserting that factors are of named types differ only in brevity of expression from propositions asserting that factors are of described types.

All such propositions are philosophers' propositions (not necessarily, of course, of professional or paid philosophers), and the converse is also, I think, true.

Now assertions about the types of factors are, as we have seen, assertions about what sorts of combinations of them with other factors would and what would not produce absurdities. And as only collocations of symbols can be asserted to be absurd or, consequently, denied to be absurd, it follows that category-propositions are semantic propositions. This does not imply that they are of the same types as the propositions of philologists, grammarians or lexicographers. There are not English category-propositions as opposed to German ones, or Occidental as opposed to Oriental. Nor does it imply that they can say nothing about the 'nature of things'. If a child's perplexity why the Equator can be crossed but not seen, or why the Cheshire Cat could not leave its grin behind it is perplexity about the 'nature of things', then certain category-propositions will give the required information about the nature of things. And the same will hold good of less frivolous type-perplexities. But what are the tests of absurdity?

CHAPTER V

IS EXISTENCE A PREDICATE?

By G. E. Moore

(This paper was written as the second part of a Symposium the whole of which was originally printed in the *Proceedings of the Aristotelian Society*, Supplementary Volume XV, in 1936. It is reprinted here without alteration. The first part — by Mr. W. Kneale — has not been included: since it has already been reprinted in Feigl and Sellars, *Readings in Philosophical Analysis*; but the references to it in Professor Moore's paper are sufficiently self-explanatory. The same applies to his use of the technical term 'propositional function'. For an explanation and discussion of the term 'sense-datum' see Mr. G. A. Paul's article 'Is there a Problem about Sense-data?' in *Logic and Language* (First Series) — EDITOR.)

I AM not at all clear as to the meaning of this question. Mr. Kneale says that existence is not a predicate. But what does he mean by the words 'Existence is not a predicate'?

In his second paragraph, he says that the word 'predicate' has two different senses, a logical sense and a grammatical one. If so, it would follow that the words 'Existence is not a predicate' may have two different meanings, according as the person who uses them is using 'predicate' in the logical or the grammatical sense. And I think it is clear that he means us to understand that when *he* says 'Existence is not a predicate', he is using 'predicate' in the logical sense, and not in the grammatical one. I think his view is that if anyone were to say 'Existence is a predicate', using 'predicate' in the grammatical sense, such a person would be perfectly right: I think he holds that existence really is a predicate in the grammatical sense. But, whether he holds this or not, I think it is clear that he does not wish to discuss the question whether it is or is not a predicate in the grammatical sense, but solely the question whether it is so in the logical one.

Now I think it is worth noticing that if we assert 'Existence is a predicate', using 'predicate' in the grammatical sense, our proposition is a proposition about certain *words*, to the effect that they are often used in a certain way; but not, curiously enough, abo. the word 'existence' itself. It is a proposition to the effect that the word 'exists' and other finite parts of the verb 'to exist', such as 'existed', 'will exist' or 'exist' (in the plural) are often the predicates (in some grammatical sense) of sentences in which they occur; but nobody means to say that the word 'existence' itself is often the predicate of sentences in which it occurs. And I think Mr. Kneale implies that, similarly, the proposition which anyone would express, if he asserted 'Existence is a predicate', using 'predicate' in the logical sense, is again equivalent to a proposition, *not* about the word 'existence' itself, but about the word 'exists', and other finite parts of the verb 'to exist'. He implies that 'Existence is a predicate', with this use of 'predicate', is equivalent to the proposition that the word 'exists', and other finite parts of the verb, often do '*stand for* a predicate in the logical sense'. It would appear, therefore, that one difference between the two different meanings of 'Existence is a predicate' is as follows: namely that, if a person who says these words is using 'predicate' in the grammatical sense, he is *not* saying that the words, 'exists', etc., ever '*stand for* a predicate in the logical sense'; whereas, if he is using 'predicate' in the logical sense, he is saying that they do (often, at least) '*stand for* a predicate in the logical sense'. What Mr. Kneale himself means by 'Existence is not a predicate' is apparently some proposition which he would express by saying: 'The words, "exists", etc., never *stand for* a predicate in the logical sense.'

What I am not clear about is as to what is meant by saying of a particular word (or particular phrase) in a particular sentence that it 'stands for a predicate in the logical sense'; nor, therefore, as to what is meant by saying of another particular word in another particular sentence that it does *not* 'stand for a predicate in the logical sense'. Mr. Kneale does, indeed, tell us that a 'predicate in the logical sense' is the same as 'an attribute'; but, though I think that the meaning of the word 'attribute' is perhaps a little clearer than that of the phrase 'predicate in the logical sense', it still seems to me far from clear: I do not clearly understand what he would mean by saying that 'exists', etc., do not 'stand for attributes'. But, from examples which he gives, it is, I think, clear that he would say that in the sentence 'This is red' the word 'red', or the phrase 'is red' (I am not clear which), does 'stand for an attribute'; and also that in the sentence 'Tame tigers growl', 'growl' so stands, and in the sentence 'Rajah growls',

'growls' does. It is, therefore, presumably some difference between the way in which 'exists', etc., are used in sentences in which they occur, and the way in which 'is red' (or 'red') and 'growl' and 'growls' are used in these sentences, that he wishes to express by saying that, whereas 'exists', etc., do *not* 'stand for attributes', these words in these sentences do. And if we can find what differences there are between the use of finite parts of the verb 'to exist', and the use of 'is red', 'growl' and 'growls', we may perhaps find what the difference is which he expresses in this way.

I

It will, I think, be best to begin with one particular use of 'exist' – the one, namely, which Mr. Kneale illustrates by the example 'Tame tigers exist'.   He clearly thinks that there is some very important difference between the way in which 'exist' is used here, and the way in which 'growl' is used in 'Tame tigers growl'; and that it is a difference which does not hold, e.g. between the use of 'scratch' in 'Tame tigers scratch' and the use of 'growl' in 'Tame tigers growl'.   He would say that 'scratch' and 'growl' both 'stand for attributes', whereas 'exist' does not; and he would also say that 'Tame tigers exist' is a proposition of a different *form* from 'Tame tigers growl', whereas I think he would say that 'Tame tigers growl' and 'Tame tigers scratch' are *of the same form*.   What difference between 'Tame tigers exist' and 'Tame tigers growl' can be the one he has in mind?

(1) That there is a difference between the way in which we use 'exist' in the former sentence and 'growl' in the latter, of a different kind from the difference between our usages of 'scratch' and 'growl' in the two sentences 'Tame tigers scratch' and 'Tame tigers growl', can, I think, be brought out in the following way.

The sentence 'Tame tigers growl' seems to me to be ambiguous. So far as I can see, it might mean 'All tame tigers growl', or it might mean merely 'Most tame tigers growl', or it might mean merely 'Some tame tigers growl'. Each of these three sentences has a clear meaning, and the meaning of each is clearly different from that of either of the two others. Of each of them, however, it is true that the proposition which it expresses is one which cannot possibly be true, unless some tame tigers do growl. And hence I think we can say of 'Tame tigers growl' that, whichever sense it is used in, it means something which cannot possibly be true unless some tame tigers do growl. Similarly I think it is clear that 'Tame tigers exist' means something which cannot possibly be true unless some tame tigers do exist. But I do not think that there is any ambiguity in 'Tame tigers exist' corresponding to that which I have pointed out in 'Tame tigers growl'. So far as I can see 'Tame tigers exist' and 'Some tame tigers exist' are merely two different ways of expressing exactly the same proposition. That is to say, it is not true that 'Tame tigers exist' might mean 'All tame tigers exist', or 'Most tame tigers exist', instead of merely 'Some tame tigers exist'. It always means just 'Some tame tigers exist', and nothing else whatever. I have said it is never used to mean 'All tame tigers exist', or 'Most tame tigers exist'; but I hope it will strike everyone that there is something queer about this proposition. It seems to imply that 'All tame tigers exist' and 'Most tame tigers exist' have a clear meaning, just as have 'All tame tigers growl' and 'Most tame tigers growl'; and that it is just an accident that we do not happen ever to use 'Tame tigers exist' to express either of those two meanings instead of the meaning 'Some tame tigers exist', whereas we do sometimes use 'Tame tigers growl' to mean 'All tame tigers growl' or 'Most tame tigers growl', instead of merely 'Some tame tigers growl'. But is this in fact the case? Have 'All tame tigers exist' and 'Most tame tigers exist' any meaning at all? Certainly they have not a clear meaning, as have 'All tame tigers growl' and 'Most tame tigers growl'. They are puzzling expressions, which certainly do not carry their meaning, if they have any, on the face of them. That this is so indicates, I think, that there is some important difference between the usage of 'exist' with which we are concerned, and the usage of such words as 'growl' or 'scratch'; but it does not make clear just what the difference is.

I think this can be made clear by comparing the expressions 'Some tame tigers don't growl' and 'Some tame tigers don't exist'. The former, whether true or false, has a perfectly clear meaning — a meaning just as clear as that of 'Some tame tigers do growl'; and it is perfectly clear that both propositions might be true together. But with 'Some tame tigers don't exist' the case is different. 'Some tame tigers exist' has a perfectly clear meaning: it just means 'There are some tame tigers'. But the meaning of 'Some tame tigers don't exist', if any, is certainly not equally clear. It is another queer and puzzling expression. Has it any meaning at all? and, if so, what meaning? If it has any, it would appear that it must mean the same as: 'There are some tame tigers which don't exist'. But has *this* any meaning? And if so, what? Is it possible that there should be any tame tigers which don't exist? I think the answer is that, if in the sentence 'Some tame tigers don't exist' you are using 'exist' with the same mean-ing as in 'Some tame tigers exist', then the former sentence as a whole has no meaning at all — it is pure nonsense. A meaning can, of course, be given to 'Some tame tigers don't exist'; but this can only be done if 'exist' is used in a different way from that in which it is used in 'Some tame tigers exist'. And, if this is so, it will follow that 'All tame tigers exist' and 'Most tame tigers exist', also have no meaning at all, if you are using 'exist' in the sense with which we are concerned. For 'All tame tigers growl' is equivalent to the conjunction 'Some tame tigers growl, and there is no tame tiger which does not growl'; and this has a meaning, because 'There is at least one tame tiger which does not growl' has one. If, therefore, 'There is at least one tame tiger which does not exist' has no meaning, it will follow that 'All tame tigers exist' also has none; because 'There is no tame tiger which does not exist' will have none, if 'There is a tame tiger which does not exist' has none. Similarly 'Most tame tigers growl' is equivalent to the conjunction 'Some tame tigers growl, and the number of those (if any) which do not growl is smaller than that of those which do' — a statement which has a meaning only because 'There are tame tigers which do not growl' has one. If, therefore, 'There are tame tigers which don't exist' has no mean-ing, it will follow that 'Most tame tigers exist' will also have none. I think, therefore, we can say that one important difference between the use of 'growl' in 'Some tame tigers growl' and the use of 'exist' in 'Some tame tigers exist', is that if in the former case we insert 'do not' before 'growl', without changing the meaning of 'growl', we get a sentence which is significant, whereas if, in the latter, we insert 'do not' before 'exist' without changing the meaning of 'exist', we get a sentence which has no meaning whatever; and I think we can also say that this fact explains why, with the given meaning of 'growl', 'All tame tigers growl' and 'Most tame tigers growl' are both significant, whereas, with the given meaning of 'exist', 'All tame tigers exist' and 'Most tame tigers exist' are utterly meaningless. And if by the statement that 'growl', in this usage, 'stands for an attribute', whereas 'exist', in this usage, does not, part of what is meant is that there is this difference between them, then I should agree that 'exist', in this usage, does not 'stand for an attribute'.

But is it really true that if, in the sentence 'Some tame tigers exist', we insert 'do not' before 'exist', withou_ changing the meaning of 'exist', we get a sentence which has no meaning whatever? I have admitted that a meaning *can* be given to 'Some tame tigers do not exist'; and it may, perhaps, be contended by some people that the meaning which 'exist' has in this sentence, where it is significant, *is* precisely the same as that which it has in 'Some tame tigers exist'. I cannot show the contrary as clearly as I should like to be able to do; but I will do my best.

The meaning which such an expression as 'Some tame tigers do not exist' sometimes does have, is that which it has when it is used to mean the same as 'Some tame tigers are imaginary' or 'Some tame tigers are not real tigers'. That 'Some tame tigers are imaginary' may really express a proposition, whether true or false, cannot I think be denied. If, for instance, two different stories have been written, each of which is about a different imaginary tame tiger, it will follow that there are at least two imaginary tame tigers; and it cannot be denied that the sentence 'Two different tame tigers occur in fiction' is significant, though I have not the least idea whether it is true or false. I know that at least one unicorn occurs in fiction, because one occurs in *Alice Through the Looking Glass*; and it follows that there is at least one imaginary unicorn, and therefore (in a sense) at least one unicorn which does not exist. Again, if it should happen that at the present moment two different people are each having an hallucination of a different tame tiger, it will follow that there are at the present moment two different imaginary tame tigers; and the statement that two such hallucinations are occurring now is certainly significant, though it may very likely be false. The sentence 'There are some tame tigers which do not exist' is, therefore, certainly significant, if it means only that there are some imaginary tigers, in either of the two senses which I have tried to point out. But what it means is that either some real people have written stories about imaginary tigers, or are having or have recently had hallucinations of tame tigers, or, perhaps, are dreaming or have dreamed of particular tame tigers. If nothing of this sort has happened or is happening to anybody, then there are no imaginary tame tigers. But if 'Some tame tigers do not exist' means all this, is it not clear that 'exist' has not, in this sentence, the same comparatively simple meaning as it has in 'Some tame tigers exist' or in 'No tame tigers exist'? Is it not clear that 'Some tame tigers do not exist', if it means all this, is not related to 'Some tame tigers exist', in the same simple way in which 'Some tame tigers do not growl' is related to 'Some tame tigers growl'?

2. There is, I think, also another important difference between this use of 'exist' and the use of 'growl', which may be brought out as follows.

Mr. Russell has said[1] 'When we say "some men are Greeks," that means that the propositional function "x is a man and a Greek" is sometimes true'; and has explained just previously that by 'sometimes true' he means 'true in at least one instance'. With this explanation of what he means by 'sometimes true', I do not think that his statement as to the meaning of 'Some men are Greeks' is strictly correct; since I think that the use of the plural implies that 'x is a man and a Greek' is true in *more* than one instance, that is to say, in at least two instances. Let us suppose that he would accept this correction and say that what 'Some men are Greeks' means is not, strictly, that 'x is a man and a Greek' is true in at least one instance, but that it is true in at least two. He has further implied[2] that to say of a propositional function that it is true in at least two instances is the same thing as to say that at least two 'values' of it are true; and he has told us[3] that the 'values' of propositional functions are propositions. With these explanations, his view would appear to be that what 'Some men are Greeks' means is that at least two propositions, related to the propositional function 'x is a man and a Greek' in some way which he expresses by saying that they are

[1] *Introduction to Mathematical Philosophy*, p. 159.   [2] Ibid., p. 158.   [3] Ibid., p. 156.

'values' of that function, are true. Now I cannot imagine what sort of propositions would be 'values' of 'x is a man and a Greek', except propositions of the following sort. There are propositions which we express by pointing at (or indicating in some other way), an object which we are seeing (or perceiving in some other way) and uttering the words 'This is a so-and-so' (or equivalent words in some other language). Let us suppose that the kind of propositions which would be 'values' of 'x is a man and a Greek' would be propositions of this sort, where the words used were 'This is a man and a Greek'. Mr. Russell's doctrine would then be that 'Some men are Greeks' means that at least two different true propositions of this sort would be made: that there must have been at least two different objects at which a man might have pointed and said truly 'This is a man and a Greek'. And, if this is his doctrine, it seems to me to be true. Surely 'Some men are Greeks' cannot possibly be true, unless there are at least two different objects, in the case of each of which a man might have seen it, pointed at it, and said with truth 'This is a man and a Greek'?

On this view 'Some tame tigers growl' means that at least two values of 'x is a tame tiger and growls' are true; and this means that there are at least two objects, in the case of each of which a man might have seen it, pointed at it, and said with truth 'This is a tame tiger and growls'. Now in this sentence 'This is a tame tiger and growls' it is clear that, except for the difference consisting in the fact that 'growls' is in the singular and 'growl' in the plural, the word 'growls' has the same meaning as has the word 'growl' in 'Some tame tigers growl'. We can say, then, that one feature about our use of 'growl' is that, if we consider a 'value' of the propositional function which is such that 'Some tame tigers growl' means that at least two values of it are true, then the singular of 'growl' can be used, with the same meaning, in the expression of such a value. And perhaps this may be part of what is meant by saying that 'growl' 'stands for an attribute'. It may perhaps be meant that to point at an object which you are seeing, and utter the words 'This object growls', is significant – that the words and gesture together do really express a proposition, true or false.

But now consider 'Some tame tigers exist'; is the same true

of 'exist' in this sentence? Mr. Russell says:[1] 'We say that "men exist" or "a man exists" if the propositional function "x is human" is sometimes true'. And he goes on to protest that though the proposition 'Socrates is a man' is *equivalent* to 'Socrates is human', it 'is not the very same proposition'. For my part I doubt whether we ever do use 'is human' in such a way that 'Socrates is human' is equivalent to 'Socrates is a man'. I think Mr. Russell is using 'is human' in a very special sense, in which nobody but he has ever used it, and that the only way of explaining how he is using it is to say that he is using it to mean precisely that which we ordinarily express by 'is a human being'. If this is so, and if we are allowed to distinguish, as I think we ought, between 'men exist' and 'a man exists', and to say that 'men exist' means, *not* ' "x is a human being" is true in at least one instance', but ' "x is a human being" is true in at least two instances', then I think his doctrine is true; provided, again, that we are allowed to regard the sort of propositions which we express, e.g. by pointing at an object which we are seeing and saying the words 'This is a human being', as being those which are values of 'x is a human being'. Surely 'Human beings exist' can be true if, and only if, there are at least two objects, such that, if a man were to see and point to one of them and utter the words 'This is a human being', he would be expressing a true proposition by what he did?

Now, if this is right, we see at once that the use of 'growl' in 'Some tame tigers growl' differs from that of 'exist' in 'Some tame tigers exist', in the respect that, while the first asserts that more than one value of 'x is a tame tiger *and growls*' is true, the second asserts, *not* that more than one value of 'x is a tame tiger *and exists*' is true, but merely that more than one value of 'x is a tame tiger' is true. Owing to this view of his that 'Some tame tigers exist' means the same as 'Some values of the propositional function "x is a tame tiger" are true', Mr. Russell has been led to say[2] 'Existence is essentially a property of a propositional function' and[3] ('It is of propositional functions that you can assert or deny existence' and[4] that it is a fallacy to transfer 'to the

[1] *Introduction to Mathematical Philosophy*, pp. 171-2.
[2] *Monist*, April 1919, p. 195.
[3] Ibid. p. 196.   [4] Ibid p. 197.

individual that satisfies a propositional function a predicate which only applies to a propositional function'; so that, according to him, existence is, after all, in this usage, a 'property' or 'predicate', though not a property of individuals, but only of propositional functions! I think this is a mistake on his part. Even if it is true that 'Some tame tigers exist' means the same as 'Some values of "x is a tame tiger" are true' it does not follow, I think, that we can say that 'exist' means the same as 'is sometimes true', and 'some tame tigers' the same as 'x is a tame tiger': indeed, I think it is clear that we can not say this; for certainly ' "x is a tame tiger" exists' would not mean the same as 'Some tame tigers exist'. But what I think does follow from this interpretation of 'Some tame tigers exist' is another thing which Mr. Russell himself holds, namely, that if a proposition which you express by pointing at something which you see and saying 'This is a tame tiger', is a 'value' of 'x is a tame tiger', then if, pointing at the same thing, you were to say the words 'This exists', and, if you were using 'exists' merely as the singular of 'exist' in the sense in which it is used in 'Some tame tigers exist', what you did would not express a proposition at all, but would be absolutely meaningless. That is to say, there is between 'Some tame tigers growl' and 'Some tame tigers exist', not only the difference that, whereas the first asserts that some values of 'x is a tame tiger *and growls*' are true, the second asserts only that some values of 'x is a tame tiger' are true; there is also the further and more important difference that, why the second asserts only that some values of 'x is a tame tiger' are true, is not because we happen to use 'This is a tame tiger' to mean the same as 'This is a tame tiger *and exists*', but because by pointing and saying 'This *exists*' we should express *no proposition at all*, so long as we were using 'exists' as the singular of the use of 'exist' with which we are concerned, whereas by pointing and saying 'This growls' we certainly should be expressing a proposition, even though we were using 'growls' merely as the singular of 'growl' with the meaning it has in 'Some tame tigers growl'. 'This is a tame tiger, *and exists*' would be not tautologous, but meaningless.

This, I think, gives us a second true thing, which may perhaps be sometimes part of what is meant by saying that 'exist', in this usage, 'does not stand for an attribute'.

II

So far I have been solely concerned with the use of 'exist' in such sentences as 'Some tame tigers exist,' and have tried to point out two differences between its use here and the use of 'growl' in 'Some tame tigers growl', which may perhaps be part of what is meant by saying that 'exist,' in this usage, does not 'stand for an attribute', whereas 'growl' does. But I cannot help thinking that there are other significant uses of 'exists'; and I want in particular, to try to point out two such, and to consider what, if anything, true can be meant by saying that in these usages also 'exists' does not 'stand for an attribute'.

1. I have just said that to point at a thing which you see and say 'This exists' seems to me to be meaningless, if 'exists' is the singular of 'exist' in the sense in which it is used in 'Tame tigers exist'; but I cannot help thinking that in the case of anything to point at which and say 'This is a tame tiger' is significant, it is also significant to point at it and say 'This exists', *in some sense or other*. My reason for thinking this is that it seems to me that you can clearly say *with truth* of any such object 'This *might* not have existed', 'It is *logically possible* that this should not have existed'; and I do not see how it is possible that 'This might have existed' should be true, unless 'This does in fact exist' is true, and therefore also significant. The statement 'It is logically possible that this should not have existed' seems to *mean* 'The sentence "This does not exist" is significant'; and if 'This does not exist' is significant, 'This does exist' must be significant too. Now I cannot help thinking that in every case in which I point at an object which I am perceiving and say significantly 'This is a tame tiger', 'This is a book', my proposition is in fact a proposition about some sense-datum, or some set of sense-data, which I am perceiving; and that part of what I am saying is that this sense-datum (or these sense-data) is 'of' a physical object. That is to say, I am saying of some sense-datum that it is 'of' a physical object in the sense in which it is true to say of an after-image which I see with my eyes shut that it is *not* 'of' a physical object. And I think that part, at least, of what we mean by 'This exists', where we are using 'this' in the same way as when we point and say 'This is a book', is 'This sense-datum is *of* a physical object', which seems to me to be certainly significant. If 'of' here stood for a

relation, we might say that 'This is a book' was short for 'The thing which this sense-datum is "of" is a book', and therefore 'This exists' short for 'The thing which this sense-datum is "of" exists'; in which case the use of 'exists' in question would be that which in *Principia Mathematica* is symbolized by E!, and there would be the same sort of reason for saying that it does not 'stand for an attribute' as in the case of the 'exist' which occurs in 'Some tame tigers exist'. I do not believe, however, that 'of' here does stand for a relation, nor therefore that 'This' in 'This is a book' can be said to be short for the sort of phrase which Russell has called 'a definite description'; and, this being so, I am not at all clear as to what that is true could be meant by saying that 'exists', in this usage, 'does not stand for an attribute'. The only suggestion I can make is this. It seems to me that 'This exists' (in this usage) always forms part of what is asserted by 'This is a book', 'This is red', etc. etc., where 'this' is used in the manner with which we are now concerned; and possibly part of what is meant by saying that 'is a book', 'is red', etc., 'stand for attributes', is that *part but not the whole* of what is asserted by any 'value' of '*x* is a book', '*x* is red', etc., is 'This exists'. In that case 'exists' in 'This exists' would not 'stand for an attribute', solely because the whole of what it asserts, and not merely a part, is 'This exists'.

2. Another reason why 'This exists', where 'this' is used as it is in 'This is a book' seems to me to be significant, is because it seems to me not only significant to say of a given sense-datum 'This *is* of a physical object' or 'This is *not* of a physical object', but also to say of the sense-datum itself 'This exists'. If this is so, we have to do with a new sense of 'exists', since certainly no part of the meaning of such an assertion with regard to a sense-datum is that it, or any other sense-datum, is 'of' a physical object. But my reason for holding that it is significant for me to say, for instance, of an after-image which I am seeing with my eyes shut, 'This exists', is similar to that which I gave in the last case: namely that it seems to me that in the case of every sense-datum which anyone ever perceives, the person in question could always say with truth of the sense-datum in question 'This might not have existed'; and I cannot see how this could be true, unless 'This does in fact exist' is also true, and therefore significant. That 'this exists' has any meaning in such cases, where, as Mr.

Russell would say, we are using 'this' as a 'proper name' for something with which we are 'acquainted', is, I know, disputed; my view that it has, involves, I am bound to admit, the curious consequence that 'this exists', when used in this way, is always true, and 'this does not exist' always false; and I have little to say in its favour except that it seems to me so plainly true that, in the case of every sense-datum I have, it is logically possible that the sense-datum in question should not have existed – that there should simply have been no such thing. If, for instance, I am seeing a bright after-image with my eyes shut, it seems to me quite plainly conceivable that I should have had instead, at that moment, a uniform black field, such as I often have with my eyes shut; and, if I had had such a field, then that particular bright after-image simply would not have existed.

But, supposing 'This exists', in this usage, has a meaning, why should we not say that 'exists' here 'stands for an attribute'? I can suggest no reason why we should not, except the same which I suggested in the last case.

CHAPTER VI

'EVERY EVENT HAS A CAUSE'

By G. J. Warnock

I

THERE is obviously something strange about the sentence 'Every event has a cause'. It is natural enough that there should sometimes be disagreement over the question whether some statement is true or false. Less commonly, but still understandably, there occur disputes about what some sentences mean, or whether they really mean anything. But in this case the situation is more complicated. Some in saying that every event has a cause (or in using more or less sophisticated variants of this) have believed without question that they were making a true statement. Others have adduced from widely diverse fields considerations which lead them to say that it is false. But views quite different from either of these have been put forward. It has been held that the statement that every event has a cause is not merely true in fact, but *necessarily* true; also that, though perhaps it is not in the ordinary way necessarily true, it is yet in some special way *unquestionable*; and also, perhaps most paradoxically, that despite appearances it is neither a true statement nor a false one, neither necessary nor unquestionable – indeed not a statement at all, but a kind of maxim, or precept, or exhortation. All this seems to show that the sentence 'Every event has a cause' is not understood as clearly as could be wished; for if it were understood it should surely be possible to decide whether what it says is contingent or necessary; or at least whether one who utters it is making a statement, adopting or commending a maxim, issuing an exhortation or expressing a resolution. Or perhaps it would be found that he is doing none of these things.

II

Those who have argued the question whether it is true or false to say that every event has a cause were often, certainly, at cross purposes. The motive for maintaining that it was true was usually the belief that every event is an instance of some scientific law, or law of nature, and could thus in principle at least be causally explained. And the motive for maintaining the contrary was not primarily the belief that this was not the case, but rather the conviction that at least some happenings can be explained by reference to the intentions, choices, and decisions of intelligent and responsible beings, or 'agents'. The contention that some events have no causes was sponsored on the assumption that only if this were so could it really be held that some events occur *because* responsible beings choose or decide to act in certain ways. However, it is by no means a clearly correct assumption that explanation of an event in terms of an agent's decision must exclude the possibility of giving a causal explanation of it as well. In order to maintain that the occupant of the next room *decided* to turn on the lights it is not necessary, nor indeed is it possible, to deny that their lighting up was an ordinary instance of the laws of electricity. And to say that the golf-ball finished short of the green because the player wanted to keep out of the bunkers does not make it either incorrect or impossible to explain its flight in terms of the elasticity of ball and club-face, the velocity of impact, and the state of atmosphere and ground.

III

This particular dispute might be continued into many further complications; but it has sometimes been swept aside as wholly misguided and inappropriate. It is, it has been argued, quite mistaken to ask whether it is true or false that every event has a cause, or what would be the consequences of affirming or denying its truth; for the alleged statement in dispute is not really a statement at all, so that questions of truth and falsity do not arise. Kant for example (in criticizing certain metaphysical arguments about a First Cause) found difficulties both in the claim that the alleged statement was true, and also in the assertion that it was false; and accordingly suggested that it must be regarded as an *injunction* to extend the search for causes as far as possible, and to seek always to make more coherent and comprehensive our formulations of natural laws.[1] Earlier, however, he had himself

---

[1] *Critique of Pure Reason*, A498 (B526).

written as if the Law of Causation were a necessary truth; and indeed it does not seem at all to resemble what would ordinarily be thought of as maxims, injunctions, or rules. 'Do not rely on defective apparatus'; 'Do not draw general conclusions from a few observations made in unfavourable conditions'; or (cf. Darwin) 'Always pay special attention to instances apparently contradicting your hypotheses' — these for example would naturally be regarded as maxims for scientists, hints on how to succeed. To attempt to formulate coherent and comprehensive statements of law, on the other hand, seems to be rather what scientists actually do (almost, what scientists do *by definition*) than something which they should be enjoined or encouraged to do. To affirm the Law of Causation would be, on this view, to urge them to carry on with their activities, not to give them maxims or tips on how to succeed. And in any case, although one who says that every event has a cause would naturally be regarded as thereby *displaying* determination to carry on the search for laws, or perhaps as urging his audience not to give up, it is still the natural view to take that he is *stating* that, if he or they persist, success will be achieved. It at least looks as if he were urging the continued search for laws only by way of stating that there are in every field natural laws to be found. There is thus no case for adopting this Kantian view, unless the natural belief that we are dealing with some kind of statement turns out to be utterly untenable; and if it turns out to be untenable, the statement-like form 'Every event has a cause' must be abandoned as muddling.

IV

Some others who have held that it is out of place to argue about the truth or falsity of this alleged statement have, I think, had the idea that the Law of Causation is to the natural sciences what the laws of logic are to deductive disciplines. It is in this sense, I believe, that one must understand the contention that this Law is and must be 'presupposed' in all scientific investigation — that it must be accepted and cannot sensibly (or 'rationally') be questioned. It might be urged that, just as one cannot profitably engage in deductive argument without accepting rules specifying the difference between valid and invalid reasoning, so one

H

cannot engage in scientific inquiry without accepting the Law of Causation. Put thus, however, this contention looks obviously wrong. The proper analogy would be that between the laws of logic and the canons of inductive argument. The pursuit of scientific inquiry certainly requires pretty general agreement on the difference between good evidence and bad, between well-established conclusions and rash hypotheses, between properly conducted tests and random gropings. But the Law of Causation has not much to do with this. For one who wishes to reject this Law need not, it would seem, deny that the grounds offered in support of most scientific conclusions are adequate; he need only maintain that there are or very well might be some cases in which no similar conclusions can be reached. This is certainly to reject the common assumption that the canons of inductive argument must be regarded as worthless unless one also accepts the Law of Causation; but this assumption is surely mistaken. It amounts to suggesting that the canons of inductive argument essentially require the guarantee, or at least the presupposition, that their observance will in principle always ensure success; but they do not in fact require so much as this. One might well recognize that to pay assiduous attention to inductive evidence is the best thing that one can do in attempting to formulate statements of law, and yet not assume that there are no cases at all in which the best attempts would be utterly baffled. It is probably true that most people who use inductive arguments do assume, or perhaps half-unconsciously take for granted, that if they try hard enough they will succeed in their quest; but it is not by any means *necessary* that they should assume this. One might well continue to do the best that one could, with failure accepted as a constant lurking possibility; and certainly one might accept without any disquiet the idea that inquirers in other fields might always fail. H. W. B. Joseph's assertion[1] that to accept this idea is to 'despair of reason and thought' is dramatic, but an exaggeration. Failure and despair in some cases are compatible with optimism and success in others.

So far, then, we have noted that the sentence 'Every event has a cause' has (often for extraneous and dubious reasons) given rise to debates about whether, as a statement, it is true or false; that it has been held to express a sort of precept or injunction – a

---

[1] *Introduction to Logic*, p. 420.

paradoxical claim on which we suspended judgment; and that it has been held to be 'unquestionable' by rational persons who wish to use inductive arguments — a suggestion that we have rejected. I wish now to examine the suggestion with which I shall be mainly concerned — the suggestion, namely that the statement that every event has a cause is *synthetic a priori*, a *synthetic necessary truth*. I hope that in the assessment of this suggestion the main source, or sources, of the difficulty will be discovered.

V

The question of synthetic necessary truth has been for some time a storm-centre in philosophy. That there should be dis-agreement here is understandable; but it seems that this question engages the emotions also. This is, I think, because upon this issue philosophers of sharply different casts of mind, however they may agree on this point or that, find themselves strongly inclined to take opposite sides. It appears to matter enormously which side is taken, and as if, here at least, the line between two opposing camps were clearly drawn out. This however is, most strikingly, not the case. Those who aver that there are synthetic necessary truths are apt to put forward the baffling contention that by some sort of insight, or intellectual gazing, we can see that some truths of fact are necessary truths; while those who contend that no synthetic truths are necessary maintain the hardly less cloudy doctrine that truths of fact can only be based on, and so might at any time be or might have been falsified by, Experience. These are large issues, and they excite strong feelings; but we must not at once range ourselves with one party or the other. Nothing but confusion can result (as it has often resulted) from considering this topic in wholly general terms, or from assuming that, whenever a claim to synthetic necessary truth is made or denied, some simple and single question is presented for decision.

To the sorts of statements which are most comfortably called synthetic it is natural also to apply such predicates as 'contingent', 'factual', 'empirical', or '*a posteriori*'; and we expect the contra-dictories of these to be of exactly the same logical character. To expressions naturally regarded as analytic we are apt to attach also such predicates as 'logically necessary', 'true by definition', and '*a priori*'; and here we expect the contradictories to be logically impossible, self-contradictory. We would hesitate to say that a statement was quite ordinarily synthetic unless it appeared also to rank as contingent, factual, and empirical; we feel uneasy in labelling an expression 'analytic' unless we can show that it is somehow necessary, true by definition; and we expect the normal behaviour of contradictories. Thus, if one refuses to submit to this dichotomy and seeks to bridge it by the phrase 'synthetic *a priori*', one's refusal may be due to a variety of discomforts. Perhaps the statement that it is proposed to call synthetic *a priori* is, though not analytic, not contingent either; perhaps it appears to be empirical but not *a posteriori*; it may seem to be necessary but not true by definition, or logically necessary and factual at the same time. The notions involved in all this are numerous, related no doubt, but nevertheless diverse. There is accordingly scope for a good many difficulties in the customary attempt to divide all significant indicative sentences into two classes; there is no good reason to suppose that in all cases we can effect a single, orderly, exhaustive, and satisfying classification; and so there are correspondingly numerous and various reasons for clutching at some such straw as 'synthetic *a priori*'. Or perhaps it resembles a smoke-screen rather than a straw; the phrase is nobody's salvation, but it serves to cloak many a tangle behind the lines.

In this case we shall consider the claim made for the sentence 'Every event has a cause', without insisting that what is said of this case has necessarily any application to other cases, and allowing that other sentences for which this claim is made may well require a very different treatment.

VI

First we must try to make clear what is or might be involved in the claim that the Law of Causation is a synthetic *a priori* truth. For saying that it is synthetic there seem to be two (related) reasons. First, the sentence 'Every event has a cause' cannot plausibly be represented as analytic; it is not like 'Every bicycle has two wheels'. For whereas, in giving the meaning of the word 'bicycle' it would be necessary to make it clear that a bicycle has two wheels, it does not seem that, in defining the word 'event', it would be correct or necessary to stipulate that every event has a cause. There is no definition of 'event' by the help of which 'Every event has a cause' can be transformed into a manifest tautology. Conversely, the sentence 'Some events have no causes' is not self-contradictory. H. A. Pritchard, indeed, claimed that to realize the truth of the Law of Causation we need only consider what we mean by 'a physical event';[1] but this is for several reasons peculiar. His claim was intended, but even if correct would fail, to support the idea that this Law is synthetic *a priori*; it does not in any case seem to be true that 'having a cause' is part of what is *meant* by 'a physical event'; and there seems to be no good reason why the events of which the Law says that every one has a cause should be only *physical* events. However, the point at present is only this — that it seems impossible to hold that 'Every event has a cause' is analytic, tautologous, true by definition; and this inclines us to conclude that it must be synthetic. For if it is not analytic what else could it be?

A second reason for inclining to this conclusion is that the Law of Causation appears to make a statement, and indeed a fundamentally important statement, about the course of nature — about what actually occurs in the universe we inhabit. It does not appear merely to illustrate, or to analyse, what we mean by the word 'event', but rather to say something of enormous importance about the way things actually are. Is it not a fundamental fact about the universe that we find in it the Rule of Law?

Such, then, are the main considerations that may lead us to say that the Law of Causation is a synthetic statement. Some would say that, if we allow these considerations to have weight, we thereby make it impossible to hold that the Law is also *a priori*; for it is sometimes argued that the expression '*a priori*' can only mean the very same as 'analytic', and hence that the expression 'synthetic *a priori*' is self-contradictory. This contention, however, is not acceptable. There may be reasons, even if not good reasons, for saying that some statements are synthetic *a priori*, and it is unhelpful, whatever suspicions we may have, to dismiss this suggestion at the outset as logically absurd; but also it is by no means obvious that 'analytic' and '*a priori*' do mean the same. Neither term is in fact quite unambiguous, but the first seems to

[1] *Kant's Theory of Knowledge*, p. 300.

be somewhat narrower than the second. Certainly, if we define
the term 'analytic' so that only those sentences are rightly so
called which can, with the help of definitions, be transformed
into formal tautologies, it will be an error to hold that only
analytic sentences are *a priori*. For there are sentences (e.g.
'Nothing can be red and green all over') which it would be
natural and proper to regard as *a priori* – anyone who knows
English knows that they are necessarily true – but which cannot
be shown to be tautologous by the use of *definitions*. In a sense,
certainly, they owe their necessary truth to linguistic rules; but
the rules governing the use of 'red' and 'green' cannot be expressed
as definitions. But quite apart from such cases as these, there are
reasons for holding that 'analytic' and '*a priori*' do not mean the
same. For to say of a statement that it is true *a priori* is to say
that it can be seen or shown to be true without appeal to empirical
evidence or tests; and though it might be that this could rightly be
said only of expressions that are in fact analytic, still to say this
would not be to say the very same thing as is said when we say
that those expressions are analytic. I suggest, then, that those who
say that the Law of Causation is, as well as a synthetic, an *a priori*
truth, may be taken to mean that what it states about the course of
nature can be seen to be true without appeal to empirical evidence;
or perhaps (though this as will be seen is a very different matter)
that we can see that no empirical evidence against it could be
found. There is no denying that this is a curious claim. If the
Law really tells us something about the course of nature, surely
we must find out whether or not it is true by discovering what
the course of nature actually is; and surely there must be something that could count against it – namely nature's not pursuing
the course that the Law says that nature does in fact pursue.
Certainly the claim is strange; but it is worth examining.

In what follows I shall try to show that, although there are
considerations that might incline us to say that the Law of
Causation is true *a priori*, these considerations in fact cancel completely the reasons that there seemed to be for saying that the
Law was a synthetic statement. This is not to say that the expression 'synthetic *a priori*' is in general and in every case self-contradictory (though I think it is always unhelpful); it is only to say
that, in the present instance, the case for applying the predicate

'synthetic' is destroyed by the case for applying the predicate 'a priori'; there may be a case for each, but not for both at once.

VII

As a preliminary move it will be desirable to re-phrase the sentence 'Every event has a cause'. For this sentence has many rather misleading features, some of which (by no means all) it will be helpful here to eliminate. It is in particular, as has often been pointed out, misleading to suggest that for any event there is some *one* other event to be described, and alone described, as its cause. Suppose, for example, that I cause my house to collapse by improvidently removing an oak beam from the cellar. Although we should no doubt ordinarily say that it collapsed *because* I thus interfered with its structure, it is obvious enough that it would not have collapsed unless the whole house was actually so constructed as to depend for its stability upon this beam. It was thus not merely my removal of the beam which occasioned its collapse, but this removal combined with the other structural features of the house. A full account of the disaster would have to include an account of these other features, as well as the statement that the beam was removed — just as a full report on an outbreak of fire would have to include an account of the inflammable materials in the area and perhaps of the conditions of atmosphere, as well as the statement that a cigarette was dropped into a waste-paper basket. The event in question (the collapse, the outbreak of fire) occurred because certain quite complex conditions were present; from these we might, as we often do, pick out as *the* cause that which was brought about immediately before the event occurred, or (sometimes) that which was unusual. (It might be said that my house collapsed *when* I removed the beam *because* I had taken to storing several tons of books in the attic.) But not uncommonly it is pointless or impossible to pick out any one occurrence as *the* cause of an event — not because the event is random or inexplicable or mysterious, but because there is no case for stressing any one in particular of the numerous conditions sufficient for its occurrence. What is important is that there should *be* conditions sufficient for its occurrence, not that it should be always possible to select some one of these as the single cause; and the statement that every event has a cause does not, presumably, claim that this is always possible. (If it did so it would be clearly synthetic, and false.)

Suppose, then, that we re-write the sentence 'Every event has a cause' in some such way as this: 'For any event E, there is some set of antecedent conditions such that, whenever these conditions obtain, an event of the kind E occurs.' (I refer to this hereafter as S.)

This is still a comparatively unsophisticated formula, and it might be criticized on various grounds which, however, are here of no great importance. Some might say that it fails to distinguish between causal and co-incidental connections – might it not happen, by sheer coincidence, that whenever certain conditions obtain a certain kind of event occurs? This version allows also the possibility that more than one set of conditions may be sufficient for the occurrence of some kinds of events, and it might be held that ideally this should be ruled out. It might also be said that, at least in some of the sciences, there is no reason for being specially interested in antecedent conditions; what we require are statements of law permitting inference from any state of a given system at any time to its state at any other time, with no special bias towards prediction or interest in the future. It might be held, too, that the vague word 'event' should be eliminated as ill-suited to scientific exactitude. All these are reasonable points in their way; but I think there is at present no reason why we should seek to translate 'Every event has a cause' into a form and vocabulary acceptable to scientists; for in the present argument nothing turns on this. The version adopted above will serve well enough, though I certainly would not deny that it might be improved upon.

VIII

Suppose one were to ask how the alleged statement S is to be verified; this at once brings out one curious feature of it. First, it is in a comparatively ordinary way of unrestricted generality. It appears to make a statement about any and every event that ever occurred, occurs, or will occur. It might thus be thought that, while we have no doubt some reason for inclining to the view that S is true, we could not possibly have good reason for affirming positively that it is true. How could we rightly venture to make positive assertions about absolutely every event? But then there is worse still to come. For it will be seen that S also makes a statement of unrestricted generality about each of an unrestricted number of events — namely that for each event there are conditions such that, whenever they obtain, an event of that kind occurs. It would thus seem that causal statements really are, as all empirical statements were once supposed to be, indefinitely vulnerable to time. If we say that conditions ABC are sufficient for the occurrence of an event E (or that A, or B, or C, is the cause of E), what we say now will have to be retracted if at any time these conditions obtain and E does not occur. We can say 'There really was a telephone here, but now it's vanished'; we cannot say 'This was the cause of E, but now it isn't'. For to say that conditions ABC may now obtain and event E not occur is to admit that we were wrong in saying earlier that ABC were its sufficient conditions. It would thus appear that even particular causal statements are indefinitely exposed to falsification; far more so then the doubly general assertion that of every event some such statement could be truly made. By this line of argument we might be led to the view that it would be unpardonably rash, almost a mere act of faith, to affirm S with confidence; one can understand why this affirmation is made, but one cannot feel much confidence in its truth.

IX

But now there is quite another side to the case. Suppose that there are indefinitely many cats, and that someone says (of all cats there ever were, are, or will be) that every cat has a tail. Here we might say that there could hardly be good reason for accepting this statement with confidence as true — after all we can only actually inspect a finite and rather small number of cats. Furthermore, we have no difficulty in saying what would show this universal statement to be false — namely the discovery of a cat without a tail — and such a discovery might be made at any time. Now it was suggested in the previous paragraph that S, being of doubly unrestricted generality, is doubly and indefinitely exposed to the risk of falsification. Suppose then that we now raise the question what would have to occur in order to establish that S is false?

A verbal answer — 'an uncaused event' — of course springs to mind. But this answer raises obvious difficulties. It is easy enough to imagine an event E, conditions sufficient for the occurrence of which have always been supposed to be ABC; and that some day these conditions may obtain and yet the event E does not occur. But clearly this has no tendency to falsify S. For it was said in S only that there are *some* conditions sufficient for the occurrence of any event; it was not specified what these conditions actually are in any instance, nor was it implied that anyone necessarily knows in any instance what conditions are sufficient. To say that there are some laws of nature does not imply that anyone knows, or indeed ever will know, what exactly they are. And thus the affirmation of S is compatible with the rejection of every particular statement of law, and every causal statement, that is or ever has been or will be asserted. If I say 'Someone now in this house has green hair', it can be shown that what I say is untrue; for everyone now in this house can be paraded and none observed to have green hair. But if I say 'There once was or is or will be, somewhere in the universe, a person who has green hair', I need never admit that I am wrong. For it could never be said that every part of the universe at every possible date had been inspected and found to contain no green-haired person. Similarly, if I were to say 'Some set of the conditions ABCDF is sufficient for the occurrence of E', it could be shown that I am mistaken. For all of the finite number of combinations could be tried and none found to be sufficient for the occurrence of E. But if I merely affirm that there are *some* conditions, and do not delimit the area of search for them at all, I need never admit that I am mistaken. For it could never be said that every conceivable factor and set of factors that might be conditions of E had been tried and rejected; and so it could always be said that the right combination of conditions had not yet been found.

Thus, there could never occur any event which it would be necessary, or even natural, to describe as an uncaused event. (There are of course events whose causes are not known.) It could never be said that among its complex and indefinitely numerous antecedents *none* could be said to be sufficient for its occurrence. And this is to say that nothing could occur which would require us to hold that S is false. Whatever occurred we might still affirm that S.

It is in this way that S resembles a tautology, an *a priori* truth. It is completely independent of the actual course of events, compatible with anything and everything that does or might happen. It calls indeed for no supporting empirical evidence, for none could count against it. It cannot be empirically tested, for no test could fail — or rather nothing could be made to count as a test. But, clearly enough, if these points were brought to support the contention that S is *a priori*, they would tell conclusively against the claim that it is synthetic. For if S can be affirmed whatever may be the course of events, it says nothing of what the course of events in fact is. It does not tell us what we shall find in our experience, for whatever we find we may assert it without fear of mistake. This is not to say, what I think is plainly untrue, that S is tautologous or analytic. It resembles a tautology in being compatible with any and every state of affairs; but it escapes the possibility of falsification not because it is necessary, but rather because it is vacuous. It is more like the assertion that there are invisible, intangible, odourless, soundless, and otherwise indetectable tigers in the garden — though it is less conspicuously vacuous than this, the reasons for its unfalsifiability being different and much less obvious.

x

All this, I think, shows that there must be something wrong with, for example, the sort of argument that Kant brings in favour of the view that S (or something like S) is a synthetic *a priori* truth.[1] Very roughly, the argument is that S lays down what is almost a defining property of human experience — unless it were the case that every event has a cause, our experience would be so unimaginably different that we could not think or speak about it in any way, there would merely be chaos and confusion. Thus, it might be contended, the fact that we can *say* that every

[1] *Critique of Pure Reason*, Second Analogy.

event has a cause, and be understood, itself shows that what we say is actually the case; for if it were not, neither this nor anything else could intelligibly be said. This sort of argument is, I believe, an exaggeration of something interesting and important. It is true that if there were *too many* random, inexplicable, quite unforeseeable happenings, we should find ourselves not merely in practical but also in linguistic difficulties. If, for example, it were the case that objects frequently changed colour in a seemingly quite random manner, we could no longer say what colour things really were, but only what colour they looked at some particular time; and this would be a nuisance, particularly in cases where colour is a criterion of identity. (There would then be no Cabbage Whites or Scarlet Ramblers.) And we could not say with confidence 'This is an apple' unless we could be sure that the object of which we spoke would behave and respond to treatment as apples do. What this shows, however, is that we could not speak and act as we do if there were *too much* disorder and chaos in our environment; it does not show that we could not tolerate any at all. Nor, of course, does it show that it must be *true* that every event has a cause; for, as we have seen, to affirm that S is compatible with any sort of happenings whatever. We would presumably be unable to speak and act as we now do if, though there were in fact conditions sufficient for the occurrence of any event, these conditions were too complex or too numerous for us to discover them. A world whose behaviour could only be rightly described in statements of law too complicated for us to formulate or comprehend would be, for our purposes, every bit as intractable as a world whose behaviour was merely random and chaotic — it would in fact be indistinguishable from such a world. There are, no doubt, some statements of fact about the world which would only be falsified by some radical change in the whole character of our experience; and it may be that some of these statements state conditions essential to the use of language (or at least to the use of any languages now used). If so, there will indeed be certain statements which, if they can be uttered at all, are thereby verified; for if their contradictories were true they could not be said. But the supposed statement that every event has a cause cannot rightly be regarded as a statement of this kind. It lays down no essential conditions; for it lays down nothing.

XI

The suggestion that the expression 'Every event has a cause' is— owing to the impossibility of describing any circumstance that could show it to be false—vacuous and utterly uninformative, may well cause some dissatisfaction. There is a natural feeling that it does say something, and furthermore something of the greatest importance. However, this feeling arises, I believe, from confusion. There are indeed certain matters of importance that abut, so to speak, on the territory of the Law of Causation; but these important matters are its neighbours, not identical with it, nor yet are they its dependants. And thus they need neither be ignored nor rejected when the Law itself is accused of vacuousness.

It is, first of all, a patently important fact that there are many people nowadays who do seek for statements of law, who do not attempt to understand, control, or alter the course of events entirely by prayers or spells or ritual performances, and who do not merely wait indifferently for what may occur. This is an important, synthetic and true statement about what many people actually do. If they did not do this or did not do it with conviction, we might properly (not by saying 'Every event has a cause') urge or encourage them to persist in their inquiries. It is a different but equally important synthetic true statement that those who seek to formulate statements of law meet with considerable, and on the whole with constantly increasing, success. (Human beings might have been much less intelligent, and the course of events might have been much more complicated.) But to say that for every event there are some conditions sufficient for its occurrence is clearly not to say that people often succeed in discovering them, nor is it to say that none will constantly elude discovery; to say that every crime is committed by somebody is not to say that no criminals go undetected nor to say that the record of the police force is good. Again, to say that correct statements of law are 'simple' is clearly to say something synthetic; and as the physicists multiply 'fundamental particles' it may well cease to be regarded as true. (A single sort of 'corpuscle' or 'atom' is not, of course, nowadays thought to be enough for all purposes). It is also synthetic to say of natural laws that they are spatially and temporally invariant; and this also, I believe, is no longer universally taken to be the case. And that the sufficient conditions for any event are to be found within a certain limited area of space and among some quite small number of possibilities, though usually and no doubt reasonably assumed, is also clearly not necessarily true.

These, then, are some of the important matters which belong in the same area as the Law of Causation; and there are no doubt others. I believe that those who attach fundamental importance to the so-called Rule of Law often have in mind some of these, and do not mean merely to utter the vacuous phrase that 'every event has a cause'. Or rather they do not think of this phrase as vacuous. It suggests that the universe is like a well-ordered house where everything runs exactly to plan and up to time; there is nothing just random and therefore unintelligible; what seems inexplicable will one day be explained. Certainly there is, as a rule, an important disagreement between one who says, and one who denies, that every event has a cause; they *intend* at any rate, to state different things. But what they actually *say* cannot be plausibly represented as stating any of the important facts mentioned in the last paragraph; and confusion is apt to result from not noticing this. For whereas these facts are indeed important and interesting, they are not necessary facts; and if we confuse them with the vacuous Law of Causation, we may come to attach to them, with resulting bewilderment, the property of being invulnerable to falsification which properly attaches alone to that vacuous Law.

XII

In conclusion, and with some trepidation, I must say something of the 'indeterminacy principle'; for it has often been said that, here at any rate, we find something that counts against the Law of Causation. It is extremely difficult for those who are not physicists to come to grips with this perplexing affair; and physicists often seem to feel a similar difficulty. The suggestion that I would offer is merely this — that although certain features of quantum physics might make it even more than usually *pointless* to insist that every event has a cause, they could not establish that this is actually a false statement. To support this I submit the following considerations. It may be that, given certain conditions, it is sometimes impossible for us actually to predict what will occur; and this may be a theoretical and not a merely practical difficulty. It may be (and this is really the same point again) that the determination of a certain quantity theoretically precludes us from determining another; and perhaps in this case we should even refuse to speak of both quantities as being determinate – what point is there in this if we cannot discover both? However, this is not to say that, given certain conditions, sometimes one thing and sometimes another occurs; it is only to say that we cannot discover whether or not this is so nor what will occur; and hence perhaps we refuse to regard the question as a proper one. But one who says that for any event at all there are some conditions sufficient for its occurrence, need not assert, as we have already seen, that anyone does or could know what these conditions are; and he need not hold that every event is in fact, or even in theory, predictable. Perhaps then he is, though doubtless rightly ignored, not flatly refuted by the contemporary physicist. If he is prepared to speak of what admittedly cannot be experimentally tested, he may remain invulnerable. I need hardly say that no great value attaches to this type of invulnerability; but I would suggest that the Law of Causation is vacuous enough to elude the attack even of this unusual and well-armed opponent. It escapes, indeed, by way of saying something that cannot in any way be tested; but it says no more than this in any case, and thus only exhibits in this unfamiliar field the same peculiarity on which it trades elsewhere. To say that the Law can be refuted *here* is to imply that elsewhere it might have been but is not; I have tried to show, however, that nowhere at all does it run the risk of refutation.

CHAPTER VII

INCOMPATIBILITIES OF COLOURS

By D. F. Pears

THE sentence 'Nothing can be red and green all over' expresses a very striking incompatibility. Few would deny that it is necessarily true or *a priori*. For if it were contingent or *a posteriori* one could look for exceptions. But anyone who began to look for exceptions would betray that he did not really understand the sentence. But why is it necessarily true? Some say that the reason is that it is analytic, claiming that all necessary truths are analytic. And since an analytic sentence is either a truth of logic or else reducible to a truth of logic by means of a definition, this is a fairly clear explanation. Others say that the reason is that it is a synthetic necessary truth, refusing to allow that all necessary truths are analytic. The positive meaning of this is sometimes taken to be that the sentence states a principle of natural necessity; which is obscure. Negatively it is always taken to mean at least that the sentence is necessarily true and yet not analytic; which, being the denial of a fairly clear thesis, is less obscure.

But perhaps the sentence is neither analytic nor synthetic. This suggestion has much to recommend it. It is diplomatic, and it avoids both the obscurity of principles of natural necessity and the implausibility of alleged definitions of 'red' or 'green'.[1] Another of its advantages is that it commends itself to common sense. For there is something very academic about the fierce debate whether the sentence owes its necessary truth to the way things behave or to the way words behave, to nature or to convention. It would seem more sensible to say that neither of these two answers is quite adequate; rather that the sentence is necessarily true because the words 'red' and 'green' pick out two classes which just do not overlap. One could say that this lack

[1] Few words are given full definitions in dictionaries, but 'red' and 'green' could not be, since they are words which are necessarily taught almost entirely by examples.

of overlap is the result of the way in which the two words are used: but since the two words pick out two classes of things, one could say equally well that it is the result of the nature of the things. Each of these two answers emphasizes one aspect of the truth. But perhaps emphasis on either side is a mistake; perhaps the culprit is neither convention alone nor nature alone.

This suggestion, however correct, is not adequate as it stands. It would not satisfy everyone who was puzzled by the problem. Some, after considering it, would re-open the question by pro-testing: 'But if it is neither analytic nor synthetic what is it? If nature and convention conspire to produce this necessary truth, then it ought to be both synthetic and analytic. But that is nonsense.' To answer this, more is needed.

What is needed as a supplement might be an account of the way we use, and learn to use, colour words. But there are grounds for thinking that a more technical approach to the problem is advisable. After all, the problem emerged because a useful tech-nique was over-worked. Accordingly this discussion may well begin almost historically, taking over the technique, and making it its first task to explain the necessary truth of the sentence, if possible, within the traditional framework, without falling back on the obscure thesis that a principle of natural necessity is involved.

Since no definition of 'red' exists the first thing to do is to try to invent one; or rather to invent a fragment of one, to the effect that 'red' means among other things 'not green'. Next the situa-tion can be exhibited schematically. One might say that the word 'red' is connected with red things by a designatory rule; and that the word 'green' is connected with green things by another, parallel designatory rule. This can be illustrated by a simple diagram of four dots arranged in a square, the two top corners being occupied by the two words, and the two lower corners being occupied by the two groups of things. Then the two vertical sides can be sketched in immediately to represent the two designatory rules. And the problem becomes: which of the two horizontal sides should be sketched in? Those who say that the sentence is analytic would sketch in the top side with a verbal rule to the effect that 'red' means among other things 'not green': while those who say that it is a synthetic necessary truth usually wish to sketch in the lower side with a principle of natural necessity.

Now there is a well-known, simple treatment which is sometimes successful with such recalcitrant sentences. For instance an entomologist who said that all Large White butterflies have two black patches on each forewing might be asked whether his statement was analytic or synthetic. Perhaps he would be unable to answer until he was told that any given use of the sentence could not be both, and which it was would depend on how the species was defined. Then he might be unwilling to answer, on the ground that he did not need to decide whether this was a defining characteristic of the species or not. If specimens with three black patches began to occur, he might say at first that they were a variety or aberration. Only if they bred true would he be likely to claim the discovery of a new species. But even about this he would prefer not to commit himself in advance. Meanwhile his answer would be that the sentence was certainly not both analytic and synthetic at once, and which it was did not matter for the moment. And this would be a perfectly satisfactory answer. One would understand the two alternatives, and also the reason for leaving the choice between them open.

But unfortunately this simple treatment will not work here. For it is not merely that 'not green' is not part of an existing definition of 'red'. Nor is it merely that one does not want to decide in advance whether or not to accept it as part of a newly invented definition. The trouble is that one does not understand what difference its acceptance would make. And since one does not understand this, one is not confronted with a genuine choice. And this is a serious difficulty. For those who say that the sentence is analytic claim that it owes its necessary truth to a verbal rule. But the suggested verbal rule seems to make no difference since, without it, the sentence already seems to be necessarily true. And it seems that this can only be because the lower side of the square is already occupied by a principle of natural necessity.

It is worth emphasizing that the failure of the simple treatment is not the result of a wildly implausible appeal to conventions. Those who say that the sentence is analytic do not suggest that it owes its necessary truth to a verbal rule which is conventional in the trivial sense in which 'yellow' might mean what 'red' now means if we adopted this different convention. For it could not matter what word was written in at the top left-hand corner, since one word at the top left-hand corner would have the same meaning as another substituted for it there, and the point at issue is how any word at the top left-hand corner gets its meaning. What they suggest is, at most, that if the sentence rested merely on the two designatory rules it would be contingent: but that in that case it would be such an excellent contingent sentence, never in fact falsified, that we might as well make it analytic by adding the verbal rule; and that this verbal rule, though conventional, would be well chosen, not all conventions being capricious.

The reason for the failure of the simple treatment is that the convention is so well chosen that it seems to make no difference at all. And the explanation of this seems to be that the lower side of the square is already occupied by a principle of natural necessity.

However, there is a possible alternative explanation. Perhaps the two designatory rules are alone sufficient to ensure the necessary truth of the sentence, so that there is no need to sketch in either the top or the lower side of the square. This solution is a fuller development of the one suggested at the beginning. If it is correct, it is a mistake to suggest that the sentence would be contingent unless either a verbal rule or a principle of natural necessity were added. The sentence will owe its necessary truth simply to the two designatory rules.

The way in which this comes about is hard to describe. Certainly it would be a mistake to describe it by saying that the sentence is analytic, since no non-ostensive definition is involved. So, if all other sentences were synthetic, it would follow that this one is synthetic: and, since it is necessary, it would be a synthetic necessary truth. But it is unwise to say this: partly because many have meant something more by it, namely that there is here a principle of natural necessity; and partly because synthetic sentences are usually taken not to include any which are true solely because of the meanings of their words. And this sentence is true solely because of the meanings of its words, and so necessarily true. For anyone who contradicted it would betray, without any possibility of an alternative plea, that he did not know the meanings of its words. But this does not imply that an alteration in language would bring about an alteration in things or that the total extinction of all speakers of all languages would effect the abolition of the differences between things. That would be an absurd error.

With equal correctness one might say that it is necessarily true because the two classes of things necessarily differ. For this description of the situation is precisely equivalent to the other. But those who adopt it must beware of a danger. It is fatally easy to talk carelessly about things in a way which suggests that they stand out there already labelled in a way which indicates their properties. And this illusion may be a source of the probably mistaken view that there is here a principle of natural necessity.[1] Of course things are what they are, and differ from one another because they possess the properties which they do possess. But to say that two classes of things necessarily differ is not only to SAY something, but also to DO something. The two classes of things can be said to differ necessarily only because they have been picked out, in the saying, by two words according to designatory rules which ensure just that. One refers airily to THE two classes, as if one could say WHICH two classes without using the words.

This crucial point is the tautology that we cannot name a class without naming it. But it is none the worse for being a tautology. It needs stating because its importance is so easily forgotten. Both geologists and philosophers can describe the world with no people in it. But geologists, who are interested only in the things in such a world, need not ask themselves how their describing was done: whereas philosophers do ask themselves just this question, and so cannot keep themselves out of their inquiry. This difference is easily overlooked, and the tautology keeps it in view.

The tautology can be generalized so as to apply not only to naming but also to thinking. One cannot think about a class without thinking about it. And if, for instance, such thinking needs a concept, then the concept will pick out the class in much the same way that the name picked it out. And the same can be said of images, and of any other suggested instrument of thought. The point is not restricted to language, but quite general.

---

[1] It would not be a mistaken view if it merely saw as real the same necessity which can be seen as verbal at least equally well, and if even such analytic sentences as 'A flower cannot be a butterfly' were included among the principles of natural necessity. And why not? It is things that we sort, even when we can explain how we sort them. But this extended use of the phrase would rob it of whatever point it is intended to convey.

It is particularly important here, because one cannot say any-thing very informative about the meanings of 'red' and 'green', but can only offer examples. But when a man shows the meaning of such a word by examples, what are the examples examples of? All one can answer is that they are examples of that feature in them in virtue of which the word is applied to them. This may sound as if it said something further; but it does not, since it is circular. Now the two words 'red' and 'green' pick out two classes of things which necessarily differ. How do they necessarily differ? One can only offer pairs of examples. But what are the pairs of examples examples of? All one can say is that they are examples of that difference between them in virtue of which the two words are applied to them. This is circular in the same way. But those who do not clearly realize that it is circular slip easily into think-ing that they have found an additional necessary difference over and above the necessary difference which is the result of the way in which the two words pick out the pairs of things. And this would be an illusion, the illusion of taking the same necessary difference twice over, once in the words and once in the things, and thinking that there were really two necessary differences. And perhaps this illusion is a source of the claim to have found a principle of natural necessity.

So long as all these errors are avoided by both sides, it does not matter which description of the situation is adopted, that which talks about words or that which talks about things. Then is the suggested solution, these errors having been removed, acceptable as it now stands?

One thing which recommends it is that it explains the emer-gence of the problem and its protracted discussion (which may stand in need of explanation in the future). For initial success in showing that many necessary truths are analytic naturally encouraged the hope that this might be done for all necessary truths. Consequently, when recalcitrant necessary truths like this one were encountered, it was felt that further analysis would discover some elusive verbal rule more convincing than the one already produced, which would show that the sentence was after all analytic. But since 'red' and 'green' are not further analysable, the discovery was not likely to be made. Yet such was the prestige of the technique that some persisted in the hopeless quest, while others announced their refusal to accept anything which might be found. And all the time it was the technique which was at fault. Either it ought to have been admitted that some necessary truths, resting on unexpandible designatory rules, are not analytic. Or else the use of ostensive definitions ought to have been allowed in the reduction of analytic sentences to truths of logic, so that these outlying cases could be taken in. (But, though the spirit of this second alternative can be understood, literally it is unintelligible, since qualities cannot appear in logic books instead of adjectives, any more than railway journeys can be stacked in automatic machines instead of tickets.)

However, the suggested solution is not acceptable as it stands. For it is inadequate in ways which there is not space to correct fully.

First of all there is something specially mysterious about this necessary truth which rests on designatory rules which cannot be expanded verbally. This can be illustrated by a series of examples arranged progressively.

About designatory rules which can be expanded verbally there is no mystery. The entomologist can name Large White butterflies, and in doing so follows a designatory rule. But he can also expand this designatory rule by stating their defining characteristics in verbal rules. And, as in the case already considered, by adopting new verbal rules he can alter the original designatory rule.

Nor is there much mystery about designatory rules which can be expanded only in a language of signs. For imagine some primitive hunter who slew mammoths of two closely resembling species and correctly sorted them into two heaps. Suppose that he had names for the two species, but not for their *differentiae*. Then he could teach an apprentice the difference between the two species only by producing pairs of examples. Would what the hunter acquired and handed on to his apprentice be for them a synthetic necessary truth? There is a slight inducement to give an affirmative answer, because, unlike the entomologist, they could not expand their designatory rules verbally. But the inducement is very slight, since if they noticed the *differentiae* they could do something almost as good. The teacher could point to the *differentia* in a specimen of one kind, then name the other species, and then shake his head and grind his teeth. And this would be almost as effective as stating the incompatibility of the possession of a certain property with membership of a certain class. The problem under discussion is not narrowly linguistic: it concerns any symbol or instrument of thought which can be made to stand for any class of things.

But now take a case where there is some mystery. A man sips two kinds of port and notices a difference between the two flavours. He may learn names for them, and assent to the proposition that they cannot both be present in the same sip, and yet he may be unable to expand his two designatory rules verbally. And this might not be the result merely of a deficient vocabulary. For there might not be anything separately noticeable in each flavour which made it the flavour that it was. Would the proposition to which he assented be for him a synthetic necessary truth? An affirmative answer is more likely here, since these two designatory rules are quite unexpandible.

Finally the necessary truth about the two colours, red and green, is even more mysterious. The colours, like the flavours, contain no separately noticeable marks. But this simplicity is more unexpected in the case of the colours, and so more baffling. It is more unexpected because sight is a successful, organizing sense, and most words for seen qualities find their places in elaborate logical networks. Also colours, unlike flavours, can be pointed to, and one is surprised by the discovery that there is a limit beyond which pointing cannot select from within a quality further separate marks of that quality. Also sight is so sharp that colours are as finely apprehended as objects, almost as if they too were independent objects:[1] and one feels that objects ought to carry separately noticeable marks. But, whatever explanations of this mysteriousness are produced, will they not all serve only to remove a strong prejudice against the view that this necessary truth rests squarely on two unexpandible designatory rules, and so leave us free to say that the two classes are different because that is how we pick them?[2]

---

[1] Not physically independent as flavours and smells are physically independent of the objects that emit them: the independence meant is of a different kind, the kind which won for colours names of their own, while many flavours and smells have to borrow the names of the objects that emit them.

[2] OBJECTION: 'Absurd! Suppose they were not picked by anybody?' REJOINDER: Then which would THEY be?'

A second inadequacy of the suggested solution is that it was not quite correct to say that there is no need for the verbal rule that 'red' means among other things 'not green'. Admittedly, if someone who had learnt the meanings of the two words by examples were asked whether the rule was valid, he would answer IMMEDIATELY that it was, and add that the question was a silly one. And it would be a silly question to ask him, since nobody who had learnt the meanings of the two words by examples would be in any danger of contravening the rule. Such a person would feel that it need not be included in his lesson. For it is usually a waste of time to indicate what a thing is not AFTER indicating what it is, unless a confusion is likely. He would not feel this so strongly if the two colours were red and orange: since the same person might well call the same thing in the same light at one time red and at another time orange (provided that he did not know that it was the same thing in the same light, and so that he was being inconsistent). But with complementary colours, like red and green, this possibility is remote. Nevertheless, it remains true that someone who contravened the verbal rule would betray that he had not really learnt his lesson. So perhaps it is unnecessary to enunciate it only because it is so necessary to have obeyed it already.

But there is a difficulty here. Possibly someone who called a thing red and green all over would not be contravening THAT verbal rule. He might be making a mistake not about the meanings of the two colour words, but about the meaning of 'all over' or of 'uniform surface colour'. A few examples will show that, if anyone with a normal experience of the full range of colours said this extraordinary thing, it would be more natural to assume that his mistake was of this other kind. Only a perverse inference would lead such a person to say it about roses seen through green glasses, or about a mixture of red and green paints. But he might say it more reasonably about green buses shining in the reflected light of red buses, or about the green glint of red ink, or about the sheen on shot silk or on a dove's throat. And if he did, it would be natural to correct him by explaining depths of colour, or by explaining the fragmentation of some fields of colour and showing him a butterfly's wing under a microscope.

However, someone who had experienced only a restricted

range of colours might really be in danger of contravening such verbal rules about colour words. A child might be taught by examples the meaning of 'red' without ever seeing anything green. Would it really know what red was before it was confronted with green which it was not? The best way to decide this would seem to be to see whether it called its first green thing red. If it did, then it could not have known what 'red' meant in spite of its previous success. But if it refused to call it red, it would not FOLLOW that it did know previously what 'red' meant. It might be said to have known previously that red was not any other colour; but this knowledge would be very thin until it was filled out by actual experience of several other colours. But when the only main experience lacking was that of green, one would be very reluctant to say that, even if tomorrow it will say that a green thing is not red, still today it does not yet really know the meaning of 'red'. The totality of colours, when learnt, form a system, and so it seems impossible fully to learn one colour without learning at least some of the others (the extreme case is the complete impossibility of learning one in a monochrome world). But it does not seem necessary to learn all the others: partly because, when a child has learnt two or three colours, it can learn the meaning of 'colour', and so perhaps of 'other colour';[1] and partly because lessons in individual colours do not impart isolated and fully developed blocks of knowledge, and, if a child does not call its first green thing red, this may be because its lessons enable it to make later discoveries about what in a way it knew before.

This partial reinstatement of the verbal rule seems to reopen the whole case. But the correction of the third inadequacy of the suggested solution may help to keep it closed.

Its third inadequacy is that it is too schematic in what it says about rules. For the way children learn is enough to show that verbal rules are not as numerous as it seems to assume. But this is not a very important point: philosophers often have to state precisely what is seldom stated, even vaguely. Also, what is

---

[1] Nobody would be surprised if a child achieved this. It is describing the achievement by stages which is difficult. For colour has no abstractible GENERIC mark: it is a concrete universal smoothly built into either red or green or one of its other species. Hence one can make oneself unable to understand the question 'Could a completely new colour be discovered?'

more important, there are no designatory rules which cannot be expanded verbally; since something which cannot be expanded verbally cannot be a rule (for instance ' "Shrill" means shrill'). And this is not just a terminological point. Calling them rules suggests wrongly that they do take analysis one stage further, in the way in which only genuine rules can, and this false suggestion may be a source of the claim that a principle of natural necessity is involved. Finally the most important fault of the schematism is that it implied that the two designatory rules are independent of the verbal rule. The falsity of this has emerged in the subsequent discussion. One does not first study examples, and then QUITE SEPARATELY learn the incompatibility. This point is worth emphasizing, since in a way it is the schema that generates the problem. If the two designatory rules were independent of the verbal rule, and if one could adopt the verbal rule without fear of having to alter either of the designatory rules, surely this could only be because there is here a principle of natural necessity?

The adoption of a misleading schematism needs some defence. Two excuses may be given for it. Without it, the emergence of the problem and its protracted discussion would go unexplained. Also, without it, both the problem and its solution might be lost from view in an apparently aimless discussion of colour words. The schema secures historical continuity, and, like scaffolding which in the end will be dismantled, it enables the case to be built up visibly in the traditional way which made its satisfactory completion seem impossible.

CHAPTER VIII

OTHER MINDS

By J. L. Austin

[This paper was written as the second part of a Symposium, the whole of which was
originally printed in the *Proceedings of the Aristotelian Society*, Supplementary Volume XX,
in 1946. It is reprinted here without significant alteration. The first part, by Mr. — now
Professor — John Wisdom, was a distillation of his very long and never concluded series of
articles on 'Other Minds', which appeared in *Mind* from 1940 onwards. As this series,
including the first part of the symposium, is now available separately (Wisdom, J., *Other
Minds*, Basil Blackwell, 1952), Professor Wisdom's paper is not included here. I hope that
— with the help of the footnotes I have added — Professor Austin's paper will be entirely
intelligible even though torn out of context. If it is not the fault is wholly mine —
EDITOR.]

I FEEL that I agree with much, and especially with the more important parts, of what Mr. Wisdom has written, both in his present
paper and in his beneficial series of articles on 'Other Minds' and
other matters. I feel ruefully sure, also, that one must be at least
one sort of fool to rush in over ground so well trodden by the
angels. At best I can hope only to make a contribution to one
part of the problem, where it seems that a little more industry still
might be of service. I could only wish it was a more central part.
In fact, however, I did find myself unable to approach the centre
while still bogged down on the periphery. And Mr. Wisdom
himself may perhaps be sympathetic towards a policy of splitting
hairs to save starting them.

Mr. Wisdom, no doubt correctly, takes the 'Predicament' to
be brought on by such questions as 'How do we know that
another man is angry?' He also cites other forms of the question — 'Do we (ever) know?', 'Can we know?', 'How can we
know?' the thoughts, feelings, sensations, mind, etc., of another
creature, and so forth. But it seems likely that each of these
further questions is rather different from the first, which alone
has been enough to keep me preoccupied, and to which I shall
stick.

Mr. Wisdom's method is to go on to ask: *Is it like the way in
which we know* that a kettle is boiling, or that there's a tea-party
next door, or the weight of thistledown? But it seemed to me that

perhaps, as he went on, he was not giving an altogether accurate account (perhaps only because too cursory a one) of what we should say if asked 'How do you know?' these things. For example, in the case of the tea-party, to say we knew of it 'by analogy' would at best be a very sophisticated answer (and one to which some sophisticates might prefer the phrase 'by induction'), while in addition it seems incorrect because we don't, I think, claim to *know* by analogy, but only to *argue* by analogy. Hence I was led on to consider what sort of thing does actually happen when ordinary people are asked 'How do you know?'

Much depends, obviously, on the sort of item it is about which we are being asked 'How do you know?' and there are bound to be many kinds of case that I shall not cover at all, or not in detail. The sort of statement which seems simplest, and at the same time not, on the face of it, unlike 'He is angry', is such a statement as 'That is a goldfinch' ('The kettle is boiling') – a statement of particular, current, empirical fact. This is the sort of statement on making which we are liable to be asked 'How do you know?' and the sort that, at least sometimes, we say we don't know, but only believe. It may serve for a stalking horse as well as another.

When we make an assertion such as 'There is a goldfinch in the garden' or 'He is angry', there is a sense in which we imply that we are sure of it or know it ('But I took it you *knew*', said reproachfully), though what we imply, in a similar sense and more strictly, is only that we *believe* it. On making such an assertion, therefore, we are directly exposed to the questions (1) 'Do you *know* there is?' 'Do you *know* he is?' and (2) '*How* do you know?' If in answer to the first question we reply 'Yes', we may then be asked the second question, and even the first question alone is commonly taken as an invitation to state not merely *whether* but also *how* we know. But on the other hand, we may well reply 'No' in answer to the first question: we may say, 'No, but I think there is', 'No, but I believe he is'. For the implication that I know or am sure is not strict: we are not all (terribly or sufficiently) strictly brought up. If we do this, then we are exposed to the question, which might also have been put to us without preliminaries, 'Why do you believe that?' (or 'What makes you think so?', 'What induces you to suppose so?', etc.).

There is a singular difference between the two forms of challenge: 'How do you know?' and 'Why do you believe?' We seem never to ask 'Why do you know?' or 'How do you believe?' And in this, as well as in other respects to be noticed later, not merely such other words as 'suppose', 'assume', etc., but also the expressions 'be sure' and 'be certain', follow the example of 'believe', not that of 'know'.

Either question, 'How do you know?' or 'Why do you believe?', may well be asked only out of respectful curiosity, from a genuine desire to learn. But again, they may both be asked as *pointed* questions, and, when they are so, a further difference comes out. 'How do you know?' suggests that perhaps you *don't* know it at all, whereas 'Why do you believe?' suggests that perhaps you *oughtn't* to believe it. There is no suggestion[1] that you *ought* not to know or that you *don't* believe it. If the answer to 'How do you know?' or to 'Why do you believe?' is considered unsatisfactory by the challenger, he proceeds rather differently in the two cases. His next riposte will be, on the one hand, something such as 'Then you *don't* know any such thing', or 'But that doesn't prove it: in that case you don't really know it at all', and on the other hand, something such as 'That's very poor evidence to go on: you oughtn't to believe it on the strength of that alone'.[2]

The 'existence' of your alleged belief is not challenged, but the 'existence' of your alleged knowledge *is* challenged. If we like to say that 'I believe', and likewise 'I am sure' and 'I am certain', are descriptions of subjective mental or cognitive states or attitudes, or what not, then 'I know' is not that, or at least not merely that: it functions differently in talking.

'But of course', it will be said, ' "I know" is obviously more than that, more than a description of my own state. If I *know*, I *can't be wrong*. You can always show I don't know by showing I am wrong, or may be wrong, or that I didn't know by showing that I might have been wrong. *That's* the way in which knowing differs even from being as certain as can be.' This must be considered in due course, but first we should consider the types of

---

[1] But in special senses and cases, there is — e.g., if someone has announced some top secret information, we can ask 'How do *you* know?', nastily.

[2] An interesting variant in the case of knowing would be 'You *oughtn't to say* (you've no business to say) you know it at all'. But of course this is only superficially similar to 'You oughtn't to believe it': you ought *to say* you believe it, if you do believe it, however poor the evidence.

answer that may be given in answer to the question 'How do you know?'

Suppose I have said 'There's a bittern at the bottom of the garden', and you ask 'How do you know?' my reply may take very different forms:

(a) I was brought up in the Fens
(b) I heard it
(c) The keeper reported it
(d) By its booming
(e) From the booming noise
(f) Because it's booming.

We may say, roughly, that the first three are answers to the questions 'How do you come to know?' 'How are you in a position to know?' or 'How do *you* know?' understood in different ways: while the other three are answers to 'How can you tell?' understood in different ways. That is, I may take you to have been asking:

(1) How do I come to be in a position to know about bitterns?
(2) How do I come to be in a position to say there's a bittern here and now?
(3) How do (can) I tell bitterns?
(4) How do (can) I tell the thing here and now as a bittern?

The implication is that in order to know this is a bittern, I must have

(1) been trained in an environment where I could become familiar with bitterns
(2) had a certain opportunity in the current case
(3) learned to recognize or tell bitterns
(4) succeeded in recognizing or telling this as a bittern.

(1) and (2) mean that my experiences must have been of certain kinds, that I must have had certain opportunities: (3) and (4) mean that I must have exerted a certain kind and amount of acumen.[1]

---

[1] 'I know, I *know*, I've seen it a hundred times, don't keep on telling me' complains of a superabundance of opportunity: 'knowing a hawk from a handsaw' lays down a minimum of acumen in recognition or classification. 'As well as I know my own name' is said to typify something I *must* have experienced and *must* have learned to discriminate.

The questions raised in (1) and (3) concern our *past* experiences, our opportunities and our activities in learning to discriminate or discern, and, bound up with both, the correctness or otherwise of the linguistic usages, we have acquired. Upon these earlier experiences depends how *well* we know things, just as, in different but cognate cases of 'knowing', it is upon earlier experience that it depends how *thoroughly* or how *intimately* we know: we know a person by sight or intimately, a town inside out, a proof backwards, a job in every detail, a poem word for word, a Frenchman when we see one. 'He doesn't know what love (real hunger) is' means he hasn't had enough experience to be able to recognize it and to distinguish it from other things slightly like it. According to how well I know an item, and according to the kind of item it is, I can recognize it, describe it, reproduce it, draw it, recite it, apply it, and so forth. Statements like 'I know *very well* he isn't angry' or 'You know *very well* that isn't calico', though of course about the current case, ascribe the excellence of the knowledge to past experience, as does the general expression 'You are old enough to know better'.[1]

By contrast, the questions raised in (2) and (4) concern the circumstances of the current case. Here we can ask 'How *definitely* do you know?' You may know it for certain, quite positively, officially, on his own authority, from unimpeachable sources, only indirectly, and so forth.

Some of the answers to the question 'How do you know?' are, oddly enough, described as 'reasons for knowing' or 'reasons to know', or even sometimes as 'reasons why I know', despite the fact that we do not ask 'Why do you know?' But now surely, according to the Dictionary, 'reasons' should be given in answer to the question 'Why?' just as we do in fact give reasons for believing in answer to the question 'Why do you believe?' However, there is a distinction to be drawn here. 'How do you know that IG Farben worked for war?' 'I have every reason to know: I served on the investigating commission': here, giving my reasons for knowing is stating how I come to be in a position to know. In the same way we use the expressions 'I know *because*

---

[1] The adverbs that can be inserted in 'How ... do you know?' are few in number and fall into still fewer classes. There is practically no overlap with those that can be inserted in 'How ... do you believe?' (firmly, sincerely, genuinely, etc.).

I saw him do it' or 'I know *because* I looked it up only ten minutes ago': these are similar to 'So it is: it *is* plutonium. How did you know?' 'I did quite a bit of physics at school before I took up philology', or to 'I ought to know: I was standing only a couple of yards away'. Reasons for *believing* on the other hand are normally quite a different affair (a recital of symptoms, arguments in support, and so forth), though there are cases where we do give as reasons for believing our having been in a position in which we could get good evidence: 'Why do you believe he was lying?' 'I was watching him very closely.'

Among the cases where we give our reasons for knowing things, a special and important class is formed by those where we cite authorities. If asked 'How do you know the election is today?', I am apt to reply 'I read it in *The Times*', and if asked 'How do you know the Persians were defeated at Marathon?', I am apt to reply 'Herodotus expressly states that they were'. In these cases 'know' is correctly used: we know 'at second hand' when we can cite an authority who was in a position to know (possibly himself also only at second hand).[1] The statement of an authority makes me aware of something, enables me to know something, which I shouldn't otherwise have known. It is a source of knowledge. In many cases, we contrast such reasons for knowing with other reasons for believing the very same thing: 'Even if we didn't know it, even if he hadn't confessed, the evidence against him would be enough to hang him.'

It is evident, of course, that this sort of 'knowledge' is 'liable to be wrong', owing to the unreliability of human testimony (bias, mistake, lying, exaggeration, etc.). Nevertheless, the occurrence of a piece of human testimony radically alters the situation. We say 'We shall never know what Caesar's feelings were on the field of the battle of Philippi', because he did not pen an account of them: *if* he *had*, then to say 'We shall never know' won't do in the same way, even though we may still perhaps find reason to say 'It doesn't read very plausibly: we shall never *really* know the

---

[1] Knowing at second hand, or on authority, is not the same as 'knowing indirectly', whatever precisely that difficult and perhaps artificial expression may mean. If a murderer 'confesses', then, whatever our opinion of the worth of the 'confession', we cannot say that 'we (only) know indirectly that he did it', nor can we so speak when a witness, reliable or unreliable, has stated that he saw the man do it. Consequently, it is not correct, either, to say that the murderer himself knows 'directly' that he did it, whatever precisely 'knowing directly' may mean.

truth' and so on. Naturally, we are judicious: we don't say we know (at second hand) if there is any special reason to doubt the testimony: but there has to be *some* reason. It is fundamental in talking (as in other matters) that we are entitled to trust others, except in so far as there is some concrete reason to distrust them. Believing persons, accepting testimony, is the, or one main, point of talking. We don't play (competitive) games except in the faith that our opponent is trying to win: if he isn't, it isn't a game, but something different. So we don't talk with people (descriptively) except in the faith that they are trying to convey information.[1]

It is now time to turn to the question 'How can you tell?' i.e. to senses (2) and (4) of the question 'How do you know?' If you have asked 'How do you know it's a goldfinch?' then I may reply 'From its behaviour', 'By its markings', or, in more detail, 'By its red head', 'From its eating thistles'. That is, I indicate, or to some extent set out with some degree of precision, those features of the situation which enable me to recognize it as one to be described in the way I did describe it. Thereupon, you may still object in several ways to my saying it's a goldfinch, without in the least 'disputing my facts', which is a further stage to be dealt with later. You may object:

(1)   But goldfinches *don't* have red heads
(1a) — But that's not a *goldfinch*. From your own description I can recognize it as a gold*crest*
(2)   But that's not enough: plenty of other birds have red heads. What you say doesn't prove it. For all you know, it may be a woodpecker.

Objections (1) and (1a) claim that, in one way or another, I am evidently unable to recognize goldfinches. It may be (1a) — that I have not learned the right (customary, popular, official) name to apply to the creature ('Who taught you to use the word "goldfinch"?'):[2] or it may be that my powers of discernment,

---

[1] Reliance on the authority of others is fundamental, too, in various special matters, e.g. for corroboration and for the correctness of our own use of words, which we learn from others.

[2] Misnaming is not a trivial or laughing matter. If I misname I shall mislead others, and I shall also misunderstand information given by others to me. 'Of course I knew all about his condition perfectly, but I never realized that was *diabetes*: I thought it was cancer, and all the books agree that's incurable: if I'd only known it was diabetes, I should have thought of insulin at once.' Knowing *what a thing is* is, to an important extent, knowing what the name for it, and the right name for it, is.

K

and consequently of classification, have never been brought sharply to bear in these matters, so that I remain confused as to how to tell the various species of small British bird. Or, of course, it may be a bit of both. In making this sort of accusation, you would perhaps tend not so much to use the expression 'You don't know' or 'You oughtn't to say you know' as, rather, 'But that *isn't* a goldfinch *(goldfinch)*', or 'Then you're wrong to call it a goldfinch'. But still, if asked, you would of course deny the statement that I do know it's a goldfinch.

It is in the case of objection (2) that you would be more inclined to say right out 'Then you don't know'. Because it doesn't prove it, it's not enough to prove it. Several important points come out here:

(*a*) If you say 'That's not enough', then you must have in mind some more or less definite lack. 'To be a goldfinch, besides having a red head it must also have the characteristic eye-markings': or 'How do you know it isn't a woodpecker? Woodpeckers have red heads too'. If there is no definite lack, which you are at least prepared to specify on being pressed, then it's silly (outrageous) just to go on saying 'That's not enough'.

(*b*) Enough is enough: it doesn't mean everything. Enough means enough to show that (within reason, and for present intents and purposes) it 'can't' be anything else, there is no room for an alternative, competing, description of it. It does *not* mean, e.g. enough to show it isn't a *stuffed* goldfinch.

(*c*) '*From* its red head', given as an answer to 'How do you know?' requires careful consideration: in particular it differs very materially from '*Because* it has a red head', which is also sometimes given as an answer to 'How do you know?', and is commonly given as an answer to 'Why do you believe?' It is much more akin to such obviously 'vague' replies as 'From its markings' or 'From its behaviour' than at first appears. Our claim, in saying we know (i.e. that we can tell) is to *recognize*: and recognizing, at least in this sort of case, consists in seeing, or otherwise sensing, a feature or features which we are sure are similar to something noted (and usually named) before, on some earlier occasion in our experience. But, this that we see, or otherwise sense, is not necessarily *describable in words*, still less describable in detail, and in non-committal words, and by anybody you please. Nearly everybody can recognize a surly look or the smell of tar, but few can describe them non-committally, i.e. otherwise than as 'surly' or 'of tar': many can recognize, and 'with certainty', ports of different vintages, models by different fashion houses, shades of green, motor car makes from behind, and so forth, without being able to say '*how* they recognize them', i.e. without being able to 'be more specific about it' — they can only say they can tell 'by the taste', 'from the cut' and so on. So, when I say I can tell the bird 'from its red head', or that I know a friend 'by his nose', I imply that there is something *peculiar* about the red head or the nose, something peculiar to goldfinches or to him, by which you can (always) tell them or him. In view of the fewness and crudeness of the classificatory words in any language compared with the infinite number of features which are recognized, or which could be picked out and recognized, in our experience, it is small wonder that we often and often fall back on the phrases beginning with 'from' and 'by', and that we are not able to *say*, further and precisely, *how* we can tell. Often we know things quite well, while scarcely able at all to say 'from' what we know them, let alone what there is so very special about them. Any answer beginning 'From' or 'By' has, intentionally, this saving 'vagueness'. But on the contrary, an answer beginning 'Because' is dangerously definite. When I say I know it's a goldfinch 'Because it has a red head', that implies that all I have noted, or needed to note, about it is that its head is red (nothing special or peculiar about the shade, shape, etc., of the patch): so that I imply that there is no other small British bird that has any sort of red head except the goldfinch.

(*d*) Whenever I say I know, I am always liable to be taken to claim that, in a certain sense appropriate to the kind of statement (and to present intents and purposes), I am able to *prove* it. In the present, very common, type of case, 'proving' seems to mean stating what are the features of the current case which are enough to constitute it one which is correctly describable in the way we have described it, and not in any other way relevantly variant. Generally speaking, cases where I can 'prove' are cases where we use the 'because' formula: cases where we 'know but can't prove' are cases where we take refuge in the 'from' or 'by' formula.

I believe that the points so far raised are those most genuinely and normally raised by the question 'How do you know?' But there are other, further, questions sometimes raised under the same rubric, and especially by philosophers, which may be thought more important. These are the worries about 'reality' and about being 'sure and certain'.

Up to now, in challenging me with the question 'How do you know?', you are not taken to have *queried my credentials as stated*, though you have asked what they were: nor have you *disputed my facts* (the facts on which I am relying to prove it's a goldfinch), though you have asked me to detail them. It is this further sort of challenge that may now be made, a challenge as to the *reliability* of our alleged 'credentials' and our alleged 'facts'. You may ask

(1) But do you know it's a *real* goldfinch? How do you know you're not dreaming? Or after all, mightn't it be a stuffed one? And is the head really red? Couldn't it have been dyed, or isn't there perhaps an odd light reflected on it?

(2) But are you certain it's the *right* red for a goldfinch? Are you quite sure it isn't too orange? Isn't it perhaps rather too strident a note for a bittern?

These two sorts of worry are distinct, though very probably they can be combined or confused, or may run into one another: e.g. 'Are you sure it's really red?' may mean 'Are you sure it isn't orange?' or again 'Are you sure it isn't just the peculiar light?'

I. REALITY

If you ask me 'How do you know it's a real stick?' 'How do you know it's really bent?' ('Are you sure he's really angry?'), then you are querying my credentials or my facts (it's often uncertain which) in a certain special way. In various *special, recognized* ways, depending essentially upon the nature of the matter which I have announced myself to know, either my current experiencing or the item currently under consideration (or uncertain which) may be abnormal, *phoney*. Either I myself may be dreaming, or in delirium, or under the influence of mescal, etc.: or else the item may be stuffed, painted, dummy, artificial, trick, freak, toy, assumed, feigned, etc.: or else again there's an uncertainty (it's left open) whether *I* am to blame or *it* is — mirages, mirror images, odd lighting effects, etc.

These doubts are all to be allayed by means of recognized procedures (more or less roughly recognized, of course), appropriate to the particular type of case. There are recognized ways of distinguishing between dreaming and waking (how otherwise should we know how to use and to contrast the words?), and of deciding whether a thing is stuffed or live, and so forth. The doubt or question 'But is it a *real* one?' has always (*must* have) a special basis, there must be some 'reason for suggesting' that it isn't real, in the sense of some specific way, or limited number of specific ways, in which it is suggested that this experience or item may be phoney. Sometimes (usually) the context makes it clear what the suggestion is: the goldfinch might be stuffed but there's no suggestion that it's a mirage, the oasis might be a mirage but there's no suggestion it might be stuffed. If the context doesn't make it clear, then I am entitled to ask 'How do you mean? Do you mean it may be stuffed or what? *What are you suggesting?*' The wile of the metaphysician consists in asking 'Is it a real table?' (a kind of object which has no obvious way of being phoney) and not specifying or limiting what may be wrong with it, so that I feel at a loss 'how to prove' it *is* a real one.[1] It is the use of the word 'real' in this manner that leads us on to the supposition that 'real' has a single meaning ('the real world' 'material objects'), and that a highly profound and puzzling one. Instead, we should insist always on specifying with what 'real' is being contrasted — not what I shall have to show it is, in order to show it is 'real': and then usually we shall find some specific, less fatal, word, appropriate to the particular case, to substitute for 'real'.

Knowing it's a 'real' goldfinch isn't in question in the ordinary case when I say I know it's a goldfinch: reasonable precautions only are taken. But when it *is* called in question, in *special* cases, then I make sure it's a real goldfinch in ways essentially similar to those in which I made sure it was a goldfinch, though corroboration by other witnesses plays a specially important part in some cases. Once again the precautions cannot be more·than reasonable, relative to current intents and purposes. And once again, in the

[1] Conjurers, too, trade on this. 'Will some gentleman kindly satisfy himself that this is a perfectly ordinary hat?' This leaves us baffled and uneasy: sheepishly we agree that it seems all right, while conscious that we haven't the least idea what to guard against.

special cases just as in the ordinary cases, two further conditions hold good:

(*a*) I don't by any means *always* know whether it's one or not. It may fly away before I have a chance of testing it, or of inspecting it thoroughly enough. This is simple enough: yet some are prone to argue that because I *sometimes* don't know or can't discover, I *never* can.

(*b*) 'Being sure it's real' is no more proof against miracles or outrages of nature than anything else is or, *sub specie humanitatis*, can be. If we have made sure it's a goldfinch, and a real goldfinch, and then in the future it does something outrageous (explodes, quotes Mrs. Woolf, or what not), we don't say we were wrong to say it was a goldfinch, *we don't know what to say*. Words literally fail us: 'What would you have said?' 'What are we to say now?' 'What would *you* say?' When I have made sure it's a real goldfinch (not stuffed, corroborated by the disinterested, etc.) then I am *not* 'predicting' in saying it's a real goldfinch, and in a very good sense I can't be proved wrong whatever happens. It seems a serious mistake to suppose that language (or most language, language about real things) is 'predictive' in such a way that the future can always prove it wrong. What the future *can* always do, is to make us *revise our ideas* about goldfinches or real goldfinches or anything else.

Perhaps the normal procedure of language could be schematized as follows. First, it is arranged that, on experiencing a complex of features C, then we are to say 'This is C' or 'This is a C'. Then subsequently, the occurrence either of the whole of C or of a significant and characteristic part of it is, on one or many occasions, accompanied or followed in definite circumstances by another special and distinctive feature or complex of features, which makes it seem desirable to revise our ideas: so that we draw a distinction between 'This looks like a C, but in fact is only a dummy, etc.' and 'This is a real C (live, genuine, etc.)'. *Henceforward*, we can only ascertain that it's a *real* C by ascertaining that the special feature or complex of features is present in the appropriate circumstances. The old expression 'This is a C' will tend as heretofore, to fail to draw any distinction between 'real, live, etc.', and 'dummy, stuffed, etc.' If the special distinctive feature is one which does not have to manifest itself in *any* definite

circumstances (on application of some specific test, after some
limited lapse of time, etc.), then it is not a suitable feature on
which to base a distinction between 'real' and 'dummy, imaginary,
etc.' All we can then do is to say 'Some Cs are and some aren't,
some do and some don't: and it may be very interesting or important whether they are or aren't, whether they do or don't, but
they're all Cs, real Cs, just the same'.[1] Now if the special feature
is one which must appear in (more or less) definite circumstances,
then 'This is a real C' is not necessarily predictive: we can, in
favourable cases, make sure of it.[2]

II. SURENESS AND CERTAINTY

The other way of querying my credentials and proofs ('Are
you sure it's the *right* red?') is quite different. Here we come up
against Mr. Wisdom's views on 'the peculiarity of a man's knowledge of his own sensations', for which he refers us to 'Other
Minds VII' (*Mind*, vol. LII, N.S., No. 207), a passage with which
find I disagree.

Mr. Wisdom there says that, excluding from consideration
cases like 'being in love' and other cases which 'involve prediction', and considering statements like 'I am in pain' which, in the
requisite sense, do *not* involve prediction, then a man *cannot* 'be
wrong' in making them, in the most favoured sense of being
wrong: that is, though it is of course possible for him to *lie* (so
that 'I am in pain' may be false), and though it is also possible
for him to *misname*, i.e. to use the word 'pawn', say, instead of
'pain', which would be liable to mislead others but would not
mislead himself, either because he regularly uses 'pawn' for
'pain' or because the use was a momentary aberration, as when I
call John 'Albert' while knowing him quite well to be John —
though it is possible for him to be 'wrong' in these two senses,
it is not possible for him to be wrong in the most favoured sense.
He says again that, with this class of statement (elsewhere called

[1] The awkwardness about some snarks being boojums.
[2] Sometimes, on the basis of the new special feature, we distinguish, not between 'Cs'
and 'real Cs', but rather between Cs and Ds. There is a reason for choosing the one procedure rather than the other: all cases where we use the 'real' formula exhibit (complicated
and serpentine) likenesses, as do all cases where we use 'proper', a word which behaves
in many ways like 'real', and is no less nor more profound.

'sense-statements'), to know directly that one is in pain is 'to say that one is, and to say it on the basis of being in pain': and again, that the peculiarity of sense-statements lies in the fact that 'when they are correct and made by X, then X knows they are correct'.

This seems to me mistaken, though it is a view that, in more or less subtle forms, has been the basis of a very great deal of philosophy. It is perhaps the original sin (Berkeley's apple, the tree in the quad) by which the philosopher cast himself out from the garden of the world we live in.

Very clearly detailed, this is the view that, at least and only in a certain favoured type of case, I can 'say what I see (or otherwise sense)' almost quite literally. On this view, if I were to say 'Here is something red', then I might be held to imply or to state that it is really a red thing, a thing which would appear red in a standard light, or to other people, or tomorrow too, and perhaps even more besides: all of which 'involves prediction' (if not also a metaphysical substratum). Even if I were to say 'Here is something which looks red', I might still be held to imply or to state that it looks red to others also, and so forth. If, however, I confine myself to stating 'Here is something that looks red to me now', then at least I can't be wrong (in the most favoured sense).

However, there is an ambiguity in 'something that looks red to me now'. Perhaps this can be brought out by italics, though it is not really so much a matter of emphasis as of tone and expression, of confidence and hesitancy. Contrast 'Here is something that (definitely) *looks to me* (anyhow) red' with 'Here is something that looks to me (something like) *red* (I should say)'. In the former case I am quite confident that, however it may look to others, whatever it may 'really be', etc., it certainly does look red to me at the moment. In the other case I am not confident at all: it looks reddish, but I've never seen anything quite like it before, I can't quite describe it – or, I'm not very good at recognizing colours, I never feel quite happy about them, I've constantly been caught out about them. Of course, this sounds silly in the case of 'red': red is so *very* obvious, we all know red when we see it, it's *unmistakable*.[1] Cases where we should not feel happy about red are not easy (though not impossible) to find.

[1] And yet she always *thought* his shirt was white until she saw it against Tommy's Persil-washed one.

But take 'magenta': 'It looks rather like magenta to me — but then I wouldn't be too sure about distinguishing magenta from mauve or from heliotrope. Of course I know in a way it's purplish, but I don't really know whether to say it's magenta or not: I just can't be sure.' Here, I am not interested in ruling out consideration of how it looks to others (looks *to me*) or considerations about what its *real* colour is (*looks*): what I am ruling out is *my being sure or certain* what it looks to me. Take tastes, or take sounds: these are so much better as examples than colours, because we never feel so happy with our other senses as with our eyesight. Any description of a taste or sound or smell (or colour) or of a feeling, involves (is) saying that it is like one or some that we have experienced before: any descriptive word is classificatory, involves recognition and in that sense memory, and only when we use such words (or names or descriptions, which come down to the same) are we knowing anything, or believing anything. But memory and recognition are often uncertain and unreliable.

Two rather different ways of being hesitant may be distinguished.

(*a*) Let us take the case where we are tasting a certain taste. We may say 'I simply don't know what it is: I've never tasted anything remotely like it before . . . No, it's no use: the more I think about it the more confused I get: it's perfectly distinct and perfectly distinctive, quite unique in my experience'. This illustrates the case where I can find nothing in my past experience with which to compare the current case: I'm certain it's not appreciably like anything I ever tasted before, not sufficiently like anything I know to merit the same description. This case, though distinguishable enough, shades off into the more common type of case where I'm not quite certain, or only fairly certain, or practically certain, that it's the taste of, say, laurel. In all such cases, I am endeavouring to recognize the current item by searching in my past experience for something like it, some likeness in virtue of which it deserves, more or less positively, to be described by the same descriptive word:[1] and I am meeting with varying degrees of success.

(*b*) The other case is different, though it very naturally combines itself with the first. Here, what I try to do is to *savour* the

[1] Or, of course, related to it in some other way than by 'similarity' (in any ordinary sense of 'similarity'), which is yet sufficient reason for describing it by the same word.

current experience, to *peer* at it, to sense it vividly. I'm not sure it *is* the taste of pineapple: isn't there perhaps just *something* about it, a tang, a bite, a lack of bite, a cloying sensation, which isn't *quite* right for pineapple? Isn't there perhaps just a peculiar hint of green, which would rule out mauve and would hardly do for heliotrope? Or perhaps it is faintly odd: I must look more intently, scan it over and over: maybe just possibly there is a suggestion of an unnatural shimmer, so that it doesn't look quite like ordinary water. There is a lack of sharpness in what we actually sense, which is to be cured not, or not merely, by thinking, but by acuter discernment, by sensory discrimination (though it is of course true that thinking of other, and more pronounced, cases in our past experience can and does assist our powers of discrimination).[1]

Cases (*a*) and (*b*) alike, and perhaps usually together, lead to our being not quite sure or certain what it is, what to say, how to describe it: what our feelings really are, whether the tickling is painful exactly, whether I'm really what you'd call angry with him or only something rather like it. The hesitation is of course, in a sense, over misnaming: but I am not so much or merely worried about possibly misleading others as about misleading myself (the most favoured sense of being wrong). I should suggest that the two expressions 'being certain' and 'being sure', though from the nature of the case they are often used indiscriminately, have a tendency to refer to cases (*a*) and (*b*) respectively. 'Being certain' tends to indicate confidence in our memories and our past discernment, 'being sure' to indicate confidence in the current perception. Perhaps this comes out in our use of the concessives 'to be sure' and 'certainly', and in our use of such phrases as 'certainly not' and 'surely not'. But it may be unwise to chivvy language beyond the coarser nuances.

It may be said that, even when I don't know exactly how to describe it, I nevertheless *know* that I *think* (and roughly how confidently I think) it's mauve. So I do know *something*. But this is irrelevant: I *don't* know it's mauve, that it definitely looks to me now mauve. Besides, there are cases where I really don't know what I think: I'm completely baffled by it.

[1] This appears to cover cases of dull or careless or uninstructed perception, as opposed to cases of diseased or drugged perception.

Of course, there are any number of 'sense-statements' about which I can be, and am, completely sure. In ordinary cases ordinary men are nearly always certain when a thing looks red (or reddish, or anyhow reddish rather than greenish), or when they're in pain (except when that's rather difficult to say, as when they're being tickled): in ordinary cases an expert, a dyer or a dress designer, will be quite sure when something looks (to him in the present light) reseda green or nigger brown, though those who are not experts will not be so sure. Nearly always, if not quite always, we can be quite, or pretty, sure if we take refuge in a sufficiently *rough* description of the sensation: roughness and sureness tend to vary inversely. But the less rough descriptions, just as much as the rough, are all 'sense-statements'.

It is, I think, the problems of sureness and certainty, which philosophers tend (if I am not mistaken) to neglect, that have considerably exercised scientists, while the problem of 'reality', which philosophers have cultivated, does not exercise them. The whole apparatus of measures and standards seems designed to combat unsureness and uncertainty, and concomitantly to increase the possible precision of language, which, in science, pays. But for the words 'real' and 'unreal' the scientist tends to substitute, wisely, their cash-value substitutes, of which he invents and defines an increasing number, to cover an increasing variety of cases: he doesn't ask 'Is it real?' but rather 'Is it denatured?' or 'Is it an allotropic form?' and so on.

It is not clear to me what the class of sense-statements is, nor what its 'peculiarity' is. Some who talk of sense-statements (or sense data) appear to draw a distinction between talking about simple things like red or pain, and talking about complicated things like love or tables. But apparently Mr. Wisdom does not, because he treats 'This looks to me now like a man eating poppies' as in the same case with 'This looks to me now red'. In this he is surely right: a man eating poppies may be more 'complex' to recognize, but it is often not appreciably more difficult, than the other. But if, again, we say that non-sense-statements are those which involve 'prediction', why so? True, if I say 'This is a (real) oasis' without first ascertaining that it's not a mirage, then I·do chance my hand: but if I *have* ascertained that it's not, and can recognize for sure that it isn't (as when I am drinking its waters), then surely

I'm not chancing my hand any longer. I believe, of course, that it will continue to perform as (real) oases normally do: but if there's a *lusus naturae*, a miracle, and it doesn't, that won't mean I was wrong, previously, to call it a real oasis.

With regard to Mr. Wisdom's own chosen formulae, we have seen already that it can't be right to say that the peculiarity of sense-statements is that 'when they are correct, and made by X, then X knows they are correct': for X may *think*, without much confidence, that it tastes to him like Lapsang, and yet be far from certain, and then subsequently become certain, or more certain, that it did or didn't. The other two formulae were: 'To know that one is in pain is to say that one is and to say it on the basis of being in pain' and that the only mistake possible with sense-statements is typified by the case where 'knowing him to be Jack I call him "Alfred", thinking his name is Alfred, or not caring a damn what his name is'. The snag in both these lies in the phrases 'on the basis of being in pain' and 'knowing him to be Jack'. 'Knowing him to be Jack' means that I have recognized him as Jack, a matter over which I may well be hesitant and/or mistaken: it is true that I needn't recognize him *by name* as 'Jack', and hence I may call him 'Alfred'), but at least I must be recognizing him correctly as, for instance, the man I last saw in Jerusalem, or else I *shall* be misleading *myself*. Similarly, if 'on the basis of being in pain' only means 'when I am (what would be correctly described as) in pain', then something more than merely *saying* 'I'm in pain' is necessary for knowing I'm in pain: and this something more, as it involves recognition, may be hesitant and/or mistaken, though it is of course unlikely to be so in a case so comparatively obvious as that of pain.

Possibly the tendency to overlook the problems of recognition is fostered by the tendency to use a direct object after the word *know*. Mr. Wisdom, for example, confidently uses such expressions as 'knowing the feelings of another (his mind, his sensations, his anger, his pain) in the way that *he* knows them'. But, although we do correctly use the expressions 'I know your feelings on the matter' or 'He knows his own mind' or (archaically) 'May I know your mind?', these are rather special expressions, which do not justify any general usage. 'Feelings' here has the sense it has in 'very strong feelings' in favour of or against something:

perhaps it means 'views' or 'opinions' ('very decided opinions'), just as 'mind' in this usage is given by the Dictionary as equivalent to 'intention' or 'wish'. To extend the usage uncritically is somewhat as though, on the strength of the legitimate phrase 'knowing someone's tastes', we were to proceed to talk of 'knowing someone's sounds' or 'knowing someone's taste of pineapple'. If, for example, it is a case of *physical* feelings such as fatigue, we do not use the expression 'I know your feelings'.

When, therefore, Mr. Wisdom speaks generally of 'knowing his sensations', he presumably means this to be equivalent to 'knowing *what* he is seeing, smelling, etc.', just as 'knowing the winner of the Derby' means 'knowing *what won* the Derby'. But here again, the expression 'know what' seems sometimes to be taken, unconsciously and erroneously, to lend support to the practice of putting a direct object after *know*: for 'what' is liable to be understood as a relative, = 'that which'. This is a grammatical mistake: 'what' *can* of course be a relative, but in 'know what you feel' and 'know what won' it is an interrogative (Latin *quid*, not *quod*). In this respect, 'I can smell what he is smelling' differs from 'I can know what he is smelling'. 'I know what he is feeling' is not 'There is an *x* which both I know and he is feeling', but 'I know the answer to the question "What is he feeling?"'. And similarly with 'I know what I am feeling': this does *not* mean that there is something which I am *both knowing and feeling*.

Expressions such as 'We don't know another man's anger in the way he knows it' or 'He knows his pain in a way we can't' seem barbarous. The man doesn't 'know his pain': he feels (not knows) what he recognizes as, or what he knows to be, anger (not his anger), and he knows that he is feeling angry. Always assuming that he does recognize the feeling, which in fact, though feeling it acutely, he may not: 'Now I know what it was, it was jealousy (or gooseflesh or angina). At the time I didn't know at all what it was, I had never felt anything quite like it before: but since then I've got to know it quite well'.[1]

---

[1] There are, of course, legitimate uses of the direct object after *know*, and of the possessive pronoun before words for feelings. 'He knows the town well', 'He has known much suffering', 'My old vanity, how well I know it!' — even the pleonastic 'Where does he feel his (= the) pain?' and the educative tautology '*He* feels *his* pain'. But none of these really lends support to the metaphysical 'He knows his pain (in a way we can't)'.

Uncritical use of the direct object after *know* seems to be one thing that leads to the view that (or to talking as though) sensa, that is things, colours, noises and the rest, speak or are labelled by nature, so that I can literally *say* what (that which) I *see*: it pipes up, or I read it off. It is as if sensa were *literally* to 'announce themselves' or to 'identify themselves', in the way we indicate when we say 'It presently identified itself as a particularly fine white rhinoceros'. But surely this is only a manner of speaking, a reflexive idiom in which the French, for example, indulge more freely than the English: sensa are dumb, and only previous experience enables *us* to identify them. If we choose to say that they 'identify themselves' (and certainly 'recognizing' is not a highly voluntary activity of ours), then it must be admitted that they share the birthright of all speakers, that of speaking unclearly and untruly.

IF I KNOW I CAN'T BE WRONG

One final point about 'How do you know?', the challenge to the user of the expression 'I know', requires still to be brought out by consideration of the saying that 'If you know you can't be wrong'. Surely, if what has so far been said is correct, then we are often right to say we *know* even in cases where we turn out subsequently to have been mistaken – and indeed we seem always, or practically always, liable to be mistaken.

Now, we are perfectly, and should be candidly, aware of this liability, which does not, however, transpire to be so very onerous in practice. The human intellect and senses are, indeed, *inherently* fallible and delusive, but not by any means *inveterately* so. Machines are inherently liable to break down, but good machines don't (often). It is futile to embark on a 'theory of knowledge' which denies this liability: such theories constantly end up by admitting the liability after all, and denying the existence of 'knowledge'.

'When you know you can't be wrong' is perfectly good sense. You are prohibited from saying 'I know it is so, but I may be wrong', just as you are prohibited from saying 'I promise I will, but I may fail'. If you are aware you may be mistaken, you oughtn't to say you know, just as, if you are aware you may break your word, you have no business to promise. But of course, being aware that you may be mistaken doesn't mean merely being aware that you are a fallible human being: it means that you have some concrete reason to suppose that you may be mistaken in this case. Just as 'but I may fail' doesn't mean merely 'but I am a weak human being' (in which case it would be no more exciting than adding 'D.V.'): it means that there is some concrete reason for me to suppose that I shall break my word. It is naturally *always* possible ('humanly' possible) that I may be mistaken or may break my word, but that by itself is no bar against using the expressions 'I know' and 'I promise' as we do in fact use them.

At the risk (long since incurred) of being tedious, the parallel between saying 'I know' and saying 'I promise' may be elaborated.[1]

When I say 'S is P', I imply at least that I believe it, and, if I have been strictly brought up, that I am (quite) sure of it: when I say 'I shall do A', I imply at least that I hope to do it, and, if I have been strictly brought up that I (fully) intend to. If I only believe that S is P, I can add 'But of course I may (very well) be wrong': if I only hope to do A, I can add 'But of course I may (very well) not'. When I only believe or only hope, it is recognized that further evidence or further circumstances are liable to make me change my mind. If I say 'S is P' when I don't even believe it, I am lying: if I say it when I believe it but am not sure of it, I may be misleading but I am not exactly lying. If I say 'I shall do A' when I have not even any hope, not the slightest intention, of doing it, then I am deliberately deceiving: if I say it when I do not fully intend to, I am misleading but I am not deliberately deceiving in the same way.

But now, when I say 'I promise', a new plunge is taken: I have not merely announced my intention, but, by using this formula (performing this ritual), I have bound myself to others, and staked

---

[1] It is the use of the expressions 'I know' and 'I promise' (first person singular, present indicative tense) alone that is being considered. 'If I knew, I can't have been wrong' or 'If she knows she can't be wrong' are not worrying in the way that 'If I ("you") know I ("you") can't be wrong' is worrying. Or again, 'I promise' is quite different from 'he promises': if I say 'I promise', I don't say I *say* I promise, I *promise*, just as if he says he promises, he doesn't say he says he promises, he promises: whereas if I say 'he promises', I do (only) say he *says* he promises — in the other 'sense' of 'promise', the 'sense' in which *I* say *I* promise, only *he* can say he promises. I *describe* his promising, but I *do* my own promising and he must do *his* own.

my reputation, in a new way. Similarly, saying 'I know' is taking a new plunge. But it is *not* saying 'I have performed a specially striking feat of cognition, superior, in the same scale as believing and being sure, even to being merely quite sure': for there *is* nothing in that scale superior to being quite sure. Just as promising is not something superior, in the same scale as hoping and intending, even to merely fully intending: for there *is* nothing in that scale superior to fully intending. When I say 'I know', I *give others my word*: I *give others my authority for saying* that 'S is P'.

When I have said only that I am sure, and prove to have been mistaken, I am not liable to be rounded on by others in the same way as when I have said 'I know'. I am sure *for my part*, you can take it or leave it: accept it if you think I'm an acute and careful person, that's your responsibility. But I don't know 'for my part', and when I say 'I know' I don't mean you can take it or leave it (though of course you *can* take it or leave it). In the same way, when I say I fully intend to, I do so for my part, and, according as you think highly or poorly of my resolution and chances, you will elect to act on it or not to act on it: but if I say I promise, you are *entitled* to act on it, whether or not you choose to do so. If I have said I know or I promise, you insult me in a special way by refusing to accept it. We all *feel* the very great difference between saying even 'I'm *absolutely* sure' and saying 'I know': it is like the difference between saying even 'I firmly and irrevocably intend' and 'I promise'. If someone has promised me to do A, then I am entitled to rely on it, and can myself make promises on the strength of it: and so, where someone has said to me 'I know', I am entitled to say *I* know too, at second hand. The right to say 'I know' is transmissible, in the sort of way that other authority is transmissible. Hence, if I say it lightly, I may be *responsible* for getting you into trouble.

If you say you *know* something, the most immediate challenge takes the form of asking 'Are you in a position to know?': that is, you must undertake to show, not merely that you are sure of it, but that it is within your cognizance. There is a similar form of challenge in the case of promising: fully intending is not enough — you must also undertake to show that 'you are in a position to promise', that is that it is within your power. Over these points

in the two cases parallel series of doubts are apt to infect philosophers, on the ground that I cannot foresee the future. Some
begin to hold that I should never, or practically never, say I
know anything — perhaps only what I am sensing at this moment:
others, that I should never, or practically never, say I promise —
perhaps only what is actually within my power at this moment.
In both cases there is an obsession: if I know *I can't be wrong*, so
I can't have the right to say I know, and if I promise *I can't fail*,
so I can't have the right to say I promise. And in both cases this
obsession fastens on my inability to make *predictions* as the root of
the matter, meaning by predictions claims to know the future.
But this is doubly mistaken in both cases. As has been seen, we
may be perfectly justified in saying we know or we promise, in
spite of the fact that things 'may' turn out badly, and it's a more
or less serious matter for us if they do. And further, it is overlooked that the conditions which must be satisfied if I am to show
that a thing is within my cognizance or within my power are
conditions, not about the future, but about *the present and the past*:
it is not demanded that I do more than *believe* about the future.[1]

We feel, however, an objection to saying that 'I know' per-
forms the same sort of function in talking as 'I promise'. It is
this. Supposing that things turn out badly, then we say, on the
one hand 'You're proved wrong, so you *didn't* know', but on
the other hand 'You've failed to perform, although you *did*
promise'. I believe that this contrast is more apparent than real.
The sense in which you 'did promise' is that you did *say* you
promised (did say 'I promise'): and you did *say* you knew. That is
the gravamen of the charge against you when you let us down,
after we have taken your word. But it may well transpire that you
never fully intended to do it, or that you had concrete reason to
suppose that you wouldn't be able to do it (it might even be
manifestly impossible), and in another 'sense' of promise you
can't then have promised to do it, so that you *didn't* promise.

Consider the use of other phrases analogous to 'I know' and
'I promise'. Suppose, instead of 'I know', I had said 'I swear':
in that case, upon the opposite appearing, we should say, exactly
as in the promising case, 'You *did* swear, but you were wrong'.

---

[1] If 'Figs never grow on thistles' is taken to mean 'None ever have and none ever will',
then it is implied that I *know* that none ever have, but only that I *believe* that none ever will.

Suppose again that, instead of 'I promise', I had said 'I guarantee' (e.g. to protect you from attack): in that case, upon my letting you down, you can say, exactly as in the knowing case 'You *said* you guaranteed it, but you *didn't* guarantee it'.[1] Can the situation perhaps be summed up as follows? In these 'ritual' cases, the approved case is one where *in the appropriate circumstances*, I say a certain formula: e.g. 'I do' when standing, unmarried or a widower, beside a woman, unmarried or a widow and not within the prohibited degrees of relationship, before a clergyman, registrar, etc., or 'I give' when it is mine to give, etc., or 'I order' when I have the authority to, etc. But now, if the situation transpires to have been in some way not orthodox (I was already married: it wasn't mine to give: I had no authority to order), then we tend to be rather hesitant about how to put it, as heaven was when the saint blessed the penguins. We call the man a bigamist, but his second marriage was not a marriage, is null and void (a useful formula in many cases for avoiding saying either 'he did' or 'he didn't'): he did 'order' me to do it, but, having no authority over me, he *couldn't* 'order' me: he did warn me it was going to charge, but it wasn't or anyway I knew much more about it than he did, so in a way he couldn't warn me, didn't warn me.[2] We hesitate between 'He didn't order me', 'He had no right to order me', 'He oughtn't to have said he ordered me', just as we do between 'You didn't know', 'You can't have known', 'You had no right to say you knew' (these perhaps having slightly different nuances, according to what precisely it is that has gone wrong). But the essential factors are (*a*) You said you knew: you said you promised (*b*) You were mistaken: you didn't perform. The hesitancy concerns only the precise way in which we are to round on the original 'I know' or 'I promise'.

To suppose that 'I know' is a descriptive phrase, is only one example of the *descriptive fallacy*, so common in philosophy. Even

[1] 'Swear' 'guarantee' 'give my word' 'promise', all these and similar words cover cases both of 'knowing' and of 'promising', thus suggesting the two are analogous. Of course they differ subtly from each other: for example, *know* and *promise* are in a certain sense 'unlimited' expressions, while when I swear I swear *upon* something, and when I guarantee I guarantee that, upon some adverse and more or less to be expected circumstance arising, I will take *some more or less definite action* to nullify it.

[2] 'You can't warn someone of something that isn't going to happen' parallels 'You can't know what isn't true'.

if some language is now purely descriptive, language was not in origin so, and much of it is still not so. Utterance of obvious ritual phrases, in the appropriate circumstances, is not *describing* the action we are doing, but *doing* it ('I do'): in other cases it functions, like tone and expression, or again like punctuation and mood, as an intimation that we are employing language in some special way ('I warn', 'I ask', 'I define'). Such phrases cannot, strictly, *be* lies, though they can 'imply' lies, as 'I promise' implies that I fully intend, which may be untrue.

If these are the main and multifarious points that arise in familiar cases where we ask 'How do you know that this is a case of so-and-so?', they may be expected to arise likewise in cases where we say 'I know he is angry'. And if there are, as no doubt there are, special difficulties in this case, at least we can clear the ground a little of things which are not special difficulties, and get the matter in better perspective.

As a preliminary, it must be said that I shall only discuss the question of feelings and emotions, with special reference to anger. It seems likely that cases where we know that another man thinks that 2 and 2 make 4, or that he is seeing a rat, and so on, are different in important respects from, though no doubt also similar to, the case of knowing that he is angry or hungry.

In the first place, we certainly do say sometimes that we know another man is angry, and we also distinguish these occasions from others on which we say only that we *believe* he is angry. For of course, we do not for a moment suppose that we *always* know, of *all* men, whether they are angry or not, or that we could discover it. There are many occasions when I realize that I can't possibly tell what he's feeling: and there are many *types* of people, and many individuals too, with whom I (they being what they are, and I being what I am) never can tell. The feelings of royalty, for example, or fakirs or bushmen or Wykehamists or simple eccentrics — these may be very hard to divine: unless you have had a prolonged acquaintance with such persons, and some intimacy with them, you are not in any sort of position to know what their feelings are, especially if, for one reason or another, they can't or don't tell you. Or again, the feelings of some individual whom you have never met before — they might be almost anything: you don't know his character at all or his tastes, you have had no experience of his mannerisms, and so on. His feelings are elusive and personal: people differ so much. It is this sort of thing that leads to the situation where we say 'You never know' or 'You never can tell'.

In short, here even more than in the case of the goldfinch, a great deal depends on how familiar we have been in our past experience with this type of person, and indeed with this individual, in this type of situation. If we have no great familiarity, then we hesitate to say we know: indeed, we can't be expected to say (tell). On the other hand, if we *have* had the necessary experience, then we can, in favourable current circumstances, say we know: we certainly can recognize when some near relative of ours is angrier than we have ever seen him.

Further, we must have had experience also of the emotion or feeling concerned, in this case anger. In order to know what you're feeling, I must also apparently be able to imagine (guess, understand, appreciate) what you're feeling. It seems that more is demanded than that I shall have learned to discriminate displays of anger in others: I must also have been angry myself.[1] Or at any rate, if I have never felt a certain emotion, say ambition, then I certainly feel an *extra* hesitation in saying that his motive is ambition. And this seems to be due to the very special nature (grammar, logic) of feelings, to the special way in which they are related to their occasions and manifestations, which requires further elucidation.

At first sight it may be tempting to follow Mr. Wisdom, and to draw a distinction between (1) the physical symptoms and (2) the feeling. So that when, in the current case, I am asked 'How can you tell he's angry?' I should answer 'From the physical symptoms', while if *he* is asked how *he* can tell he's angry, he should answer 'From the feeling'. But this seems to be a dangerous over-simplification.

---

[1] We say we don't know what it must feel like to be a king, whereas we do know what one of our friends must have felt when mortified. In this ordinary (imprecise and evidently not whole-hog) sense of 'knowing what it would be like' we do often know what it would be like to be our neighbour drawing his sword, whereas we don't know (can't even guess or imagine), really, what it would feel like to be a cat or a cockroach. But of course we don't ever 'know' what in our neighbour accompanies the drawing of his sword in Mr. Wisdom's peculiar sense of 'know what' as equivalent to 'directly experience that which'.

In the first place, 'symptoms' (and also 'physical') is being used in a way different from ordinary usage, and one which proves to be misleading.

'Symptoms', a term transferred from medical usage,[1] tends to be used only, or primarily, in cases where that of which there are symptoms is something undesirable (of incipient disease rather than of returning health, of despair rather than of hope, of grief rather than of joy): and hence it is more colourful than 'signs' or 'indications'. This, however, is comparatively trivial. What is important is the fact that we never talk of 'symptoms' or 'signs' except *by way of implied contrast with inspection of the item itself*. No doubt it would often be awkward to have to say exactly where the signs or symptoms end and the item itself begins to appear: but such a division is always implied to exist. And hence the words 'symptom' and 'sign' have no use except in cases where the item, as in the case of disease, is liable to be *hidden*, whether it be in the future, in the past, under the skin, or in some other more or less notorious casket: and when the item is itself before us, we no longer talk of signs and symptoms. When we talk of 'signs of a storm', we mean signs of an impending storm, or of a past storm, or of a storm beyond the horizon: we do *not* mean a storm on top of us.[2]

The words function like such words as 'traces' or 'clues'. Once you know the murderer, you don't get any more clues, only what were or would have been clues: nor is a confession, or an eye-witness' view of the crime, a particularly good clue — these are something different altogether. When the cheese is not to be found or seen, then there may be traces of it: but not when it's there in front of us (though of course, there aren't, then, 'no traces' of it either).

For this reason, it seems misleading to lump together, as a general practice, all the characteristic features of any casual item as 'signs' or 'symptoms' of it: though it is of course sometimes

---

[1] Doctors nowadays draw a distinction of their own between 'symptoms' and '(physical) signs': but the distinction is not here relevant, and perhaps not very clear.

[2] There are some, more complicated, cases like that of inflation, where the signs of incipient inflation are of the same nature as inflation itself, but of a less intensity or at a slower tempo. Here, especially, it is a matter for decision where the signs or 'tendencies' end and where the state itself sets in: moreover, with inflation as with some diseases, we can in some contexts go on talking of signs or symptoms even when the item itself is quite fairly decidedly present, because it is such as not to be patent to simple observation.

the case that some things which could in appropriate circumstances be called characteristics or effects or manifestations or parts or sequelae or what not of certain items may *also* be called signs or symptoms of those items in the appropriate circumstances. It seems to be this which is really wrong with Mr. Wisdom's paradox[1] about looking in the larder and finding 'all the signs' of bread, when we see the loaf, touch it, taste it and so on. Doing these things is not finding (some) signs of bread at all: the taste or feel of bread is not a sign or symptom of bread at all. What I might be taken to mean if I announced that I had found signs of bread in the larder seems rather doubtful, since bread is not normally casketed (or if in the bin, leaves no traces), and not being a transient event (impending bread, etc.), does not have any normally accepted 'signs': and signs, peculiar to the item, have to be more or less normally accepted. I might be taken to mean that I had found traces of bread, such as crumbs, or signs that bread had at one time been stored there, or something of the kind: but what I could *not* be taken to mean is that I had seen, tasted, or touched (something like) bread.

The sort of thing we do actually say, if the look is all right but we haven't yet tasted it, is 'Here is something that looks like bread'. If it turns out not be bread after all, we might say 'It tasted like bread, but actually it was only bread-substitute', or 'It exhibited many of the characteristic features of bread, but differed in important respects: it was only a synthetic imitation'. That is, we don't use the words sign or symptom at all.

Now, if 'signs' and 'symptoms' have this restricted usage, it is evident that to say that we only get at the 'signs' or 'symptoms' of anything is to imply that we never get at *it* (and this goes for '*all* the signs' too). So that, if we say that I only get at the *symptoms* of his anger, that carries an important implication. But *is* this the way we do talk? Surely we do not consider that we are never aware of more than *symptoms* of anger in another man?

'Symptoms' or 'signs' of anger tend to mean signs of *rising* or of *suppressed* anger. Once the man has exploded, we talk of something different — of an expression or manifestation or dis-

---

[1] [In 'Other Minds III' he had discussed the logic of a possible complaint, from a man who was actually looking at, touching, smelling, tasting, bread, that nevertheless, though admittedly all the *signs* of bread were present still it might not be quite safe to say that there actually *was* bread there. — EDITOR.]

play of anger, of an exhibition of temper, and so forth. A twitch
of the eyebrow, pallor, a tremor in the voice, all these may be
symptoms of anger: but a violent tirade or a blow in the face
are not, they are the acts in which the anger is vented. 'Symptoms'
of anger are not, at least normally, contrasted with the man's own
inner personal feeling of anger, but rather with the actual display
of anger. Normally at least, where we have only symptoms to
go upon, we should say only that we *believe* that the man is
angry or getting angry: whereas when he has given himself away
we say that we *know*.[1]

The word 'physical' also, as used by Mr. Wisdom in contrast
to 'mental', seems to me abused, though I am not confident as
to whether this abuse is misleading in the current case. He evidently does not wish to call a man's feelings, which he cites as a
typical example of a 'mental' event, *physical*. Yet this is what we
ordinarily often do. There are many physical feelings, such as
giddiness, hunger or fatigue: and these are included by some
doctors among the physical signs of various complaints. Most
feelings we do not speak of as either mental or physical, especially
emotions, such as jealousy or anger itself: we do not assign them
to the *mind* but to the *heart*. Where we do describe a feeling as
mental, it is because we are using a word normally used to
describe a physical feeling in a special transferred sense, as when
we talk about 'mental' discomfort or fatigue.

It is then, clear, that more is involved in being e.g., angry
than simply showing the symptoms and feeling the feeling. For
there is also the display or manifestation. And it is to be noted
that the feeling is related in a unique sort of way to the display.
When we are angry, we have an impulse, felt and/or acted on,
to do actions of particular kinds, and, unless we suppress the
anger, we do actually proceed to do them. There is a peculiar
and intimate relationship between the emotion and the natural

---

[1] Sometimes, it is said, we use 'I know' where we should be prepared to substitute
'I believe', as when we say 'I know he's in, because his hat is in the hall': thus 'know' is
used loosely for 'believe', so why should we suppose there is a fundamental difference
between them? But the question is, what exactly do we mean by 'prepared to substitute'
and 'loosely'? We are 'prepared to substitute' *believe* for *know* not as an *equivalent* expression but as a weaker and therefore preferable expression, in view of the seriousness with
which, as has become apparent, the matter is to be treated: the presence of the hat, which
would serve as a proof of its owner's presence in many circumstances, could only through
laxity be adduced as a proof in a court of law.

manner of venting it, with which, having been angry ourselves, we are acquainted. The ways in which anger is normally manifested are *natural* to anger just as there are tones *naturally* expressive of various emotions (indignation, etc.). There is not normally taken to be[1] such a thing as 'being angry' apart from any impulse, however vague, to vent the anger in the natural way.

Moreover, besides the natural expressions of anger, there are also the natural *occasions* of anger, of which we have also had experience, which are similarly connected in an intimate way with the 'being angry'. It would be as nonsensical to class these as 'causes' in some supposedly obvious and 'external' sense, as it would be to class the venting of anger as the 'effect' of the emotion in a supposedly obvious and 'external' sense. Equally it would be nonsensical to say that there are three wholly distinct phenomena, (1) cause or occasion (2) feeling or emotion and (3) effect or manifestation, which are related together 'by definition' as all necessary to anger, though this would perhaps be less misleading than the other.

It seems fair to say that 'being angry' is in many respects like 'having mumps'. It is a description of a whole pattern of events, including occasion, symptoms, feeling and manifestation, and possibly other factors besides. It is as silly to ask 'What, really, *is* the anger *itself?*' as to attempt to fine down 'the disease' to some one chosen item ('the functional disorder'). That the man himself feels something which we don't (in the sense that he feels angry and we don't) is[2] evident enough, and incidentally nothing to complain about as a 'predicament': but there is no

[1] A new language is naturally necessary if we are to admit unconscious feelings, and feelings which express themselves in paradoxical manners, such as the psycho-analysts describe.

[2] In the absence of Mr. Wisdom's variety of telepathy. [Professor Wisdom wrote: 'Likewise we can imagine a man doing what we now can seldom do, something which people have called "looking into the mind of another". This man doesn't examine present symptoms and predict how the patient will go on. He sees scenes in a glass or in his mind's eye and knows they are what another sees, he feels distress and knows that another is in distress. If this is to be called seeing what another sees or feeling what he feels, if this would be real knowledge of the thoughts and feelings of another, then when someone says "We cannot know the feelings of others" what he refers to is the familiar fact that few of us can do this' — EDITOR.] There is, it seems to me, something which does actually happen, rather different from Mr. Wisdom's telepathy, which does sometimes contribute towards our knowledge of other people's feelings. We do talk, e.g. of 'feeling another person's displeasure', and say, e.g. 'his anger could be felt', and there seems to be something genuine about this. But the feeling we feel, though genuine 'feeling', is *not*, in these cases, displeasure or anger, but a special *counterpart* feeling.

call to say that 'that' ('the feeling')[1] *is* the *anger*. The pattern of events whatever its precise form, is, fairly clearly, peculiar to the case of 'feelings' (emotions) — it is not by any means exactly like the case of diseases: and it seems to be this peculiarity which makes us prone to say that, unless we have had experience of a feeling ourselves, we cannot know when someone else is experiencing it. Moreover, it is our confidence in the general pattern that makes us apt to say we 'know' another man is angry when we have only observed parts of the pattern: for the parts of the pattern are related to each other very much more intimately than, e.g. newspapermen scurrying in Brighton are related to a fire in Fleet Street.[2]

The man himself, such is the overriding power of the pattern, will sometimes accept corrections from outsiders about his own emotions, i.e. about the correct description of them. He may be got to agree that he was not really angry so much as, rather, indignant or jealous, and even that he was not in pain, but only fancied he was. And this is not surprising, especially in view of the fact that he, like all of us, has primarily learnt to use the expression 'I am angry' of himself by (*a*) noting the occasion, symptoms, manifestation, etc., in cases where other persons say 'I am angry' of *themselves* (*b*) being told by others, who have noted all that can be observed about *him* on certain occasions, that 'You are angry', i.e. that he should say 'I am angry'. On the whole, 'mere' feelings or emotions, if there are such things genuinely detectable, are certainly very hard to be sure about, even harder than, say, tastes, which we already choose to describe, normally, only by their occasions (the taste 'of tar', 'of pineapple', etc.).

All words for emotions are, besides, on the vague side, in two ways, leading to further hesitations about whether we 'know' when he's angry. They tend to cover a rather wide and ill-defined variety of situations: and the patterns they cover tend to be, each of them, rather complex (though common and so not difficult to recognize, very often), so that it is easy for one of the more or less necessary features to be omitted, and thus to

---

[1] The 'feelings', i.e. sensations, we can observe in ourselves when angry are such things as a pounding of the heart or tensing of the muscles, which cannot in themselves be justifiably called 'the feeling of anger'.

[2] It is therefore misleading to ask 'How do I get from the scowl to the anger?'

give rise to hesitation about what exactly we should say in such an unorthodox case. We realize, well enough, that the challenge to which we are exposed if we say we *know* is to *prove* it, and in this respect vagueness of terminology is a crippling handicap.

So far, enough has perhaps been said to show that most of the difficulties which stand in the way of our saying we know a thing is a goldfinch arise in rather greater strength in the case where we want to say we know another man is angry. But there is still a feeling, and I think a justified feeling, that there is a further and quite *special* difficulty in the latter case.

This difficulty seems to be of the sort that Mr. Wisdom raises at the very outset of his series of articles on 'Other Minds'. It is asked, might the man not exhibit all the symptoms (and display and everything else) of anger, even *ad infinitum*, and yet still *not* (really) *be* angry? It will be remembered that he there treats it, no doubt provisionally, as a difficulty similar to that which can arise concerning the reality of any 'material object'. But in fact, it has special features of its own.

There seem to be three distinguishable doubts which may arise:

(1) When to all appearances angry, might he not really be labouring under some other emotion, in that, though he normally feels the same emotion as we should on occasions when we, in his position, should feel anger and in making displays such as we make when angry, in this particular case he is acting abnormally?

(2) When to all appearances angry, might he not really be labouring under some other emotion; in that he normally feels, on occasions when we in his position should feel anger, and when acting as we should act if we felt anger, some feeling which we, if we experienced it, should distinguish from anger?

(3) When to all appearances angry, might he not really be feeling no emotion at all?

In everyday life, all these problems arise in special cases, and occasion genuine worry. We may worry (1) as to whether someone is *deceiving* us, by suppressing his emotions, or by feigning emotions which he does not feel: we may worry (2) as to whether we are *misunderstanding* someone (or he us), in wrongly supposing that he does 'feel like us', that he does share emotions like ours: or we may worry (3) as to whether some action of another person is really deliberate, or perhaps only involuntary or inadvertent in some manner or other. All three varieties of worry may arise, and often do, in connection with the actions of persons whom we know very well.[1] All work together in the feeling of loneliness which affects everybody at times. Any or all of them may be at the bottom of the passage from Mrs. Woolf.[2]

None of these three special difficulties about 'reality' arises in connection with goldfinches or bread, any more than the special difficulties about, e.g. the oasis arise in connection with the reality of another person's emotions. The goldfinch cannot be assumed, nor the bread suppressed: we may be deceived by the appearance of an oasis, or misinterpret the signs of the weather, but the oasis cannot lie to us and we cannot misunderstand the storm in the way we misunderstand the man.

Though the difficulties are special, the ways of dealing with them are, initially, similar to those employed in the case of the goldfinch. There are (more or less roughly) established procedures for dealing with suspected cases of deception or of misunderstanding or of inadvertence. By these means we do very often establish (though we do not expect *always* to establish) that someone is acting, or that we were misunderstanding him, or that he is simply impervious to a certain emotion, or that he was not acting voluntarily. These special cases where doubts arise and require resolving, are contrasted with the normal cases which hold the field[3] *unless* there is some special suggestion that deceit, etc., is involved, and deceit, moreover, of an intelligible kind in the circumstances, that is, of a kind that can be looked into because motive, etc., is specially suggested. There is no suggestion that I *never* know what other people's emotions are, nor yet that in particular cases I might be wrong for no special reason or in no special way.

Extraordinary cases of deceit, misunderstanding, etc. (which are themselves not the normal), do not, *ex vi termini*, ordinarily occur: we have a working knowledge of the occasions for, the temptations to, the practical limits of, and the normal types of

[1] There is, too, a special way in which we can doubt the 'reality' of our own emotions, can doubt whether we are not 'acting to ourselves'. Professional actors may reach a state where they never really know what their genuine feelings are.
[2] [Professor Wisdom had quoted a paragraph from *Jacob's Room*. — EDITOR.]
[3] 'You cannot fool all the people all of the time' is 'analytic'.

deceit and misunderstanding. Nevertheless, they *may* occur, and there may be varieties which are common without our yet having become aware of the fact. If this happens, we are in a certain sense wrong, because our terminology is inadequate to the facts, and we shall have thenceforward to be more wary about saying we know, or shall have to revise our ideas and terminology. This we are constantly ready to do in a field so complex and baffling as that of the emotions.

There remains, however, one further special feature of the case, which also differentiates it radically from the goldfinch case. The goldfinch, the material object, is, as we insisted above, uninscribed and *mute*: but the man *speaks*. In the complex of occurrences which induces us to say we know another man is angry, the complex of symptoms, occasion, display and the rest, a peculiar place is occupied by the man's own statement as to what his feelings are. In the usual case, we accept this statement without question, and we then say that we know (as it were 'at second-hand') what his feelings are: though of course 'at second-hand' here could not be used to imply that anybody but he could know 'at first-hand', and hence perhaps it is not in fact used. In unusual cases, where his statement conflicts with the description we should otherwise have been inclined to give of the case, we do not feel bound to accept it, though we always feel some uneasiness in rejecting it. If the man is a habitual liar or self-deceiver, or if there are patent reasons why he should be lying or deceiving himself on this occasion, then we feel reasonably happy: but if such a case occurred as the imagined one[1] where a man, having given throughout life every appearance of holding a certain point-less belief, leaves behind a remark in his private diary to the effect that he never did believe it, then we probably should not know what to say.

I should like to make in conclusion some further remarks about this crucial matter of our believing what the man says about his own feelings. Although I know very well that I do not see my way clearly in this, I cannot help feeling sure that it is fundamental to the whole Predicament, and that it has not been given the attention it deserves, possibly just because it is so obvious.

---

[1] [Professor Wisdom had considered the case of a man who persistently claimed that he believed that flowers feel. — EDITOR.]

The man's own statement is not (is not treated primarily as) a sign or symptom, although it can, secondarily and artificially, be treated as such. A unique place is reserved for it in the summary of the facts of the case. The question then is: 'Why believe him?'

There are answers that we can give to this question, which is here to be taken in the general sense of 'Why believe him ever?' not simply as 'Why believe him this time?' We may say that the man's statements on matters other than his own feelings have constantly been before us in the past, and have been regularly verified by our own observations of the facts he reported: so that we have in fact some basis for an induction about his general reliability. Or we may say that his behaviour is most simply 'explained' on the view that he does feel emotions like ours, just as psycho-analysts 'explain' erratic behaviour by analogy with normal behaviour when they use the terminology of 'unconscious desires'.

These answers are, however, dangerous and unhelpful. They are so obvious that they please nobody: while on the other hand they encourage the questioner to push his question to 'profounder' depths, encouraging us, in turn, to exaggerate these answers until they become distortions.

The question, pushed further, becomes a challenge to the very possibility of 'believing another man', in its ordinarily accepted sense, at all. What 'justification' is there for supposing that there is another mind communicating with you at all? How can you know what it would be like for another mind to feel anything, and so how can you understand it? It is then that we are tempted to say that we only mean by 'believing him' that we take certain vocal noises as signs of certain impending behaviour, and that 'other minds' are no more really real than unconscious desires.

This, however, is distortion. It seems, rather, that believing in other persons, in authority and testimony, is an essential part of the act of communicating, an act which we all constantly perform. It is as much an irreducible part of our experience as, say, giving promises, or playing competitive games, or even sensing coloured patches. We can state certain advantages of such performances, and we can elaborate rules of a kind for their 'rational' conduct (as the Law Courts and historians and psychologists work out the rules for accepting testimony). But there is no 'justification' for our doing them as such.

FINAL NOTE

One speaker at Manchester[1] said roundly that the real crux of the matter remains still that 'I ought not to say that I know Tom is angry, because I don't introspect his feelings': and this no doubt is just what many people do boggle at. The gist of what I have been trying to bring out is simply:

(1) *Of course* I *don't* introspect Tom's feelings (we should be in a pretty predicament if I did).

(2) *Of course* I *do* sometimes know Tom is angry.
Hence

(3) to suppose that the question 'How do I know that Tom is angry?' is meant to mean 'How do I introspect Tom's feelings?' (because, as we know, that's the sort of thing that knowing is or ought to be), is simply barking our way up the wrong gum tree.

---

[1] [Where the Symposium was held. — EDITOR.]

CHAPTER IX

ON GRADING [1]

By J. O. Urmson

A. An Outline of Some Typical Grading Situations

IF you have an apple tree you know very well that all the apples
will not be worth eating and that in a normal season there will
be more apples on the tree which are fit for eating than you can
eat immediately on ripening. Therefore, when you gather your
crop, you will probably divide it into three lots — the really good
apples, the not-so-good but edible, and the throw-outs. The
good ones you will store (or perhaps sell some at a high price),
the not-so-good you will use at once (and perhaps sell some at a
lower price), the throw-outs you will throw out, or give to your
pigs, or sell at a very low price for someone else's pigs. Let us
call this process by the name which, in more complicated forms,
it bears in the packing sheds of commercial growers — *grading*.
Let us call *grading labels* the adjectives which we apply to the
different grades as names of those grades — good, bad, indifferent;
first-rate, second-rate, third-rate; high quality, medium quality,
low quality; and so on.

In the sequel I intend to extend the expressions 'grading'
and 'grading labels' beyond their normal employment to cover
operations and words which, from the viewpoint from which I
shall discuss them, seem to me to be essentially similar to grading
in its narrower sense. There will be no harm in this if we realize
that we are doing it and if we make sure that the other operations
and words are really essentially similar to the more obvious cases
of grading.

First I will make a series of fairly non-controversial remarks
about the more obvious and unmysterious cases of grading.

(1) Often, instead of carrying out the physical process of

[1] Many of my Oxford colleagues will notice unauthorized borrowings, sometimes
involving distortions, from their theories. Mr. Hare suffers worst; I have had the benefit
of many discussions on this subject with him. Professor Austin suffers next worst, but
many others will notice minor peculations.

grading, which may be futile or impossible, we do something which I shall call mental grading (on the analogy of 'mental' arithmetic). For example, a permanent-way inspector examining railway sleepers will presumably grade them mentally in such grades as 'in good condition', 'in fair condition' and 'unserviceable'. But though he does not rip the sleepers from the track and put them in piles he is clearly not doing something importantly different from physical grading. Mental grading is obviously more common than physical grading. We shall not often need to distinguish them.

(2) Grading and the application of grading labels are common activities. Inspectors of goods, tea-tasters and the like (and examiners) do it professionally; we all need to do it for the ordinary purposes of life.

(3) In the case of physical grading one can learn to carry out the physical processes correctly, in some cases at least, without any previous knowledge of the objects being graded and with absolutely no knowledge of the opinions about and attitude towards the objects being graded of the person from whom one learns to carry out the processes, or, for that matter, of anybody else. Thus, for example, a person who had never seen an apple before, nor tasted one, and who knew nothing of your, or anybody else's, opinions about and attitude towards apples, would, with reasonable intelligence, and after a period of observation, learn to help you to put the apples into the correct piles merely by watching you do it. The greater his intelligence and the longer his apprenticeship, the more nearly infallible he would become; of course, there would be marginal cases in which he would differ from you, but in these you might as easily have differed from yourself. An instructive point should, however, be noticed here. Without further information our intelligent apprentice, although he would have learnt to grade the apples, or sleepers, in the sense in which a parrot can learn to speak English, might realize no more than the parrot that he was grading. He might not guess but that he was playing some rather tedious game, or tidying up, just as if he were sorting out white and black draughts pieces, or assisting in some scientific classification; he need not speculate on what he is doing at all. As we might say that the parrot was not really speaking English,

knowing just what we meant to convey by this, so we might say that the apprentice, unlike you, was not really grading. This state of affairs would be particularly likely to occur if you either did not tell him what grading labels you were employing, or else used such words as are not usually used for grading purposes.

Clearly the same possibilities and limitations would occur in the case of mental grading providing that the apprentice heard the grading labels used with reference to the various objects without recognizing them as grading labels.

One moral of this is quite obvious; grading, like speaking English in the sense in which parrots cannot speak English, or lying, or committing murder, is something which you cannot in a full sense do without understanding what you are doing. The other moral, equally obvious, is that grading is quite different from tidying up or scientific classification, but the difference lies in the purpose of the grader, not in its external form.

(4) It is perhaps instructive to notice a possible half-way house between your situation as a fully conscious grader and that of your ignorant and inexperienced, but intelligent and observant, apprentice. Suppose that you use the grading labels 'good', 'indifferent' and 'bad' of your piles of apples; then (more on this topic later), since they are adjectives, which are consecrated to use as grading labels, your apprentice, in addition to his former capacity of going through the right motions, will presumably also realize that he is grading. What he will lack which you have will be firstly an understanding of why you grade one pile more highly than another, though he will be able to distinguish the sets and know which you grade more highly, and secondly any conviction whether he would himself choose to grade on your principles if left to himself. Here too, for these reasons, there would be some point, though not as much as in the case imagined in (3) above, in saying that the apprentice is not really grading. Compare with this our tendency to say that the person who merely echoes conventional moral judgments correctly is not really making moral judgments, remembering especially what Plato has to say of those who have only opinion and not knowledge in moral matters.

(5) In our examples we have considered cases of grading, mental and physical, where we have dealt with a large number

of objects of a certain type, such as apples or railway sleepers. These are perhaps the only cases which can properly be called grading. But we do sometimes apply the same grading labels to single objects without explicit reference to any others, but using the same criteria. I cannot see any important difference in the two situations, and I shall refer to this type of situation as grading as well as the other. This is one of the ways in which, as I admitted, I intend to stretch the word.

(6) Finally, it should be clear that, whatever else there may be that is puzzling about grading, in ordinary typical cases, at least, there is no puzzle about or doubt that it is a business done in accordance with principles and which one can learn to do in the way other people do it. There is no doubt that even the most ignorant apprentice can learn how to go through the right motions by watching other people do it. As a spokesman of the Ministry of Agriculture has wisely said, 'proficiency in grading to the most rigid standards is easily acquired in practice, although a precise, and at the same time simple, definition of those standards in words or pictures is a matter of difficulty'.

B. TYPES OF GRADING LABELS

Before trying to throw any further light on the nature of grading and its difference from other language-using procedures such as scientific classification it would be advisable to examine a little more closely the grading labels which we use in grading.

(1) It is clearly possible, and often done, to employ *ad hoc*, without abuse of one's language, a very wide range of words (marks, etc.) as grading labels, including made-up words and words which sometimes are used for purposes other than grading. For example, I might use 'red', 'white', 'blue' in this way, or 'class X', 'class Y', 'class Z', where it would be necessary explicitly to say what order of merit they convey; I could equally well use 'red' for the best and 'green' for the worst, or vice versa. Still avoiding controversial issues, it might none the less be worth pointing out here one of the advantages of the use of *ad hoc* labels. More professional grading labels naturally tend to become emotionally charged for good or ill, especially extreme ones; using *ad hoc* grading labels in their place is a

way of ensuring objective unbiased calm. It is easier to hand back a paper to a pupil marked 'δ' than marked 'stupid and worthless'.

(2) But there is also a large class of words, called 'professional' in the preceding paragraph, which are used almost exclusively, or quite exclusively, as grading labels. Some obvious examples are 'first class', 'third rate', 'good', 'indifferent' 'bad', 'medium quality'. These can be used as grading labels without explicit warning; they themselves give warning, if it is not otherwise evident, that the object of the exercise *is* grading. Furthermore, it is easy and natural to choose sets whose order is clearly defined. It would be an abuse of language to use 'indifferent' of a higher grade than 'good'. It is indeed almost a necessary professional qualification of grading words to show their order; not so invariably (nor would we wish it), some show also their absolute position in the hierarchy of grades immediately. Thus 'first rate', 'second rate', 'third rate' show both order and absolute position – therefore they require careful handling as more precise tools do. But, whereas 'good', 'bad', and 'indifferent' show their order, they do not show their absolute position. This has to be determined from time to time, if precision is required. 'Good' for example can be at the top of a hierarchy or quite low down. Many parents have received school reports in which their children's work has been graded in different subjects as V.G., or G., or F., and, at the bottom will appear some such list as

> E. = Excellent
> V.G. = Very Good
> G. = Good
> F. = Fair
>> etc.

One obvious trick of sellers of graded wares is to use 'good' very nearly at the bottom and a number of superlatives above it.

(3) Some words which are professionally used mainly or exclusively as grading labels can be used in grading many different kinds of objects, persons, activities, etc. This applies, for example to 'good', 'bad' and 'indifferent'. Other professional grading words, which, for this and other reasons to be given below, may be called 'specialized', are restricted to one or a few types of

objects. For example, the terms 'Super', 'Extra Fancy', and 'Domestic' are, so far as I know, used as an ordered series with absolute position only of commercial consignments of apples. No doubt they could be used in a slightly less specialized way of other merchandise. Some, at least, of them could only be used very abnormally and metaphorically for people or activities.

An especially interesting and important set of specialized grading labels must be mentioned here. In calling them grading labels at all I acknowledge my second stretch of the word 'grading' and I must defend it. 'Rash', 'brave', 'cowardly', 'extravagant', 'liberal', 'mean', 'boorish', 'eligible (bachelor)', 'arrogant' are examples. Aristotle, in Books III and IV of the *N.E.* and Theophrastus in his *Characters* give numerous examples of such grading labels and seek to set out the criteria for their employment. As Aristotle noticed, we tend to have explicit grading labels only for some positions in some of the implied scales. Similarly 'indifferent' is a more sophisticated word than 'good' and 'bad'; it tends not to be used in popular discourse. They can be recognized as grading labels in that they show order of merit.[1]

If an Army Company Commander were, as a preliminary to choosing a band of men for an important operation, to go through his Company roll marking each man as 'rash', 'brave' or 'cowardly' we would surely not find it abnormal to say he was grading them (from a specialized point of view). If one were merely to say 'He is a brave man' one would not normally call it grading; but I cannot see that the stretch of the word so to call it is harmful. One resistance to calling 'brave' a grading label arises from the fact that being more specialized than 'good' it enables one to predict more accurately, though in a narrower field, the behaviour of a man so graded. This inclines people to think that it is a descriptive word in the way that 'ferocious' normally is. But this is just a mistake; the resistance must be overcome. It would be better to regard 'brave' as a grading label restricted to human behaviour in tight places, whereas 'good' grades in all places, including tight ones.

(4) As would be expected, specialized grading labels show

---

[1] Ἔνια γὰρ εὐθὺς ὠνόμασται συνειλημμένα μετὰ τῆς φαυλότητος. Aristotle, *N.E.*, 1107 a 9. Aristotle unfortunately says this of a few words and does not see that it applies to nearly everything which he discusses in this work.

absolute position as well as order more explicitly and more frequently than more general ones.

(5) In addition to professional and *ad hoc* grading words there are a number of what we might call enthusiastic amateurs — words of which it is difficult to say whether they function as grading labels or in ordinary classification. Sometimes they are obviously being used for the one purpose, sometimes for the other; often we seem to be killing two birds with one stone and grading and classifying at the same time. Examples of such words would be (*a*) *valuable*; contrast 'Her jewels were in bad taste but valuable' with 'That was valuable information'; (*b*) *nonsensical*, especially as it occurs in the works of some Logical Positivists — it is often hard to say whether a Logical Positivist who states that ethical statements are nonsensical wishes thereby to rate them lower than scientific statements, or merely to note a difference of logical type; one often suspects he is doing both. *Normal* is another example.

Conversely, even the most professional grading labels can be used sometimes practically descriptively — almost entirely so in the case of 'I walked a good four miles'; and often 'He gave him a good hiding' is used more to indicate severity than propriety.

There is nothing surprising or disconcerting in this. It will be convenient in the main, however, to examine typical, unequivocal examples of grading situations. One should be aware of marginal cases, but one should not harp on them.

(6) Apart from these marginal cases a further qualification must be made. Sometimes I merely describe an object and do not grade it explicitly when clearly my prime object is to grade. Thus two of the criteria for being a boor which Theophrastus gives us in his *Characters* are singing in one's bath and wearing hobnailed boots. Now I might mention that a man sings in his bath and wears hobnailed boots and not say that he is a boor although my prime object was to grade him as a boor. The reverse, too, can no doubt happen. In the packing sheds an employee might mention that a certain proportion of a batch of apples was Extra Fancy when his prime object was to give the implied descriptive information. Or I might tell you that a man has a good complexion primarily to enable you to recog-

nize him. It seems worth while explicitly to make this point because when made it is clearly not a damaging admission. If I distinguish commands from descriptions it would not be damaging to admit that I might say 'The door is open' with the prime intention of getting you to shut it.

(7) A further reason for distinguishing specialized from more general grading labels is that the specialized ones tend to have more clear cut and explicit criteria for their employment. This can best be illustrated by an actual example, so I will now quote from a Government publication the directions for the use of the grading labels *Super* and *Extra Fancy*, which were mentioned in (3) and which have been established by regulations made under the Agricultural Produce (Grading and Marketing) Acts of 1928 and 1931.[1] For brevity's sake the criteria for the grades *Fancy* and below are not quoted here. They are similar in principle and are given in full in the original document.

DEFINITIONS OF QUALITY
SUPER GRADE (DESSERT APPLES ONLY)

Size. — Each apple not less that $2\frac{1}{2}$ in. in diameter. The apples in any tray to be closely uniform in size and not to vary by more than $\frac{1}{8}$ in. in diameter.

Ripeness. — Each apple to have reached that stage of maturity which allows the subsequent completion of the ripening process.

Shape. — Each apple to be of good shape.

Blemish (other than russet). — Each apple to be entirely free from all blemishes including mechanical injuries, bruises and apple-scab.

Russeting. — Russeting in which the apple is cracked, and corky russeting, are not permitted on any apple. Solid russeting in the stem cavity and lightly dispersed russeting sprinkled over an aggregate of one-eight of the surface are permitted.

Colour. – Closely uniform in any tray.

Condition. – The apples in any tray to be closely uniform in stage of maturity.

EXTRA FANCY GRADE

Size. — Dessert. — Each apple not less than $2\frac{1}{4}$ in. in diameter. Cooking. — Each apple not less than $2\frac{1}{2}$ in. in diameter. — The apples in any container to be reasonably uniform in size and not to vary more than $\frac{1}{4}$ in. in diameter.

Ripeness. — Each apple to have reached that stage of maturity which allows the subsequent completion of the ripening process.

Shape. — No apple to be mis-shapen or malformed.

Blemish (other than russet). — Each apple to be free from such blemishes, bruises and other mechanical injuries as may affect keeping quality during the period which normally elapses between the time of packing and retail sale.

Uncracked apple-scab on any one dessert apple not to exceed $\frac{1}{8}$ in. square in the aggregate, and no one scab to be larger than $\frac{1}{16}$ in. square (a pin head).

Uncracked apple-scab on any one cooking apple not to exceed $\frac{1}{8}$ in. square in the aggregate and no one scab to be more than $\frac{1}{4}$ in. in diameter.

[1] *Apple Packing*, Bulletin number 84 of the Ministry of Agriculture and Fisheries, Appendix I. Published by H.M. Stationery Office.

Other superficial, non-progressive blemishes on any one apple not to exceed 4 in. square in the aggregate on dessert apples and ⅔ in. square in the aggregate on cooking apples.

Russeting. — Russeting in which the apple is cracked is not permitted. Solid or corky russeting in the stem cavity and eye basin is permitted. Dispersed russeting, together with solid russet spots not exceeding ⅓ in. in diameter sprinkled over an aggregate of one-third of the surface, is permitted.

Colour. — Dessert apples in any container to be reasonably uniform in colour.

Condition. — Dessert apples in any container to be reasonably uniform in stage of maturity.

(8) Many grading labels which have a specialized meaning can also in isolation be used more generally. 'Super', in slang usage, is an example. This constitutes a further reason for the use in technical contexts of *ad hoc* grading labels. Since these have no conventional criteria for employment there is no danger of confusing a general with a specialized employment as would be possible in the case of such a statement as 'That was a super consignment of apples'.

(9) In addition to the general philosophical problem of the nature of grading, the more general (less specialized) grading labels raise special problems of their own. It is perhaps partly for this reason that philosophers, who relish difficulties, have concentrated their attention on such general grading labels as 'good' and 'bad'. (There seems to be no good reason why they have neglected 'indifferent'.) One unfortunate result of concentrating on examples which raise special problems in contexts (ethical ones) which are especially complicated has been that the *general* problem of the nature of grading has been made to appear vastly more difficult than it is.

As a matter of fact 'first class' raises practically all the special problems which 'good' does, but for convenience I will now mention some of these special problems using 'good' as my example.

(*a*) Granted that 'good' is a grading label, is it used so generally because the criteria for its employment (corresponding to the technical criteria for the use of Extra Fancy) are very general, or because a different set of criteria is used in each different type of context (one set for apples, one for cabbages, one for guns, one for moral agents, and so on)?

(*b*) Granted that there are criteria for the use of some specialized grading labels which it would be linguistic eccentricity not to accept, is it so obvious that in every situation there are accepted criteria for the use of the label 'good', whether general or specially adapted to the context? Certainly if there are any criteria for the employment of the label 'good' they will be vague; but are there any, however vague, which are generally accepted? (This will be recognized as the familiar ethical difficulty about moral relativity.)

(c) Do there not appear to be many meanings of 'good'? Even if it turns out to be a grading label with accepted, though vague, criteria in some contexts (e.g. apple grading) may there not be others where, though not used as a natural description (as in 'good hiding'), it is not used as a grading label either?

(10) These special difficulties about such very general labels as 'good' must be admitted to infect more specialized grading labels in some cases, since many of them conceal a reference to good amongst their criteria. For example, in the show ring some of the criteria for judging animals are such pedestrian questions as whether this bit of the body is in line with that. But nearly always, I suspect, certainly in some cases, points are given for something like 'good general appearance' or 'good bearing in the ring'. See also the example of grading standards given in B(4) above.

C. The General Nature of Grading

In B we outlined some of the special problems about 'good'. Some of the most famous conundrums were missing, but this was partly because they apply to all grading labels. The basic problem *why* I grade higher a truthful man than a liar, or regard a whole apple as better than a pest-infested one, applies equally to the question why the criteria for Super should not be exchanged for the criteria of Extra Fancy. I shall start, therefore, by dealing with some of the general questions about grading, avoiding the special problems raised by 'good' and kindred words as long as I conveniently can.

Let us take a symbolic instance where X is a specialized label and A, B and C are the acknowledged natural criteria for its application. Let us further concentrate just on elucidating the question of how logically the use of a sentence 'This is X' differs from other uses of sentences, and how much and in what way it resembles some other uses. Thus for the present such questions as *why* A B C are the criteria for X will be disregarded.

The first thing which seems clear is that the question whether this is X is, granted the acknowledged criteria, as definitely decidable as are the empirical questions whether this is A, or B, or C. Of course, if A = 'not less than 2 inches in diameter', then the question whether this is X might be disputed in a marginal case because it might be disputed whether it *is* not less than 2 inches in diameter. But this kind of uncertainty obviously need not detain us now. The point is that if this has the empirical characters A, B, C, then it merits the grading label X, and if not, not; and this, in the required sense, is a decidable issue.

The facts noticed in the last paragraph tempt us to say that 'This is X' is just an ordinary empirical statement, that X is just an abbreviation for A B C; the relation of 'Super' to its criteria will be the same as 'Bramleys' to *its* criteria. But this doctrine, which will be recognized as a close relation of the doctrine of ethical naturalism, surely does not survive much reflection. At this stage we may merely note that the puzzle of how our intelligent apprentice was to distinguish apple grading from sorting out black and white draughts pieces is in effect repudiated by this naturalistic doctrine with the answer that there is no real distinction. And this is obviously false.

A second possible theory of the relation of X to A B C is a close relation of the doctrine of ethical intuitionism. Having rejected naturalism, but recognizing the close connection between X and A B C, we shall say, on this view, that X-ness (say, Extra Fanciness) is a non-natural, intuitable, toti-resultant character supervening on situations in which A B C are present, necessarily, but synthetically, connected with A B C. (If X-ness had been goodness and A knowledge this would not have been too much of a parody of intuitionism.) One negative argument for the view is that we have seen that naturalism fails, and that since the question whether this is X is decidable (objective) subjectivism will not do; nor, clearly, is it plausible to regard 'This is an Extra Fancy consignment of apples' as a squeal of delight. So in default of other theories Intuitionism stands. More positively we may say that 'Extra Fancy' is an adjective used in true or false statements; it must stand for some character; but it is not possible to see, hear, smell, Extra Fanciness, so it must be a non-natural character. Though I clearly do not accept this theory, I shall not attack it; probably even those who support it in the case of 'goodness' would not wish to support it in the case of Extra Fanciness or Full Fruit Standardness. The reason for mentioning it as a theoretical possibility is that all the arguments of Moore and Ross can be converted to apply in all cases of grading labels. It is hard to see why it should be true of 'goodness' but not of 'Extra Fanciness'.

I suppose that a case can be made for a Stevensonian[1] analysis in all grading situations. In stressing the close relation between X and A B C, it will be said, we have been concentrating on the second pattern of analysis too closely. Why the equivalence between X and A B C does not hold will become clear if we consider the neglected first pattern of analysis. To call an apple Extra Fancy would perhaps be to express a special type and degree of approval and call for it from others. Grading words will differ from others by the possession of a special emotive charge.

Certainly it cannot be denied that amongst words which are or become highly charged emotively are the more extreme of the more general grading labels ('good' and 'bad', but not so much 'indifferent', for obvious reasons). But we have already noticed that one extremely valuable use of *ad hoc* grading words is that by using them it is possible to grade without emotional repercussions.[2] It is perfectly intelligible that professional grading words should normally be emotively significant; it is true that we often exploit this emotive significance;[3] but to the true nature of grading these facts appear to be quite peripheral.

But all these three views, naturalism, intuitionism and the emotive theory have seized on some points of importance (so, we shall see later, have ordinary subjectivism and utilitarianism). Naturalism rightly emphasizes the close connection between the grading label and the set of natural characters which justify its use; intuitionism rightly emphasizes that this close connection is not identity of meaning and insists on the different logical

---

[1] C. L. Stevenson, *Ethics and Language*. (Yale University Press, 1944).
[2] See B (1).   [3] See B (2).

character of grading labels and natural descriptions. Both rightly stress the objective character of grading. The emotive theory, agreeing with intuitionism about the fault of naturalism, rightly stresses that the intuitionist cure of suggesting that grading labels are a special kind of non-natural descriptive adjective will not do.

At some stage we must say firmly (why not now?) that to describe is to describe, to grade is to grade, and to express one's feelings is to express one's feelings, and that none of these is reducible to either of the others; nor can any of them be reduced to, defined in terms of, anything else. We can merely bring out similarities and differences by examples and comparisons. That, too, in the end, would presumably be the only way of bringing out the difference between asking questions and giving orders (here, again, the marginal case such as 'Won't you go now?' must not be overstressed).

We can, for example, tell stories of people sorting out mixed piles of fruit into apples, plums and pears, and of people sorting mixed piles of apples into Blenheims, Bramleys, etc., and notice the difference between this activity and that of people who sort piles of mixed fruit into good, bad and indifferent piles, or Super, Extra Fancy, etc., piles. We can tell stories comparing also the distinction between mental classification and grading. Also, since philosophers are wedded to the expectation that indicative sentences will all be used for describing things, it will be as well to remind them of other non-descriptive (and non-emotive) uses of indicative sentences — Austin's performatory sentences, for example.[1]

Or let us go back to the problem of the relation between the natural criteria A B C and the grading label X which they justify. Is the sentence 'Anything which is A B C is X' analytic or synthetic? We have already noticed the naturalistic difficulties involved in answering 'analytic'; but yet the pointlessness, the impossibility, of maintaining that a thing is X if it is not A B C or denying that it is X if it is A B C makes the answer 'synthetic' equally unplausible.[2] But if we see that grading is different from

---

[1] [See Vol II, Ch. VIII, pp. 143ff. — EDITOR.]
[2] This will have to be modified later. See pp. 181-2. But this modification does not detract from the force of the argument in this context, where the acceptance of A B C as criteria is not being questioned.

ordinary description we can understand why this dilemma is insoluble; for the question whether the connection between two sets of characteristics is analytic or synthetic is a question which is designed to be asked where the related characters are descriptive. If not pressed too hard, the analogy of the relation between possession of the legal qualifications for a right or privilege and the possession of that right or privilege illuminates better the relation between natural criteria and grade far better than the analogy of expanded descriptive phrases and defined abbreviations. For to assert the possession of the legal qualifications for a certain right (say the vote), e.g. that one is a British subject twenty-one or more years old, not a peer, not mad, etc., is not to assert analytically the possession of the legal right; but to assert the legal right is not to assert the possession of any additional characteristics of a descriptive kind beyond these qualifications.[1] There are, of course, differences too; otherwise, being graded and possessing rights would be indistinguishable.

It may also be helpful to compare and contrast grading and choosing:

(*a*) There is an analogy between examining various objects and then saying 'I'll have that one' — which is a choice not a prediction — and mental grading.

(*b*) There is an analogy between examining various objects and then picking one out to have and physical grading.

There is a difference also in these cases which can be put by saying that between examining and choosing one grades, and chooses on the basis of one's grading.

Therefore (*c*) we may make up a more artificial example. Two captains picking sides will normally pick them on their estimate of the grade of the candidates for selection. But suppose there were certain rules for picking sides (say, that you have to pick the person who is first in alphabetical order) so that there would be a right and wrong way of picking your side. This example brings out the logical disparity which there can be between a non-descriptive activity like taking as a member of your side and the descriptive criteria for picking, and to that extent should make the relation between a grading label and its criteria less mysterious. It is not surprising that there should be

[1] [See Vol I, Ch. VIII. — EDITOR.]

a close connection between such an activity as picking something and the rules in accordance with which it is done and yet it be impossible to ask whether this connection is analytic or synthetic; the same thing should not be mysterious in regard to the natural criteria and physical grading. And if we see the unimportance of the difference between choosing something and saying 'I will have this' (we cannot ask whether the rule for choosing *entails* 'I will have this one'), we might also see how unimportant is the difference between grading and applying a grading label. Of course, choosing in accordance with a rule is very different in many ways from grading; the analogy which I want to stress is between the relation of rule to choice and criteria to grade label.

As a final attempt to bring out the general nature of grading it might be worth considering the word 'approve' for a while. It has been used frequently in recent philosophy to elucidate some specific grading situations.

Many philosophers recently[1] have been examining the distinction in English between the present perfect tense (I sit, I run, I play) and the present continuous tense (I am sitting, running, playing). It is obvious that they have very different uses. Some verbs appear to have no present continuous, nor does their use in the present perfect appear similar to the use of other verbs in either the present perfect or present continuous tense (I know, I believe, I regret). 'I approve' seems also to be such an anomalous verb. It is, indeed, possible to use its present continuous tense but an example will show how anomalous such a usage is: suppose Smith has to obtain your approval if he wishes to do a certain thing. Then you will signify your approval by writing 'I approve' (not 'I am approving'). Now supposing someone were to dash into your room and say 'What are you doing?' just while you are writing these words, you might possibly answer 'Oh, I'm just approving Smith's application'. Here 'I am approving' describes what I am doing, but the doing which I describe is not asserting, expressing, evincing or having any feeling or emotion or state of mind. I am writing 'I approve' and it is this action which I describe when I say 'I am approving'. To say, or write, 'I approve', however, is not to describe anything at all — it

---

[1] I have learnt something about this from Professors Ryle and Austin. I do not know who owns the patent.

can be described but is not itself a case of describing. In the case above it is something like giving your authority for an action.

Our other uses of 'approve' differ from this in many ways, but at least resemble it in that they are not descriptive uses.[1] Suppose, for example, someone says 'On the whole, I approve of the licensing laws'. Clearly this is not so absurd a thing to say as to give his authority for something which does not need his authority. A better suggestion is that he is grading the licensing laws as being on the whole at least satisfactory. He might change his mind and henceforth disapprove, but this kind of change of mind is not the correction of a factual error.

I do not wish to examine further the logic of approval for its own sake. I agree, however, with the subjectivists and emotivists in considering that the analogy between approving and grading is illuminating – but not in the way they think, in that I deny that 'I approve' is a description of the subjective events or that 'Please approve' is a request to have certain feelings.

That is all I can do in the way of a logical description of grading. Before going on to consider such other general problems as how we get the criteria in order to start grading we may first consider some of the special problems about 'good' and other very general grading labels.

D. SOME SPECIAL PROBLEMS ABOUT 'GOOD'

We shall start with the assumption (to be argued later) that 'good' is a grading label applicable in many different types of contexts, but with different criteria for employment in each. Now first it must be pointed out that such general grading labels have a character equivalent to the vagueness and open texture to which Dr. Waismann has drawn attention[2] in the case of ordinary descriptive words. Take the example of an apple again; what are the criteria for its being good? First no doubt it must have a pleasant taste and straightway we have a case of a vague and open textured criterion. A pleasant taste for whom? it will be asked; and there is no definitely right answer. But we must

---

[1] If I say 'I approve – do so as well' there is no descriptive element in my statement.
[2] *Proceedings of the Aristotelian Society*, Supplementary Volume for 1945. [Reprinted as Vol. I, Ch. VII. — EDITOR.]

not exaggerate this vagueness. For if we answer 'to a majority of apple eaters' there is nothing seriously wrong with the answer as there would be if we answered 'to the Archbishop of Canterbury' or 'to squirrels'. But can we guarantee that it will be a stable majority? Clearly not; but this should not be philosophically worrying; the simple fact is that but for the contingent fact that there is such a stable majority we should have to give up grading apples altogether or else give up using pleasant taste as one of the criteria for grading apples.[1]

The writings of some philosophers seem to suggest that pleasant taste is the only criterion of goodness in apples,[2] but this is surely false. Other criteria are size, shape, keeping quality, nutritive value, pleasing appearance and, perhaps, feel. Now we have already noticed vagueness and open texture within one criterion. But the list itself has the same properties. No one can give the precise list; some will omit a criterion I have given, add another, vary the emphasis, and none of them need be wrong (though we could produce a list which would be certainly wrong). And it is always possible to think of something else which might be taken as a criterion or which has been implicitly used as such and not been noted. But surely as long as we recognize this it need not worry us any more than the vagueness of the criteria for the use of descriptive adjectives. 'Good' is *very* vague – so is 'bald', or 'middle-aged'. So long as there is a general consensus in the employment of criteria all is well. If, as sometimes happens in the case both of vague descriptions and of vague grading labels, this consensus is missing, communication becomes uncertain (democratic, body-line bowling).

In contrast with the apple consider a cabbage (the contrast could be made much greater). Many of the criteria will be quite different from those in the case of apples – firm heart, a bright green or bluish-green colour, few spreading outer leaves, long-standing, etc.

Now, if the grading label 'good' were, in each of these and

---

[1] As a matter of fact in the technical grading of apples taste is not used as a criterion. This, no doubt, is partly because you cannot both taste and sell whole, partly because the taste of varieties is constant and it is assumed that only varieties will be further graded which have already survived the test of taste.

[2] ' "This is good", may mean "This is pleasant" as when we say "This is good cheese"' Paton, *Proceedings of the Aristotelian Society*, Supp. Vol. XXII, p. 110.

all other cases, merely shorthand for the sum of the criteria (naturalism) we should have the absurd situation that 'good' was a homonym with as many punning meanings as the situations it applied to; it could not significantly be used of a theatrical performance in the sense in which it is used of an apple. This, granted our present assumptions, constitutes a most graphic refutation of naturalism. On the other hand, to regard the relation between 'good' and the criteria for a good apple as synthetic is equally absurd. If someone were to admit that an apple was of 2 inches diameter, regularly shaped, of pleasing taste, high vitamin content and pest-free, nor claimed that it lacked some other essential characteristic but none the less denied that it was a good apple it would not merely be empiri-cally surprising; it would involve a breakdown in communication.

The obvious naturalistic reaction to this, which, though for different reasons, might be shared by other schools of thought, would be to deny any assumption that the criteria are different in each different type of situation. 'The real criteria', they might say, 'for the employment of "good" are much more general than you have made it appear. The criteria which a show judge might mention for a good Shorthorn cow or a cutler for a good knife are not the real criteria of goodness. The real criterion is easy production of a desired end, approximate or ultimate, in each case. 'The so-called criteria', they might say, 'of the judge and the cutler are really no more than signs or symptoms that the object in question will satisfy this general criterion.' 'We must distinguish', they might add, 'the various senses of "good," provisionally limiting ourselves to the modest distinction of good as a means and good as an end. Then there will be one general criterion of good as a means — already given, and one for good as an end which is perhaps something like "worth choosing for its own sake". Perhaps, on reflection', they conclude, 'we might wish to distinguish other senses, but we do not require the myriad of punning senses you suggested but only a few which in any case will be paronyms, not homonyms.'

No doubt this presentation of their argument could be bettered in many details, but it is not in detail that I wish to attack it, so perhaps it will suffice. Let me first admit that if one examines the kinds of thing which one employs as criteria, then, though this may not be the best way of putting it, one possible division of the criteria employed is into criteria which we choose for themselves and others which we choose for their consequences. Some criteria, too, as Plato pointed out in the *Republic*, we choose both for themselves and their consequences. Let me also admit that some criteria are less central than others, that some *are* used mainly as signs of the presence of criteria more difficult to detect in themselves. But these admissions in no way justify a distinction of two senses of 'good' – good as a means and good as an end. Firstly, the criteria which we employ for the grading label 'good' in any given case will usually include criteria of both types, and of Plato's dual type; if there are indeed any things for the goodness of which all criteria fall into either class these are limiting cases and not normal types. It would be a great mistake to imagine that farmers, cutlers and fruit growers value their products only as means to ends; and the consumer pays less for an unsightly vegetable because it *is* unsightly and not because of any detrimental effects of unsightliness. If I am asked whether a good apple is good as a means or as an end I should not know how to answer; it is not a real question. But the division of *criteria* which we have admitted would only justify a distinction of two senses of 'good' if it were logically impossible to mix the two sets of criteria, if at all.

It might perhaps be replied to this, though even before argument it is not very plausible, that all we have shown is that normally anything which we grade as good we call good in both senses of the word at once – *that* was why I could not answer in which sense of 'good' the apple was good. Still I have not established that there really are different sets of criteria for different types of situation. Let us answer that, even if an apple, *per impossibile*, satisfied all the criteria which we require for good as an end and good as a means in the case of cabbages, it would not be a good apple. Though we have agreed that some criteria are less central than others, there still remains a hard core of criteria which have to be satisfied in each different case, which cannot be generalized into any one or two formulae. Why an apple which tasted like a good cabbage would certainly be a very bad apple we have not yet ventured to discuss; but a very bad apple it certainly would be; I cannot see how my

N

imaginary opponents would be able to explain this fact, which seems to require different criteria for goodness in apples and cabbages (and *a fortiori* in men and guns). Omitting consideration of certain cant or slang phrases I see no reason for thinking that there is more than one sense of the word 'good'. On the other hand, since I deny an analytic identity of meaning between criteria and grading labels I still hold that the criteria are, as the facts seem to require, different in each situation.

I add at this stage two small points which perhaps illuminate and are illuminated by the above discussion.

1. Suppose that I, ignorant of horses, point to a horse in a field and say 'That's a good horse'. In a way we want to say that I know what I mean — after all I know how to use the various words and understand their syntax. But in a way we might want to say that I do not really know what I mean. For suppose that an expert had said 'That's a good horse'. Now, looking at it once, and at a distance, he may be mistaken; he needs more facts than he has in order to be confident of the truth of his statement. But the kind of lack of confidence which I ought to feel is quite different; for, unlike the expert, I will not be enabled by further examination of the horse to decide at all whether it is a good horse. And because I have made a statement which I just do not know how to verify or falsify (in the way grading statements are verified and falsified) we tend, as I suggested, to say that I did not really know what I meant.

2. Grading statements being, as I maintain, objectively decidable, they are, for many reasons, more important and impressive than mere indications of personal likes and dislikes. We therefore tend to use them when all we are really entitled to do is to state our likes and dislikes. Thus I might easily say 'That's a good horse' being ignorant of the criteria for a good horse and therefore really only entitled to say that I like the look of it. We really know this, as becomes clear when we reflect that only a very conceited person would chance his arm by saying 'That's a good horse' unless he knew or believed that his companion was as ignorant of horses as he was. We might say it to a city clerk — but not to a Newmarket trainer. These considerations help, I think, both to bring out the difference between grading and expressing one's likes, and to explain why some

people, observing that we naughtily interchange them, tend to confuse them.

So much for the way we use such general grading labels as 'good' and how their use differs from that of more specialized grading labels, though the distinction is not a hard and fast one.

E. THE ESTABLISHMENT OF GRADING CRITERIA

So far we have confined our study of grading to cases where it is fairly clear that there are criteria for grading, and without asking whether there must always be accepted criteria, or why the accepted criteria are accepted. We have certainly said nothing whatsoever to deal with such special problems as that raised by the moral reformer, who is often clearly intelligible and yet may almost be defined as the man who does not accept the accepted criteria. I cannot pretend to offer a complete answer to these problems, but there are a few things which are perhaps worth saying about them.

The first point to be made is that the question whether there are any objective and accepted criteria for grading and how they function, which we have just left, is a quite different problem from the problem why we employ and accept these criteria. This, I think, has not always been fully realized; but certain theories could be much more powerfully stated if they took it into account.

Subjectivism, in its traditional varieties as an account of how we use the word 'good' in general, for example, is usually stated in a manner which makes it an utterly absurd view. To say that there are no objective criteria, that there is no right or wrong opinion about whether this is good cheese or (to take a case of something which is clearly not good as a means) a good lap-dog, seems quite preposterous. Anyone who knew about cheese or dogs would laugh at you. It is equally preposterous, as Broad points out,[1] to hold that a statement that some cheese is good is a statistical statement about peoples' likes and dislikes, passions and emotions. But if we remodel this latter subjectivist theory and treat it not as a theory about the way we use the word 'good'

[1] See his essay on Hume in *Five Types of Ethical Theory*. I do not necessarily agree that Hume held this preposterous view.

but as a theory about how the criteria for grading cheese or lap-dogs come to be accepted and established, it becomes a much more plausible theory. The theory will now admit our account of how we use the word 'good'; its contribution will be as follows: it is a fact that there is a stable majority (we need not now settle among which people the majority will be) who prefer, like, choose, cheese with the characteristics A B C. Then A B C become the characteristics which are accepted even by the minority, for grading cheese. Thus even if one happens to hate all cheese, one will still be able sensibly to distinguish good from bad cheese; *mutatis mutandis* the same applies to lap-dogs or anything else. Before the acceptance of such conventional criteria for good cheese the question whether some sample of cheese is good will have no answer.[1] After their acceptance the question will have a definite answer. This seems to me, thus recast as an answer to a different question, a very formidable theory. In the case of cheese it is just about right.

But few philosophical theories have the monopoly of all truth; any rival which survives long does so because it has got hold of some important point. But most of the prevalent philosophical theories about the meaning of 'good' can be recast as theories of how we arrive at criteria of goodness.

Now, *a priori* there is no reason why there should be any one answer to the question why we accept the criteria which we do accept. We might adopt some criteria for certain reasons and some for others. Consider a utilitarian theory of goodness, for example, recast as a theory that we choose the criteria we do choose because things satisfying these criteria in a high degree subserve more easily the ends for which we employ them. As a general theory this is no doubt lamentably inadequate, but as an account of why we employ *some* criteria (e.g. sharpness in the case of a knife) it seems very plausible, and I have no doubt that if it makes this limited claim it is correct.

Or consider social theories of goodness (especially moral goodness) which hold that a man or form of behaviour is good in so far as he or it contributes to sòcial life and well-being. Once again, considered as an account of why we accept *some* of the criteria of goodness, I have no doubt that it is of value. No

---

[1] See pp. 182-3 below on this point.

doubt truthfulness as a criterion of a good man is at least in part accepted for this kind of reason. And if anyone wishes to maintain that this is a *rational* ground for accepting the criterion, why not?

I have no doubt that there are other reasons for accepting criteria for grading, but we cannot aim at a complete catalogue; in no circumstance could we have a right to regard any catalogue as complete. No doubt some criteria for some things are retained for all kinds of odd reasons. Perhaps few people nowadays could imagine why a family is better if the names of more of its former members and their interrelationships are recorded.

But what of matters where there is not complete agreement on the criteria for grading something? This is a situation which surely does sometimes arise. If the disagreement is minor it matters no more than minor disagreements about the requirements for baldness. But disagreement is admittedly not always minor; the slayer and eater of aged parents and the moral reformer now rear their (respectively) ugly and reverend heads.

Schematically, the main patterns of moral and other grading disagreements seem to be as follows:

(1) We accept roughly or exactly the same criteria of goodness (or of being first class, etc.) but haven't yet examined them all. When one says of some object under discussion that it is good and the other says that it is bad, we will be speculating on partial evidence. We can settle the question by examining the other agreed criteria. This raises no problems, and its frequent occurrence is therefore insufficiently noticed by philosophers.

(2) We accept the same criteria but it is a marginal case. Here perhaps we shall never settle our agreement. But this raises no more problems than the unsettlable dispute as to who won a close race. Such disputes quite often occur and naturally last longer and attract more attention than the first type.

(3) We have no agreement, or very little, on criteria. Here we just cannot settle our problems for the overwhelmingly good reason that we cannot discuss them. We shall normally assume that we have the same criteria and talk at cross purposes until we find that we cannot settle our dispute. We shall then either recognize what has happened and try to reach some agreed criteria failing which further discussion will be worthless, i.e.

we shall stop discussing the undiscussable question whether this O is good and discuss the question how to grade Os. The reasons we shall offer for accepting the criteria we propose will be such as were mentioned in our last discussion. Or if we do not recognize our predicament we shall think each other stupid and/or dishonest and fall back on rhetoric and abuse.

(4) We may have important disagreements on criteria and Jones, the reformer, may know it. He may then openly reveal himself as not asking the question whether a thing is good or not by accepted standards, but as advocating new standards, new criteria. In this case it will be clear that we are not arguing whether a thing is good or bad in the ordinary way as in (1) and (2) above but arguing what criteria to use in order to argue that kind of question. More likely, and perhaps not so clear-headedly, he will use the rhetorical device of talking as though his proposed new criteria were the accepted criteria; this is one of the most effective methods of getting new criteria accepted.[1] This trick is commonly employed not merely by moral reformers but also by advertisers – they try to make you accept the characteristics of their wares as criteria of goodness in that class of merchandise by pretending that everyone (or all the best people) knows that these *are* the accepted criteria. If people do not recognize this device for what it is, it may either be successful with enough people to get the standards actually changed or else we shall go through all the trying manœuvres of type (3) above.

It should be added that criteria of grade can change without the impetus of a militant reformer. No doubt 'eligible' was a grading word as applied to bachelors in the eighteenth and nineteenth centuries. No doubt also the criteria of eligibility gradually shifted, under the pressure of social evolution, from such things as a baronetcy and land to a good job and railway shares.

If this rough schema of disagreements be accepted (in practice of course the types will be complicated and mixed up with each other) the answer to the problem of disagreement about grading criteria seems to be this: grading words can only be *used* success-fully for communication where criteria are accepted. Where they are not there can only be confusion and cross purposes

---

[1] Stevenson, *Ethics and Language*, Ch. IX 'Persuasive Definitions' is very relevant here.

until it is seen that the only discussion possible between such people is what criteria for grading to adopt – grading words must then be discussed, not used.

The need for agreed criteria can perhaps be further illustrated in the following way. There are situations in which we do not naturally use grading words at all and where, therefore, there are no accepted criteria for grading. Consider for example the prime numbers. So far as I know, no one has yet graded the prime numbers as good and bad, or first and second class, and so far as I know there are no criteria for doing so. Unless my inadequate mathematical training misleads me, I suggest that if anyone were to say '17 is an exceptionally bad prime number' there would be a complete failure to communicate – a failure not due to anybody's ignorance or incapacity. Only after criteria were adopted (I cannot imagine what in this case they would possibly be unless superstitious astrological ones) would such a statement be of any use in communication. (Whether it would therefore be previously meaningless may be left to the reader to decide.)

But the extreme vagueness of the criteria in some grading situations undoubtedly makes it appear that there are no criteria to philosophers who like and expect things to be clear cut. Pre-eminently people might think this to be the case with the moral goodness of a person. We cannot hope to deal adequately with this point now but a few observations might be permitted and must suffice.

A good man, without further qualification, obviously must fulfil different criteria in different contexts (for club and church membership, for example). This appears to be so even if we qualify our grading label and write 'morally good'. In some contexts, one might almost say, the criteria of moral goodness in earlier twentieth-century England can be roughly specified as being conformity to Ross's list of *prima facie* duties. In other contexts what a man does will be less important and why he does what he does more important ('Motive not action makes a man good or bad'). Roughly the way to find out what criteria are being employed is to ask why the man has been graded thus. But however the criteria may vary from context to context they must and can be recognized for effective communication; without it we tend all too often merely to 'recite Empedoclean verses'.

A further resistance to recognizing the ordinary grading mechanism as operating in morals is set up by the undoubted fact that moral grading is so much more important; we feel so much more strongly about the attainment of high moral grades than others. Being a good cricketer is excellent in its way, but not vital; being a good citizen, a good father, a good man, is very different. This creates the impression that to call someone a good man is logically different from calling him a good cricketer. The one point I shall make about this is that in grading people in non-moral matters and in grading things we are dealing with dispensable qualifications in people and dispensable things. But moral grade affects the whole of one's life and social intercourse — a low grade in this makes other high gradings unimportant. The nearest approach to morals in indispensability is made by manners; and surely it is significant that we feel next most strongly after morals about manners — indeed there is a borderline where it is hard to distinguish which we are dealing with. But when we acknowledge these facts we surely give no reason for expecting a logical difference as well.

F. The Relation between Alternative Sets of Grading Criteria

Now for the final problem; when there are differences of opinion about what grading criteria to adopt in a given situation is there not a right and wrong about it; can we not say that these are the right, these are the wrong criteria; or are we to say that the distinction, for example, between higher and lower, enlightened and unenlightened, moral codes is chimerical? In some cases we would perhaps be content to admit that there was no right or wrong about it; the differences in criteria arise from different interests, different environments, different needs; each set is adequate to its own sphere. But in others we certainly do not want to say this; the distinction, for example, between higher and lower moral codes cannot be lightly brushed aside. Roughly the question of whether we wish to decide this issue appears to depend largely on whether the simultaneous use of different sets of grading criteria by juxtaposed groups is in departmental, dispensable matters, or in all-embracing matters such as moral codes (more or less enlightened) and manners (more or less polished or cultivated).

This problem is clearly a large one which for adequate treatment would require a book in itself. We can here only sketch a method of dealing with it.

Clearly when we debate which of two moral codes is more enlightened there is no ultimate court of appeal, no umpire, unless some agreed revealed religious code is treated as a *deus ex machina*. Nor will it do to say that 'more enlightened' means the same as 'the one I advocate'. This is shown by the fact that though I cannot admit that the code I advocate is less enlightened than yours, I can admit that it may be; just as I cannot admit that my present belief about anything is mistaken, but can admit that it may be.

The important clue for dealing with this problem is to notice that *enlightened, unenlightened, higher, lower* are grading labels. Of course, we cannot, when debating what criteria to use for moral grading, grade the criteria morally. But we can grade them by enlightenment provided, of course, that the disputants have an agreed set of criteria of enlightenment. We cannot hope now to give a complete and clear list of these criteria; no doubt they are vague; and it is easier to employ criteria than to recognize them. But surely one criterion would be that the reasons for adopting the criteria are not superstitious or magical; that some reasons can be given would seem to be another. Again, the contrast between the health, wealth and happiness of people living under different moral codes cannot prove the superiority of one code over another, but it does seem to be a criterion of enlightenment. The misery of slaves, for example, is surely a potent cause for the rejection of a moral code as unenlightened in which a slave owner or trader is a good man.

If people have not agreed criteria for enlightenment, I do not know what one can do about it. All co-operative activities, all uses of language, must start from some agreed point. One needs a fixed point to move the world with one's lever.

Finally two postscripts.

(1) I am not wedded to the words 'grade' and 'criterion'. I use 'grade' rather than 'evaluate', for example, largely because 'evaluate' tends to be associated with a special kind of theory.

Again, in the Government directions for grading apples the word 'standard' is used as a synonym for my word 'criterion'. Possibly it is better in some ways but has the dangerous overtone for philosophers of 'moral standard'.

(2) Nothing has been said in this paper about 'right', 'wrong' and cognate words. The discussion has ranged widely enough without that. But it might be as well to make it quite clear that I do not regard them as grading labels. They function quite differently, and what I have said does not apply to them.

CHAPTER X

HISTORICAL EXPLANATION

By A. M. MacIver

THE ultimate stuff of history is the countless individual doings of individual human beings through the ages, together with such natural events and facts as have conditioned those human doings – events such as the normal alternation of fair and foul weather or the cycle of the seasons, as well as earthquakes, inundations and droughts, and facts such as the fact that here is sea and there is dry land, this land is fertile and that is barren, this has coal and iron and that has none. But these natural facts and events are important to the historian only in so far as they condition human doings. The actual individual doings, on the other hand, collectively make up his subject-matter.

This is a plain fact which Idealist philosophers of history, with their slogan that 'all history is contemporary history', completely overlook. Oakeshott or Collingwood calls the history (let us say) of the Peloponnesian War a 'mode of experience', meaning by this his own experience in his twentieth-century Oxford or Cambridge college room, forgetting that what made the history was experience all right, but the experience of thousands of poor devils two dozen centuries ago. The Idealist philosophers have unthinkingly transferred to history an argument that was plausible enough when applied to physical science. It is easy to argue that atoms and electrons are mere postulates of theory; nobody has ever met one in the flesh; to say that they have such and such characters, or behave in such and such ways, is only to say that this is what physicists at present find it convenient to suppose. But, whatever may be the case with atoms and electrons, human beings are not mere creatures of theory. To say that we are now doing whatever we are actually doing, and for the reasons for which we are actually doing it, is not to say merely that this is what some future historian is going to find it convenient for his purposes then to suppose. And, by parity of reasoning, whatever men were doing a thousand years ago does not depend upon what historians find it convenient to suppose now.

Individual human doings collectively make up the stuff of history. What each one of us is doing here and now is part of the subject-matter of the history that will be written in the future. If what we were all doing now were different, the history of this period would be different. But history is not itself the record of all these doings. The historian selects and (what is more important) generalizes. It is thanks to this that the proposition that 'all history is contemporary history' is not patently absurd, because it is true that each historian selects and generalizes with reference to his own contemporary interests. But his generalizations are true or false in proportion as they represent or misrepresent all the individual doings and happenings. (This is the foundation-stone upon which I am going to build the whole of my argument in this paper – a stone which the builders of philosophies of history hitherto have, so far as I can understand them, almost universally rejected.) To show up by contrast the character of all actual written history, we may perhaps find it convenient to suppose an ideal written history, which would tell the whole story of everything that ever happened to every human being, which we might call 'the Book of the Recording Angel'. The function of the historian (we might then say) is not, indeed, to copy out extracts from the Book of the Recording Angel, but it is to make an intelligent précis of some part of it. This is not to depreciate the work of the historian. The function of the Recording Angel could, after all, in a fully mechanized Heaven, be performed by an electrical device, whereas the making of the historian's précis requires intelligence. But, though the précis may be made for some particular purpose and omit what is not relevant to that purpose, it must not misrepresent the contents of the original.

But, although all history rests upon this same foundation and all actual history generalizes, there are many different levels of historical generality. What I have called 'the Book of the Recording Angel' may be regarded as the ideal limit to which history approximates as generalization tends to zero. At the lowest level of generality of all kinds of historical writing is biography – particularly that kind of biography which hardly professes to be more than a collection of anecdotes about its subject arranged in chronological order. This hardly generalizes at all: it differs from the Book of the Recording Angel itself only in that it selects, and that according to no fixed principle other than the accidental limitations of the writer's sources of information. Almost at the other extreme stands the sort of general world history which knows no epochs except the great technological revolutions which completely transformed the whole background of human life, for which hardly anything worth mentioning happened between the discovery of the smelting of metals at the close of the Neolithic Age and the perfection of the steam engine by James Watt. Slightly (but only slightly) less general than this is Marxian history, which considers events only in so far as they have affected or followed from changes in the large-scale organization of society for the production, distribution and consumption of economic goods. History at all these different levels is (that is to say, can be) equally good history. We do not get a better or a worse view of a field according as we take a bird's eye, or a man's eye, or a worm's eye view of it, though we get a different view; and yet they are all views of the same field.

Serious trouble only begins when levels are not distinguished. From this many futile disputes arise. Take for example the question, still often eagerly disputed, whether the acts of individuals determine the course of history. Obviously they do. The only proper question is: How much? History is nothing but the resultant of all the acts of millions of individuals, but the consequences of some individual acts are still distinguishable after a considerable lapse of time, while the consequences of others blend together almost immediately. The fact that John Smith at a particular time on a particular morning hurried to the local branch of his own bank and withdrew a much larger sum than he would normally have withdrawn, because he had heard that another bank had failed or was about to fail, goes down to history only as part of the fact that there was a run on the banks in that week, which precipitated a world financial crisis; John Smith's contribution can no longer be distinguished. On the other hand, the fact that General Brown, overcome by a fit of pessimism, surrendered the strategically vital fortress of which he was in command, when a more resolute general could have held it until relief arrived, perhaps led immediately to the loss of the war and a whole string of consequences, all of which can be traced back to that single act. Certainly the loss of the war will have other contributory causes. General Brown's surrender would perhaps not have had this result if the relieving force had been in a position immediately to retrieve the situation, but in fact it was not, because it was inadequately armed, because there had been financial corruption in the quartermaster-general's department, the causes of which corruption ramify back into the whole political and social history of the country. Still the fact remains that General Brown need not have capitulated, and that, if he had not, the war could have been won, so that the loss of the war and all that followed from it was the direct consequence of this individual act of capitulation. (The case might equally have been that of an unknown private soldier, who might have prevented the enemy from gaining what proved to be a vital point, though in that case it would probably escape mention in the history-books, for the question is only whether a chain of consequences could be traced back to an individual act, if it were known.) It is possible that, if General Brown had not capitulated unnecessarily, some other commander on the same side would have done so, but this is not certain and anyhow he might not have surrendered such a vitally important position. As, however, we take a broader and a broader view, such possibilities may begin to accumulate into probabilities. If General Brown was constitutionally liable to fits of pessimism, he should never have been appointed to command a strategically vital fortress in time of war. A country whose administration made such unwise appointments might by good luck come successfully through one war, but would hardly survive a series of wars if it persisted in the habit. Where such appointments are favoured by persistent conditions, such as the general decay of a social class from which military officers continue to be drawn, resulting in turn from a cause such as the ruin of a country's agriculture by the appearance of a more powerful competitor on the world market, it may be possible to predict that such a country will ultimately either be conquered in war or else succumb without fighting; though not precisely how or when.

We can see how this bears upon that favourite example in arguments about the influence of 'great men' in history – the part played by Julius Caesar in the history of the Roman Empire. It is almost certain that, if Julius Caesar had died in infancy, someone else would have unified the Mediterranean world under a single autocratic monarchy. The situation was ripe for it. Both Sulla and Pompey had already very nearly achieved it. As seen by the universal historian who thinks in no time-unit less than a century and no social unit smaller than a whole civilization, the picture would be just the same even if Julius Caesar had never lived. For those who take a closer view, however, the picture would have been very different. If Caesar had not lived, Rome might have had to wait another generation or even longer for a man who combined the necessary ambition with the necessary abilities, and the resulting prolongation of senatorial anarchy might have had effects which would have been felt for centuries. For his actual contemporaries the difference would have been all-important.

History at different levels has different periods and different turning-points. For his own subjects the death of an individual autocrat may mark an epoch, but for later historians it may be some event in the middle of his reign, perhaps hardly noticed by contemporaries, which marks the end of one period, which began long before he was born, and the beginning of another, which continued long after he was dead, the death of the ruler himself being something quite insignificant. Marx, though he introduced the conception of the Industrial Revolution, attached no particular importance to the introduction of power-driven machinery. His historical researches were mainly concerned with the transition from feudalism to capitalism, with the ultimate object of applying the lesson to predict the course of the expected subsequent transition from capitalism to socialism. Most interesting to him was the change in the distribution of social force which came when production for profit took the place of production for use. The introduction of power-driven machinery appears in his account as a mere incident in the subsequent development – just one of the devices by which capitalists, in a competitive economy, sought to turn the labour-power of the workers to more and more profit. Marx duly considers its multifarious social repercussions, but, from his point of view, none of them is so important as the introduction, centuries earlier, of the new economic motive of profit. If, however, we try to look at the history of the last few hundred years through the eyes of historians living thousands of years hence, we can see at once that the difference made by the transition from feudalism to capitalism will then have become almost imperceptible, but differences made by the introduction of power-driven machinery will be impossible to overlook. Yet this does not mean either that Marx was mistaken or that the historians of the future will be mistaken, but only that history divides into different periods at different levels of historical generality.

Now we can introduce the subject of 'historical explanation'. By this we must understand, I think, only such explanation as is part of the historian's business as such, and not include any further explanations in which use happens to be made of the historian's results. In this sense, whatever 'historical explanation' may be, it is not the scientific sort of 'explanation' described in Mill's *System of Logic*, Book III, chapter xii – the discovery of hitherto unknown universal laws of which particular phenomena are instances, and the resolution of universal laws into mere special cases of other universal laws even more general. When we say that history 'generalizes', we do not mean that it seeks to establish universal laws. We contrast the 'generality' of historical statements with the individuality of the facts on which they are based, meaning that they are related to those facts as the general proposition 'I possess some philosophical books' is related to the individual facts (my possession of this copy of Plato's *Republic*, and that copy of Kant's *Critique*, and so forth) which make it true. In logical terminology, the historical proposition is 'general', but 'particular', not 'universal'. A typically historical statement is 'The Normans defeated the English at Hastings in 1066'. The battle itself was a vast medley of individual actions and experiences – this man shooting this arrow, that man avoiding it or being hit by it, horses stumbling, men feeling pain or fear or exultation – but the historical statement takes it as a whole and selects for mention just that aspect of it which bears upon the historian's purpose – in this case, the fact that as a result the Duke of Normandy was able to make himself King of England.

It is not the business of the historian to 'generalize' in any other sense than this.

To say this is not to give orders to historians. It is only to put a limitation on the use of the word 'history' in this discussion, which is, I think, supported by ordinary usage. I think that most people would agree, for example, that in Toynbee's *Study of History*, while many of the 'annexes' and incidental digressions are real 'history', the body of the work is not — it is a new sort of 'science'. Its object is 'explanation' in Mill's sense — to discover the hitherto unknown laws governing the establishment and disintegration of civilizations. This is something which only a trained historian can attempt, since it demands an immense equipment of historical knowledge, but, when he attempts it, he is going beyond history. It is possible — we may grant this hypothetically, without committing ourselves — that historical research is wasted if its results are not afterwards applied in this way; but, even so, the application is not historical research itself, any more than the collection of social statistics is by itself the formulation of a social policy, even if it is true that statistics are wasted unless made the basis of a policy. It would be 'historical explanation' to account for the rise of the Sumerian, or the fall of the Minoan, civilization, but it is 'scientific explanation' to account for the rise and fall of civilizations as such. Even if 'historical explanation' is (as it may be) explanation by reference to universal laws, it differs from 'scientific explanation' in taking the laws as known and concentrating upon the analysis of the particular event, asking which of the known laws actually account for it, and how, and in connection with what other particular events. This is what a historian ordinarily does whenever he professes to 'explain' an event, or the origin of an institution, or any of the other things which it is thought to be his business to explain, and I take it that the question which we are intended to answer here is, what sort of an explanation this is (or can be.)

Half of the correct answer to this question is, I submit, that there is a different historical explanation appropriate to every different level of historical generality. Even in the Book of the Recording Angel there will be explanation as well as simple narrative. It will say, not merely 'Napoleon was annoyed', but 'Napoleon was annoyed because his breakfast coffee had been

o

weaker than he liked it'. This 'because' raises familiar philosophical problems. It suggests some such major premiss as 'All
human beings are annoyed whenever they do not get exactly
what they like', but we know that this is not in fact universally
true. It is in a more recondite manner than this that the luke-
warmness of the coffee 'explains' Napoleon's irritation. But I will
assume that the nature of this sort of 'explanation' is a question
for another symposium. It is not these problems, concerning
the kind of 'explanation' appropriate to individual human actions,
which are troubling us when we are puzzled about specifically
'historical explanation'. We are thinking of explanation at
higher levels of historical generality. But the second half of my
answer to this, the question which concerns us here and now, is
that correct explanation at these higher levels can be nothing
but the reflection of correct explanation at the individual level.
Individual acts have individual causes. This I take as acknowledged, whatever the philosophical difficulties concerning the
precise kind of causation involved. Just as the historical *statement*
summarizes a large number of individual acts, representing a
character which runs through them all — perhaps the way in
which they all contributed to a particular result — neglecting
all their multitudinous features which were irrelevant to this,
so in the historical *explanation* some of the individual causes of
the individual acts disappear as unimportant, but others add up
to something which can be stated generally. Its validity consists
in representing fairly the balance of the underlying causes. The
difference between a correct explanation and an incorrect one,
at any particular level of historical generality, corresponds to the
difference, in optics, between an undistorted and a distorted
picture, at any particular degree of reduction of scale, at which
some details inevitably disappear.

Historical explanation becomes confused whenever there is
confusion of levels. Perhaps for brevity's sake we must sometimes say such things as that Mr. Jones votes Conservative because
he is a business man; but it is always dangerous. Mr. Jones votes
Conservative for his own personal reasons, which can be indicated
(though not without already generalizing) by saying that he was
brought up as a Conservative, that all his friends are Conservatives, that his business experience has drawn his attention

to the considerations in favour of the Conservative policy and
against the Socialist, that nothing has ever happened to induce
him to pay equal attention to the considerations on the other
side, and that he is more biased than he himself realizes in favour
of a political policy which would tend to his personal advantage.
Other business men like Mr. Jones also vote Conservative, each
for his own reasons, but all for similar reasons, because their
situations are similar. This is the basis for the legitimate historical
generalization that 'business men vote Conservative because the
Conservative Party represents their class interests'. But it is
confusion of levels to use this generalization to explain individual
behaviour. Marxist historians are frequently guilty of this confusion, which results in absurd notions of 'economic determinism',
implying that it is impossible for an individual to have any
political opinions which are not those of his economic class.
Idealist historians may commit the same confusion, implying
that no individual can make his own judgments but that they
are forced upon him by the Spirit of the Age. For events at
the individual level explanations must be found at the same level.
But the generalization that the Conservative Party is the party
of the business men can legitimately be used (say) to explain
the decline of the Conservative Party as a natural consequence
of the decreasing importance of private, as compared with
public, enterprise in the national economy. This is (that is to say
may be, provided that the facts support it) a valid historical
explanation at what we may call the 'Marxist' level of historical
generality.

In historical explanation at all levels above the purely individual,
whatever is unimportant is disregarded. This sounds subjective,
but in fact there is no subjectivity in it, apart from the subjectivity
of the motive dictating choice of a particular level. The test of
importance, at any particular level, is a purely quantitative one.
Factors are important in proportion as their influence is felt all
over the field under examination. This is forgotten by those
who object against the Marxian conception of history that it
neglects all the spiritual achievements of mankind. So it does;
but only because they are actually negligible at the level of
generality with which it is concerned. In the case of every individual there are respects in which he resembles all or very many of

his contemporaries and differs noticeably from any man of another period, and other respects in which he differs from all his contemporaries and may perhaps most nearly resemble some individuals of other periods. What are called the great spiritual achievements of mankind represent that individual distinction which sets the great man apart as much from his contemporaries as from any predecessors or successors. But this individual distinction has comparatively little influence on the course of history. What influence it does have may be called 'vertical' rather than 'horizontal'; that is to say, the great mind influences only comparatively few individuals in any particular generation, but continues to exert that influence (generally through the survival of writings, though it might be by an oral tradition) through many centuries. The influence of Plato or Aristotle in philosophy would be an obvious example. This sort of influence is imperceptible at the level of generality of Marxian history.

This is concerned with the general state of a whole society at a particular date, and its relation to the general state of the same society at an earlier or later date, and cannot be expected to attend to the achievements of individuals, however 'great', except in so far as they were immediately responsible for large-scale social changes which would not have occurred without them. And this happens even less often that it appears to do, for a movement may bear the name of a great individual, yet the part which it played in history may have comparatively little to do with him. Thus it would be absurd to deny that there is a Christian tradition which has done more to form our present ways of thinking and feeling than any other intellectual influence from the past, and equally absurd to deny that a great deal in Christianity derives from Christ, but it may well be doubted whether it is this part of Christianity which has ever had most general influence. What has determined the course of history, viewed on any large scale, at any particular period, has not been Christianity as such, but, if anything, the Christian Church as it was at that period, focusing a mass of beliefs of very varied origins, some of them old, some comparatively new (though perhaps expressed in old terms), traditions, moral intuitions, prejudices, considerations of sectional interest, and personal ambitions, in which the immediate contemporary interests of the clergy and the faithful bulk much larger than the general Christian heritage. Marxist historians can fairly be criticized for claiming (as they often seem to do) that history cannot legitimately be studied except at their own chosen level, but not for insisting that, at that level, it is only 'materialist' explanations which really explain. This is a simple consequence of the fact that men are more often bad than good, and more often stupid than intelligent, so that the acts of the exceptional individuals disappear from view as soon as the human scene is contemplated from any distance.

But there is also a level at which ideas have a history of their own, which is the level at which Idealist historians prefer to work. This is quite as legitimate as working at any other level, so long as it is remembered that 'absolute mind' is only a logical construction — that this sort of history is only another set of historical generalizations from the same mass of individual acts and thoughts of which we suppose the whole story written in the Book of the Recording Angel. New conceptions and methods of approach to intellectual questions are introduced by individuals, become fashionable and are very widely applied, until finally they are found for one reason or another unsatisfactory and gradually abandoned. Changes in material conditions can exert an influence here, because they may raise new problems which the old conceptions and methods cannot solve, thus hastening their abandonment; but the importance of this is probably much exaggerated by Marxists, and the Idealist historians may often be justified in disregarding it. In any case it is very naive to think that methods and conceptions will ever be abandoned merely because problems have arisen which they cannot solve. The fact that the old methods cannot solve the new problems will not be recognized. It will be alleged that they have in fact been solved already, or else that, though not solved yet, they will be solved soon, still by the old methods, or perhaps that they are completely insoluble. What forces the abandonment of old methods and conceptions is always the invention of new methods and conceptions which prove their superiority in competition, and this requires a certain lapse of time and may have to wait for the appearance of some individual of genius. In such a case it is not misrepresentation of the facts, provided that it is recognized as being representation at a very high level of generality, to tell the whole story in terms of problems, criticisms and suggested solutions – a doctrine failing to stand up to criticism, thus producing a problem, to which various tentative solutions are offered until finally the solution is found which is associated with a great name.

But it must be owned that Idealist philosophers of history show a disposition to suppose that the history of ideas must itself be 'ideal', in the sense of describing what they think ought to have happened rather than what actually did. When the individual of genius appears, he may not be immediately recognized, and will certainly not be recognized universally. Every educated person now knows something about the greatest thinkers of the past, but the minor writers are read only by historical specialists, and the great mass of the public, which wrote nothing, tends to become quite forgotten, and in consequence we are apt to remember those who were immediately influenced by a great mind and forget that there were many at the time who never tried to think for themselves hard enough to become aware that there was anything unsatisfactory about the conceptions and methods to which they had been brought up – to whom the views of the great man were nothing but unintelligible newfangled nonsense. I may be unfair to Collingwood, but it has sometimes seemed to me that, in his account of the 'presuppositions' of different historical periods, he considered only those outstanding philosophers whose achievement was so permanent that their works are still compulsory reading for 'Greats' at Oxford. But this is to confuse what the men of a period actually presupposed with what they *would* have presupposed if they had realized that Descartes (or whoever it might be) had solved their problems, when in fact most of them did not. And this seems to have tempted Idealist philosophers of history into an account of 'historical explanation' which is inadequate even to the history of ideas, to which the Idealist conception of history properly applies. They think that they have 'explained' the acceptance of a doctrine when they have shown that it solved a certain problem. But to show that the doctrine actually solved the problem is logic, not history. The historical question is, how it came to be accepted, which is not accounted for by the mere fact that it solved the problem, for a problem may be solved and the solution never be generally acknowledged, while conversely doctrines may be generally accepted which conspicuously fail to solve very urgent problems.

Practising historians may be expected to dislike an account of 'historical explanation' which reminds them that history rests on facts in the shape of actual human doings. This is the skeleton in their cupboard, and they prefer Idealist or Marxist theories of history, which enable them to keep the door shut on it. We may expect criticism on lines familiar to philosophers, being that used against all representative theories of perception and correspondence theories of truth. It will be said that our test of historical truth is a test which can never be made. We can never check a historical generalization against the individual facts on which it is based, because we are never presented with both together. For immediate contemporary history or at least that small section of it which we are ourselves actually living through – we have the individual facts, but it is notorious that we always find them so complex and confusing that we cannot at the time summarize them in any general historical statement. Historical generalization becomes possible as the events recede into the past, but then the individual facts are no longer there for comparison with the generalization. From some arguments in this vein it is difficult to see what is meant to follow, if not that a historian is a purely imaginative writer like a novelist, though this is not, I think, a conclusion which any practising historian would welcome. But all that is in fact shown is that the historian's conclusions rest wholly on circumstantial evidence and are peculiarly fallible. What is asked of him is nothing resembling the absurdity demanded by crude representative theories of perception – that it should be decided by mere inspection of 'representative ideas' whether or not they are good copies of 'things in themselves' which nobody has ever had knowledge of. The historian cannot pretend that he has no knowledge of any individual human action, since he is acquainted at least with his own actions and those of his friends, and we only ask him never to forget that the justification for all his statements (if they have any) is nothing but the similar actions of similar human beings, even if they lived a long time ago and in very different circumstances. Owing to lack of imagination, or simple ignorance, he may make what would have seemed to those about whom he is talking absurd mistakes concerning what they did or the reasons why they did it, and the mistakes may be inevitable in the sense that he has no evidence which should have enabled him to avoid them, but in the case of each particular mistake he might always have had such evidence that he would not have made it. He cannot claim that any of his statements is wholly true to the facts, but he also cannot pretend that there is any impassable barrier making it impossible for him to have known more of the facts than he actually does. It is true that he cannot check his statements by the facts, but only by the evidence, which is a different thing. The facts are individual, but historical evidence is often already at a high degree of generality — for example, memoirs and dispatches, not to speak of the writings of previous historians (what are called 'authorities'). Practising historians, therefore, naturally prefer what we may call 'coherence theories', according to which historical truth consists in agreement with the evidence, which they have before them, rather than with the facts, which they have not. This makes things much easier for them, just as it would be easier for the members of a jury if they could only feel that it was their duty merely to give a true verdict according to the evidence. But in fact every juryman feels that he would be giving an unjust verdict if he condemned a man who was actually innocent, whatever the evidence. If the verdict is according to the evidence, that makes its injustice excusable, but does not make the defendant justly condemned, if he has not in fact committed the crime. Similarly the historical statement which is the most probable on the evidence available may be the best that can reasonably be expected of the historian, but, if it misrepresents the facts, it is not true. As for Idealist talk of 'so-called historical facts' being nothing but what historians have said, that is only a device to increase the self-satisfaction of historians by enabling them to forget that, however near they may come to the real facts, they might always have come nearer.

These are topical questions now, not only in philosophy (owing to the publication of the posthumous works of Collingwood) but also in politics. The doctrine that 'all history is contemporary history' might seem nothing more than a stimulating paradox when enunciated by Croce or Collingwood, but we may well feel doubtful about it when we see how it is officially adopted and acted upon in the Soviet Union. In 1917, according to all contemporary accounts, from whatever source they emanated, without distinction of politics, Lenin's principal lieutenant in the Russian Revolution was Trotsky; but, according to the history of the Revolution as now taught in Russia and to Communists throughout the world, the second part was played by Stalin, of whom hardly any mention will be found in documents of the time. This is perfectly in accordance with the principles of the Idealist philosophers of history, according to whom what happened in the past is nothing but whatever it suits our purposes now to suppose to have happened then. Being themselves quiet Bourgeois Liberals, they thought only of quiet Bourgeois Liberal purposes and their conception of history remained mild and inoffensive. But now it has suddenly grown teeth, when it is found to have the consequence that the Battle of Hastings might come to have been fought, not in 1066, but in 1067, or perhaps even in this present year 1947, and to have been won, not by the Normans, but by the English, or perhaps even by the Russians, if that happened to be demanded by the 'Party Line' in the twentieth, or the twenty-first, or the twenty-second century. I do not mean to imply that a doctrine ought to be rejected merely because it has received its final polish in Russia; but Russian ruthlessness in drawing logical conclusions does seem to me to have put it beyond doubt that this conception of history is radically false, although, as half-heartedly presented by Croce and Collingwood, it could still seem plausible.

At the root of this false conception lie, I think, two closely connected false assumptions. We are concerned with them here only as affecting history, but their influence is actually much more extensive. One is the assumption that, because we can never hope to free our opinions from all trace of error, therefore there is no truth, or the word 'truth' must be re-defined and re-applied to lend dignity to favoured errors. People like to think of the truth as something which they can hope some day actually to attain — not as something which will always be beyond them, even if they can always come nearer and nearer to it — and they are ready to re-define the term 'truth' to gratify this inclination. Historians do not like to think that their ideal is undistorted representation of actual past human doings, since this is something which one can do better than another, but none can do perfectly. They prefer to make their criterion of 'historical truth' agreement with the available evidence and the needs of their own time, success in this being in principle attainable. Yet it is surely obvious that a judgment may be the best that could possibly be made in certain particular circumstances, and yet false. We find it quite natural to say that the judgments of a particular historian are sound within certain limits, but in certain respects distorted by his nineteenth-century prejudices. In these respects we consider his judgments mistaken, without thinking that, living in the nineteenth century, he could have been expected to judge differently. Most of us are ready to allow that our own judgments are probably similarly distorted by twentieth-century prejudices, although we cannot say in what respects, since otherwise we should already have corrected them. When we say that they are distorted, we mean that they misrepresent the facts. If we did not recognize the ideal of correspondence with the facts, we could only say that the judgment would have been false if it had been made in the present century, but it was not, and in its own century it was true. Collingwood does say things like this when he remembers his own philosophical position, but sooner or later his natural good sense asserts itself and then we find him stating roundly that we can now see that on some points past historians were mistaken, though owing to causes which they could not help, such as lack of evidence.

The other false assumption is that, because no judgment can ever be wholly free from bias, therefore a less biased judgment is no better than a more biased one. In fact it is possible, even if difficult, to reduce one's own bias, though certainly not to eliminate it completely, and, other things being equal, the judgment is the more likely to be true, the less the amount of bias. (We may reflect that the world has come to a pretty pass when anything so obvious need be said, but every philosopher knows that this does not now go without saying.) But modern philosophies of history encourage historians to glory in their own bias and exaggerate it, and to approve or condemn other historians purely according as they do or do not share the same bias. There is Communist history, Fascist history and Liberal history, and it is approved or condemned as Communist or Fascist or Liberal according to the allegiance of the critic. Thought on this subject is almost always confused by considerations of the desirability of passionate convictions for resolute action, in which it is generally forgotten that, the more fervent the heart, the greater the need of a cool head. Marx himself (though not some modern Marxists) was well aware of this; just because he was devoted heart and soul to the Socialist cause, he insisted that an investigation of the means by which Socialism could be attained must be true to the facts and undistorted by wishful thinking; hence his life-long war against 'Utopian Socialists'. A historian may be none the worse for studying the past with an eye to applications in the present, but we must distinguish two very different kinds of application. There is narration of past events in such a way as to encourage present supporters and discourage opponents, distorting wherever necessary for this purpose; this is 'history' according to the prescription of the Idealist philosophers, whose criterion is contemporary needs, and in fact it is not history at all, but propaganda. (Idealist philosophers will indignantly deny that this is what they mean, and I know quite well that it is not what they intend, but in that case they ought to be more careful about what they say.) The other kind of application is the discovery that something happened in the past which may serve as a guide to action in the present — indicating, for example, the likely consequences of a particular course of action. This sort of application I have already described as going beyond the business of the historian as such, since it implies the detection of universal laws in the historical process, but it does make use of the historian's results. What is important for our purposes here is that it is a sort of application which would be impossible with purely Idealist 'history'. The contemporary application depends upon the historical representation being true to the facts, in the sense of what really happened in the past; otherwise it would be merely misleading. In history we may say that pure Idealism meets its Waterloo, because in history we cannot do without 'things in themselves', and the problem has to be faced, how they are 'represented'.

CHAPTER XI

MATHEMATICS AND THE WORLD

By Douglas Gasking

My object is to try to elucidate the nature of mathematical propositions, and to explain their relation to the everyday world of counting and measurement — of clocks, and yards of material, and income-tax forms. I should like to be able to summarize my views in a few short phrases, and then go on to defend them. Unfortunately I cannot do this, for, as I shall try to demonstrate, I do not think any short statement will do to express the truth of the matter with any precision. So I shall proceed by approximations — I shall discuss several different views in the hope that in showing what is right and what is wrong with them, clarification will come about.

The opinions of philosophers about the nature of mathematical propositions can be divided, as can their opinions about so many things, into two main classes. There are those who try to analyse mathematical propositions away — who say that they are *really* something else (like those writers on ethics who say that goodness is really only pleasure, or those metaphysicians who say that chairs and tables are really groups of sensations, or colonies of souls). I shall call such 'analysing-away' theories 'radical' theories. On the other hand there arc those who insist that mathematical propositions are *sui generis*, that they cannot be analysed into anything else, that they give information about an aspect of reality totally different from any other (compare those philosophers who maintain, e.g. that goodness is a simple unanalysable quality, or those realists who maintain that a chair is a chair, an external material substance, known, perhaps, by means of sensations, but not to be confused with those sensations). For convenience, I shall call these types of theory which oppose any analysing-away, 'conservative'. I should maintain that in general what I call 'conservative' opinions in philosophy are perfectly correct, but rather unsatisfactory and unilluminating, whereas opinions of the 'radical' type are untrue, but interesting and illuminating.

I shall start by considering the 'radical' theories about the nature of mathematics. Those I know of fall into two main types. (1) Some people maintain that a proposition of mathematics is *really* a particularly well-founded empirical generalization of a certain type, or that it is logically on the same footing as a very well-established scientific law. Mill's theory was of this type, and many scientists I have talked to have tended to have similar opinions. Let us call these 'empirical' theories about mathematics. (2) Then, on the other hand, there is a great variety of theories usually called 'conventionalist', which analyse away mathematical propositions into propositions about the use of symbols. Examples: 'By a mathematical proposition the speaker or writer merely expresses his intention of manipulating symbols in a certain way, and recommends or commands that others should do likewise'. 'A mathematical proposition is really an empirical proposition describing how educated people commonly use certain symbols.' 'A mathematical proposition is really a rule for the manipulation of symbols.' (Ayer, for example, and C. I. Lewis have expressed opinions of this general type.)

First for the 'empirical' theories. According to these a mathematical proposition just expresses a particularly well-founded empirical generalization or law about the properties and behaviour of objects, obtained by examining a large number of instances and seeing that they conform without exception to a single general pattern. The proposition '7 + 5 = 12', for instance, just expresses (on one version of this theory) the fact of experience that if we count up seven objects of any sort, and then five more objects, and then count up the whole lot, we always get the number twelve. Or again, it might be maintained that the geometrical proposition 'Equilateral triangles are equiangular' just expresses the fact that wherever, by measurement, we find the sides of a triangle to be equal, we will find, on measuring the angles with the same degree of accuracy, that the angles are equal too. It is contended that such propositions are essentially like, for example, Boyle's Law of gases, only much better founded.

But '7 + 5 = 12' does not mean the same as the proposition about what you get on counting groups. For it is true that 7 + 5 does equal 12, but it is not true that on counting seven objects and then five others, and then counting the whole, you

will always get twelve. People sometimes miscount, and sometimes the objects counted melt away (if they are wax) or coalesce
(if they are globules of mercury). Similarly the geometrical
proposition that equilateral triangles are equiangular does not
mean the same as the proposition that any triangle which is
equilateral by measurement will be found to be equiangular when
measured. The former is true; the latter false. We sometimes
make mistakes with our rulers and protractors.

To this it might be objected that this shows that the empirical
proposition offered as a translation of the mathematical one is
not a correct translation, but that it has not been demonstrated
that it is impossible to find an empirical proposition about counting and measurement, which is a correct translation. Let us try
some alternatives, then. It might be suggested that '7 + 5 = 12'
means 'If you count *carefully and with attention*, you will get such
and such a result'. But, even with the greatest care in counting,
mistakes sometimes happen at any rate with large numbers.
Shall we then say: '7 + 5 = 12' means 'If you count *correctly* you
will get such and such results'? But, in the first place, even if
you count objects correctly, you do not always get a group of
seven objects and a group of five adding up to twelve. It sometimes happens that a person correctly counts seven objects, then
correctly counts five, and then correctly counts the total and gets
eleven. Sometimes one of the objects does disappear in the course
of counting, or coalesces with another. And even if this were
not so, the suggested translation would not give you a simple
empirical proposition about what happened when people counted,
as a translation of 7 + 5 = 12, but would give you a mere
tautology. For what is the criterion of correctness in counting?
Surely that when you add seven and five you should get twelve.
'Correctness' has no meaning, in this context, independent of the
mathematical proposition. So our suggested analysis of the
meaning of '7 + 5 = 12' runs, when suitably expanded:
'7 + 5 = 12' means 'If you count objects *correctly* (i.e. in such a
way as to get 12 on adding 7 and 5) you will, on adding 7 to 5,
get 12'.

No doubt there *are* important connections between mathematical propositions, and propositions about what results people
will usually get on counting and measuring. But it will not do

to say that a mathematical proposition means the same as, or is equivalent to, any such empirical proposition, for this reason: A mathematical proposition is 'incorrigible', whereas an empirical proposition is 'corrigible'.

The difference between 'corrigible' and 'incorrigible' propositions can best be explained by examples. Most everyday assertions that we make, such as that 'Mr. Smith has gone away for the day', are corrigible. By this I mean simply that, whenever we make such an assertion, however strong our grounds for making it, we should always freely withdraw it and admit it to have been false, *if* certain things were to happen. Thus my assertion, that Smith is away for the day, is corrigible, because (although I may have the excellent grounds for making it that when I met him in the street this morning he said he was on his way to the railway-station) if, for example, I were to go to his room now and find him sitting there, I should withdraw my assertion that he was away and admit it to have been false. I should take certain events as proving, if they happened, that my assertion was untrue.

A mathematical proposition such as '$7 + 5 = 12$', on the other hand, is incorrigible, because no future happenings whatsoever would ever prove the proposition false, or cause anyone to withdraw it. You can imagine any sort of fantastic chain of events you like, but nothing you can think of would ever, if it happened, disprove '$7 + 5 = 12$'. Thus, if I counted out 7 matches, and then 5 more, and then on counting the whole lot, got 11, this would not have the slightest tendency to make anyone withdraw the proposition that $7 + 5 = 12$ and say it was untrue. And even if this constantly happened, both to me and to everyone else, and not only with matches, but with books, umbrellas and every sort of object – surely even this would not make us withdraw the proposition. Surely in such a case we should not say: 'the proposition "$7 + 5 = 12$" has been empirically disproved; it has been found that $7 + 5$ really equals 11'. There are plenty of alternative explanations to choose from. We might try a psychological hypothesis, such as this: we might say that it had been discovered by experiment that everyone had a curious psychological kink, which led him, whenever he performed counting operations of a certain sort, always to miss out one of the objects in his final count (like the subject in some experiments on hypnosis who, under suggestion, fails to see any 't's on a printed page). Or we might prefer a physical hypothesis and say: a curious physical law of the universe has been experimentally established, namely, that whenever 5 objects are added to 7 objects, this process of addition causes one of them to disappear, or to coalesce with another object. The one thing we should *never* say, whatever happened, would be that the proposition that $7 + 5 = 12$ had been experimentally disproved. If curious things happened, we should alter our physics, but not our mathematics.

This rather sweeping assertion that mathematical propositions are completely incorrigible is, I think, an over-simplification, and needs qualifying. I shall mention the qualifications later, rather than now, for simplicity of exposition. So if you will accept it for the moment as very nearly true, I should like to draw your attention to certain of its consequences. A *corrigible* proposition gives you some information about the world — a completely *incorrigible* proposition tells you nothing. A corrigible proposition is one that you would withdraw and admit to be false if certain things happened in the world. It therefore gives you the information that *those* things (i.e. those things which would make you withdraw your proposition *if* they happened) will *not* happen. An incorrigible proposition is one which you would never admit to be false *whatever* happens: it therefore does not tell you *what* happens. The truth, for example, of the corrigible proposition that Smith is away for the day, is compatible with certain things happening (e.g. your going to his room and finding it empty) and is not compatible with certain other happenings (e.g. your going to his room and finding him there). It therefore tells you what sort of thing will happen (you will find his room empty) and what sort of thing will not happen (you will not find him in). The truth of an incorrigible proposition, on the other hand, is compatible with any and every conceivable state of affairs. (For example: whatever is your experience on counting, it is still true that $7 + 5 = 12$). It therefore does not tell you which events will take place and which will not. That is: the proposition '$7 + 5 = 12$' tells you nothing about the world.

If such a proposition tells you nothing about the world, what,

then, is the point of it – what does it do? I think that in a sense
it is true to say that it prescribes what you are to *say* – it tells
you *how to describe* certain happenings. Thus the proposition
'7 + 5 = 12' does not tell you that on counting 7 + 5 you will
not get 11. (This, as we have seen, is false, for you sometimes
do get 11.) But it does *lay it down*, so to speak, that *if* on counting
7 + 5 you do get 11, you are to describe what has happened in
some such way as this: *Either* 'I have made a mistake in my counting' *or* 'Someone has played a practical joke and abstracted one of
the objects when I was not looking' *or* 'Two of the objects have
coalesced' *or* 'One of the objects has disappeared', etc.

This, I think, is the truth that is in the various 'conventionalist'
theories of mathematics. Only, unfortunately, the formulae
expressing such theories are usually misleading and incorrect.
For example, to say that: 'a mathematical proposition merely
expresses the speaker's or writer's determination to use symbols
in a certain way', is obviously untrue. For if it were true, and if
I decided to use the symbol '+' in such a way that 5 + 7 = 35,
I would then be speaking truly if I said '5 + 7 = 35'. But this
proposition is not true. The truth of any mathematical proposition does not depend on my decision or determination. It is
independent of my will. This formula neglects the 'public' or
'over-individual' character of mathematics.

Or, consider the formula: 'A mathematical proposition is
really an empirical statement describing the way people commonly use certain symbols'. This, I think, is nearer. But it is
open to the following obvious objection: If '7 + 5 = 12' were
really an assertion about the common usage of symbols, then it
would follow that 7 + 5 would not equal 12 if people had a
different symbolic convention. But even if people did use symbols in a way quite different from the present one, the fact which
we now express by '7 + 5 = 12' would still be true. No change
in our language-habits would ever make this false.

This objection is, I think, sufficient to show that the suggested
formula is untrue, as it stands. But we should be blind to its
merits if we did not see *why* it is that no change in our language-
habits would make the proposition '7 + 5 = 12' untrue. The
reason is this: As we use symbols at present, this proposition is
incorrigible – one which we maintain to be true whatever

P

happens in the world, and never admit to be false under any circumstances. Imagine a world where the symbolic conventions are totally different — say on Mars. How shall we *translate* our incorrigible proposition into the Martian symbols? If our translation is to be correct— if the proposition in the Martian language is to mean the same as our '$7 + 5 = 12$', it *too* must be incorrigible — otherwise we should not call it a correct translation. Thus a correct Martian translation of our '$7 + 5 = 12$' must be a proposition which the Martians maintain to be true whatever happens. Thus '$7 + 5 = 12$,' and any correct translation into any other symbolic convention will be incorrigible, i.e. true whatever happens. So its truth does, in a sense, depend on the empirical fact that people use symbols in certain ways. But it is an inaccurate way of stating this fact to say that it describes how people use symbols.

A better formulation is: 'A mathematical proposition really expresses a rule for the manipulation of symbols'. But this, too, is unsatisfactory, and for the following reason: To say that it is a 'rule for the manipulation of symbols' suggests that it is entirely arbitrary. A symbolic rule is something which we can decide to use or not, just as we wish. (We could easily use 'hice' as the plural of 'house', and get on as well as we do now.) But, it seems, we cannot just change our mathematical propositions at will, without getting into difficulties. An engineer, building a bridge, has to use the standard multiplication tables and no others, or else the bridge will collapse. Thus which mathematical system we use does not seem to be entirely arbitrary — one system works in practice, and another does not. Which system we are to use seems to depend in some way not on our decision, but on the nature of the world. To say that '$7 + 5 = 12$' really expresses a rule for the use of symbols, suggests that this proposition is just like ' "house" forms its plural by adding "s" '. But there *is* a difference between the two, and so the formula is misleading.

I want to conclude this paper by considering in some detail the objection that you cannot build bridges with any mathematics, and that therefore mathematics does depend on the nature of reality. Before doing so, however, I should like to mention the type of theory I called 'conservative'. We saw that the (radical) theory, that mathematical propositions are 'really' empirical propositions about the results of counting, is untrue. But there is a close connection between the two sorts of proposition, and therefore the 'empirical' theory, although untrue, has a point. It emphasizes the connection between mathematical propositions and our everyday practice of counting and calculation; thus it serves as a useful corrective to that type of theory which would make mathematics too abstract and pure — a matter of pure intellect and Platonic 'Forms', far from the mundane counting of change. Similarly the various 'conventionalist' theories are also, strictly speaking, untrue, but they too have their point. Mathematical propositions in certain respects are *like* rules for the use of symbols, *like* empirical propositions about how symbols are used, *like* statements of intention to use symbols in certain ways. But conventionalist formulae are untrue because mathematical propositions are not *identical* with any of these. They are what they are; they function in the way they do, and not exactly like any other sort of proposition.

And this it is which makes that sort of theories I have called 'conservative' perfectly correct. Mathematical propositions are *sui generis*. But merely to say: 'They are what they are' is not very helpful. Nor is it any better if this is dressed up in learned language: e.g. 'Mathematical propositions state very general facts about the structure of reality; about the necessary and synthetic relations between the universals number, shape, size, and so on'. If you are inclined to think that such answers as this, to the question 'What are mathematical propositions about?', are informative and illuminating, ask yourself: 'How does my hearer come to understand the meaning of such phrases as "structure of reality", "necessary relations between universals", and so on? How were these phrases explained to him in the first place?' Surely he was told what was meant by 'necessary relation between universals', by being told, for example, that colour, shape, size, number, etc., are universals, and that an example of a necessary relation between universals would be 'everything that has shape has size', '2 + 2 = 4', 'two angles of an isosceles triangle are equal', and so on. These phrases, such as 'necessary relation between universals', are *introduced* into his language *via* or *by means of* such phrases as '2 + 2 = 4'; they are introduced *via* mathematical propositions, among others. To use an expression

of John Wisdom's,[1] they are 'made to measure'. So to tell someone that mathematical propositions are 'so-and-so' does not help,
if, in explaining what is meant by 'so-and-so', you have to introduce mathematical propositions, among others, as illustrative
examples. Compare giving a 'conservative' answer to the question 'What are mathematical propositions?' with the following
example: A child learns the meaning of the words 'see', 'can't
see', 'blindfolded' etc., before he learns the meaning of the word
'blind'. The latter word is then introduced into his vocabulary
by the explanation: 'A blind man is one who can't see in broad
daylight even when not blindfolded'. If the child then asks of a
blind man 'Why can't he see in broad daylight even when not
blindfolded?', it is not much use answering 'Because he is blind'.
Like the 'conservative' answer in philosophy, it may serve to
stop any further questions, but it usually leaves a feeling of
dissatisfaction.

Then what sort of answer *can* be given to one who is puzzled
about the nature of mathematics? Mathematical propositions
are what they are, so any radical answer equating them with
something else, such as symbolic rules, or statements of the results
of counting and measurement, or of common symbolic usage,
will be untrue. Such answers will be untrue, because the two sides
of the equation will have different meanings. Similarly conservative answers will be unhelpful, because the two sides of the equation will have the same meaning. The definiens will be useless,
because it will contain terms which are introduced into the language *via* the definiendum, and can only be explained in terms
of it. It is 'made to measure'. No simple formula will do. The
only way of removing the puzzle is to describe the use and function of mathematical propositions in detail and with examples.
I shall now try to do this, to some extent, in considering the
natural objection to the strictly untrue but illuminating theory:
'Mathematical propositions express rules for the manipulation
of symbols'. The objection is that symbolic rules are essentially
arbitrary, whereas mathematics does, to some extent at least,
depend not on our choice of symbolic conventions, but on the
nature of reality, because only our present system gives useful

[1] My debt to the lectures of Wisdom and Wittgenstein, in writing this paper, is very
great.

results when applied to the practical tasks of the world. Against this, I shall maintain that we could use *any* mathematical rules we liked, and still get on perfectly well in the business of life.

Example 1. 6 × 4, according to our current multiplication table, equals 24. You might argue: this cannot be merely a conventional rule for our use of symbols, for if it were we could use any other rule we liked, e.g. 6 × 4 = 12, and still get satisfactory results. But if you tried this alternative rule, you would, in fact, find your practical affairs going all wrong. A builder, for example, having measured a room to be paved with tiles, each one yard square, and having found the length of the sides to be 6 yards and 4 yards, could not use the alternative table. He could not say to himself: 'The room is 6 by 4; now 6 × 4 = 12, so I shall have to get 12 tiles for this job.' For, if he did, he would find he had not enough tiles to cover his floor.

But the builder could quite easily have used an arithmetic in which 6 × 4 = 12, and by measuring and counting could have paved his room perfectly well, with exactly the right number of tiles to cover the floor. How does he do it? Well, he:

(1) Measures the sides, and writes down '4' and '6'.
(2) Multiplies 4 by 6 according to a 'queer' multiplication table which gives 4 × 6 = 12.
(3) Counts out 12 tiles, lays them on the floor. And they fit perfectly.

The 'queer' multiplication table he uses gives 2 × 2 = 4, 2 × 4 = 6, 2 × 8 = 10, 4 × 4 = 9, 4 × 6 = 12, etc. The number found by multiplying a by b according to *his* table, is that which in *our* arithmetic we should get by the formula:

$$(a + 2)(b + 2) / 4$$

And he could pave any other size of floor, using the queer multiplication table described, and still always get the right number of tiles to cover it.

How is this possible? He measures the sides of the room with a yardstick as follows: He lays his yardstick along the longer side, with the '0' mark of the yardstick in the corner, and the other end of the stick, marked '36 inches', some distance along the stick. As he does this, he counts 'one'. He then pivots the yardstick on the 36 inches mark, and swings it round through two right angles, till it is once more lying along the side of the room—this time with the '36 inches' mark nearer to the corner from which he started, and the 'o' mark further along the side. As he does this, he counts 'two'. But now the direction of the stick has been reversed, and it is the convention for measuring that lengths should always be measured in the same direction. So he pivots the stick about its middle and swings it round so that the '36' mark is now where the 'o' mark was, and vice versa. As he does this, he counts 'three'. He then swings the stick round through two right angles, pivoting on the '36' mark, counting 'four'. He then reverses its direction, as before, counting 'five'. He swings it over again, counting 'six'. It now lies with its end in the corner, so he writes down the length of the side as 'six yards'. (If we had measured it in our way, we should have written its length down as four yards.) He then measures the shorter side in the same way, and finds the length (using his measuring technique) to be four yards. (We should have made it three.) He then multiplies 4 by 6, according to his table, making it 12, counts out 12 tiles, and lays them down. So long as he uses the technique described for measuring lengths, he will always get the right number of tiles for any room with his 'queer' multiplication table.

This example shows you that we use the method we do for multiplying lengths to get areas, because we use a certain method of measuring lengths. Our technique of calculating areas is relative to our technique of measuring lengths.

Here you might say: Admitting that this is true, it is still the case that mathematics is not arbitrary, for you could not use the method of measuring we do, *and* a different multiplication table, and *still* get the right number of tiles for our room. Can't we? Let's see.

Example 2. Suppose our 'queer' multiplication table gave $3 \times 4 = 24$. The builder measures the sides of a room exactly as we do, and finds that they are 3 yards and 4 yards, respectively. He then 'multiplies' 3 by 4, and gets 24. He counts out 24 tiles, places them on the floor, and they fit perfectly, with none over. How does he do it?

He measures the sides as we do, and writes down '3' and '4'. He 'multiplies' and gets 24. He then counts out 24 tiles as follows:

He picks up a tile from his store, and counts 'one'. He puts the tile on to his truck and counts 'two'. He picks up another tile and counts 'three'. He puts it on his truck and counts 'four'. He goes on in this way until he reaches a count of 'twenty-four'. He then takes his 'twenty-four' tiles and paves the room, and they fit perfectly.

This example shows that our technique of calculating areas is relative both to a certain technique of measurement, *and* to a certain technique of counting.

At this stage you might make a further objection. You might say: Mathematics *does* tell you something about the world, and is not an arbitrary rule of symbolic usage. It tells you that *if* you both count and measure lengths in the way we do, you will not get the right number of tiles for a room unless you multiply the lengths according to our present table. It is not arbitrary, because if, for example, you measure the sides of a room as we do, and find them to be 4 and 3, and if you count tiles as we do, you would get the wrong number of tiles to pave your room if you used some other multiplication table — say one in which $3 \times 4 = 24$. I maintain, on the contrary, that we could quite well use such a 'queer' table, and count and measure as at present, and still get the right number of tiles. To help us to see what is involved here, let us consider a rather analogous case.

Example 3. Imagine that the following extraordinary thing happened. You measure a room normally, and find the sides to be 6 and 4. You multiply normally and get 24. You then count out 24 tiles in the normal way. (Each tile is 1×1.) But when you come to try and lay the tiles in the room, you find that you can only get 12 such tiles on to the floor of the room, and there are 12 tiles over. What should we say if this happened?

The first thing we should say would be: 'You must have made a mistake in your measuring' or 'You must have made a slip in multiplying' or 'You must have counted your tiles wrongly, somehow'. And we should immediately check again the measurements, calculations and counting. But suppose that, after the most careful checking and re-checking, by large numbers of highly qualified persons, *no* mistake at all of this sort can be found anywhere. Suppose, moreover, that this happened to everyone constantly, with all sorts of rooms and tiles. What should we say then? There are still a number of ways in which we might explain this curious phenomenon. I shall mention two conceivable hypotheses:

(1) Measuring rods do not, as we supposed, stay a constant length wherever they are put. They stay the same size when put against things the same length as themselves, and also when put against things larger than themselves running from north to south. But when put against things larger than themselves running east-west, they always contract to half their previous length (and this contraction happens so smoothly that we never notice it). Thus the room is in fact 6 by 2 yards, i.e. 12 square yards, and twelve tiles are needed. When the measuring rod is put along the north-south wall of six yards' length, it stays a yard long, and so we get a measurement of 6. When, however, it is put along the shorter east-west wall it contracts to half a yard in length, and can be put four times along the two-yard wall. If you now say the dimensions are 6 and 4, and multiply to get 24, you are overestimating the real area.

(2) An alternative hypothesis: When we measure the room our yardstick always stays a constant length, and thus the area of the room is really 24 square yards. But since we can only get 12 tiles in it, each tile being 1 yard square, it follows that the tiles must *expand*, on being put into the room, to double their area. It is just a curious *physical* law that objects put into a room double their area instantaneously. We do not see this expansion because it is instantaneous. And we can never measure it, by measuring the tiles, first out of the room and then inside, because our yardstick itself expands proportionately on being taken into the room.

This example (which might easily have been put in much more detail with *ad hoc* hypotheses to cover every discrepancy) shows that, however much the practical predictions of builders' requirements are upset when we use our present multiplication table, this need never cause us to alter our present rules for multiplication. Anomalies are accounted for by saying our knowledge of the relevant *physical* laws is defective, not by saying that the multiplication table is 'untrue'. If, when working things out in the usual way, we found that we had constantly 12 tiles too many, we should not say that we had been wrong in thinking that $6 \times 4 = 24$. We should rather say that we had been wrong in thinking that physical objects did not expand and contract in certain ways. If things go wrong, we always change our physics rather than our mathematics.

If we see, from Example 3, what we should do if things went wrong when we used our present arithmetic, we can now answer the objection it was intended to throw light on. The objection was this:

'It is wrong to say that we could use any arithmetic we liked and still get on perfectly well in our practical affairs. Mathematics is not a collection of arbitrary symbolic rules, therefore, and does tell us something about, and does depend on, the nature of reality. For if you *both* count and measure as we do, *and* use a "queer" multiplication table, you won't get the right number of tiles to pave a room. Thus the proposition "$3 \times 4 = 12$" tells you that for a room 3 yards by 4, measured normally, you need neither more nor less than 12 tiles, counted normally. Its truth depends on this fact about the world'.

But I deny this. I say we could have

(1) used our present technique of counting and measurement,

(2) multiplied according to the rule $3 \times 4 = 24$ (for example),

(3) and still have got exactly the right number of tiles to pave our room.

I therefore say that $3 \times 4 = 12$ depends on *no* fact about the world, other than some fact about the usage of symbols.

Example 4. Imagine that we did use a 'queer' arithmetic, in which $3 \times 4 = 24$. If this was our universally accepted and standard arithmetic, we should treat the proposition '$3 \times 4 = 24$' *exactly* as we now treat the proposition '$3 \times 4 = 12$' of our present standard arithmetic. That is to say, if we did use this queer system, we should stick to the proposition '$3 \times 4 = 24$' no matter *what* happened, and ascribe any failure of prediction of builders' requirements, and so on, *always* to a mistaken view of the physical laws that apply to the world, and *never* to the untruth of the formula '$3 \times 4 = 24$.' This latter proposition, if it *were* part of our mathematical system, would be *incorrigible*, exactly as '$3 \times 4 = 12$' is to us now.

In Example 3 we saw what would be done and said if things went wrong in using '3 × 4 = 12'. Now *if* 3 × 4 = 24 were our rule, and incorrigible, and *if* in using it we found ourselves getting the wrong practical results, we should do and say exactly the same sort of thing as we did in Example 3. Thus, assuming that our rule is 3 × 4 = 24, a builder measures his floor normally and writes down '3' and '4.' He multiplies according to his table and gets 24. He counts out 24 tiles normally and tries to put them in the room. He finds that he can only get 12 tiles in. What does he say? He *does not* say 'I have proved by experiment that 3 × 4 does not equal 24', for his proposition '3 × 4 = 24' is *incorrigible*, and no event in the world, however extraordinary, will ever lead him to deny it, or be counted as relevant to its truth or falsity. What he does say is something like this: 'The area of the room is *really* 24 square yards. Since I can only get 12 yard square tiles into it, it follows that the tiles must expand to double their area on being put into the room'. (As we have seen, he might use other hypotheses, e.g. about the behaviour of measuring rods. But this is probably the most convenient.)

Thus we could easily have counted and measured as at present, *and* used an arithmetic in which 3 × 4 = 24, *and* have got perfectly satisfactory results. Only, of course, to get satisfactory practical results, we should use a physics different in some respects from our present one. Thus a builder having found the area of a room to be 24 square yards would never attempt to put 24 tiles in it, for he would have learnt in his physics lessons at school that tiles put in a room double in area. He would therefore argue: 'Since the tiles double in area, I must put half of 24 tiles, or 12 tiles, in the room'. He would count out 12 tiles and pave the room perfectly with them.

But even here an obstinate objector might admit all this, and still maintain that mathematics was not an arbitrary convention; that it did depend on certain facts about the world. He might say ' "3 × 4 = 12" is true, and it is true because of this fact about the world, namely that *if* tiles and rulers do not expand and contract (except slightly with changes in temperature), and if we measure and count normally, we need exactly 12 tiles, no more and no less, to pave a room that is 3 by 4. And "3 × 4 = 24" is false, because of the "brute fact" that *if* tiles, etc., don't expand,

and *if* you measure and count normally, 24 tiles are too many to pave a room that is 3 by 4'.

The point that is, I think, missed by this objection could be brought out by asking: 'How do we *find out* whether a tile or a yardstick has or has not expanded or contracted?' We normally have two ways of doing so. We can *watch* it growing bigger or smaller. Or we can *measure* it before and after.

Now in the case described in example 4, where our queer arithmetic gives 3 × 4 = 24, and things double in area on being put in a room, how do we find out that the things do expand? Not by watching them grow — *ex hypothesi* we do not observe this. Nor by measuring them before and after. For, since we assume that a measuring rod *also* expands on being taken into the room, the dimensions of the tile as measured by a yardstick outside the room are the same as its dimensions as measured by the same (now expanded) yardstick inside the room. In this case we find out that the tiles expand by *measuring, counting and calculating in a certain way* — by finding that the tiles each measure 1 × 1, that the room measures 3 × 4, or 24 square yards, and that we can only get 12 tiles in it. This is our sole *criterion* for saying that the tiles expand. That the tiles expand *follows from* our queer arithmetic. Similarly, as we do things at present, our criterion for saying that tiles do not expand, is that when 12 tiles measuring 1 × 1 are put into a room 3 × 4, or 12 square yards, they fit exactly. From our present arithmetic, it follows that tiles do not expand.

In Example 4, where we have a 'queer' arithmetic in which 3 × 4 = 24, and a 'queer' physics, it is a 'law of nature' that tiles expand on being put into a room. But it is not a 'law of nature' which describes what happens in the world. Rather is it a law 'by convention', analogous to that law of our present physics which says that when a body falls on the floor with a certain downward force, the floor itself exerts an equal force in the opposite direction. It is just put into the system to balance our calculations, not to describe anything that happens.

This last objection might have been put in a slightly different form. It might have been said: ' "3 × 4 = 12" does describe and depend on the nature of reality, because it entails a certain purely empirical proposition about what does and does not happen, namely the complex proposition: "It is not the case *both* that tiles do not expand *and* that we need less than 12 tiles to pave a floor measuring 3 by 4" '. But I should maintain that this complex proposition (of the form 'Not both p and q') is not empirical; that it does not describe anything that happens in the world, because it is incorrigible. Nothing whatsoever that we could imagine happening would ever lead us, if it happened, to deny this complex proposition. Therefore it does not tell us what happens in the world. The simple propositions which are elements in this complex one— the propositions 'Tiles do not expand' and 'We need less than 12 tiles to pave a 3 by 4 floor'— are both of them corrigible, and both describe the world (one of them falsely). But the complex proposition that they are not both true is incorrigible, and therefore, for the reasons given earlier, does not describe or depend on the nature of the world. There is nothing out of the ordinary about this. The propositions 'My curtains are now red over their whole surface', and 'My curtains are now green all over' are both of them corrigible propositions, descriptive of the world. (One is true, the other false, as a matter of fact.) But the complex proposition 'My curtains are not both red and green over their whole surface' is incorrigible, because nothing would ever make me deny it, and it is therefore not descriptive of the world.

I have talked, throughout the paper, as if mathematical propositions were completely incorrigible, in the sense that *whatever* queer things happened, we should *never* alter our mathematics, and always prefer to change our physics. This was a convenient over-simplification that must now be qualified. I maintain that we *need* never alter our mathematics. But it might happen that we found our physical laws getting very complicated indeed, and might discover that, by changing our mathematical system, we could effect a very great simplification in our physics. In such a case we might decide to use a different mathematical system. (So far as I can understand, this seems to be what has actually happened in certain branches of contemporary physics.) And mathematics does depend on and reflect the nature of the world at least to this extent, that we would find certain systems enormously inconvenient and difficult to use, and certain others relatively simple and handy. Using one sort of arithmetic or geometry, for example, we might find that our physics could be reduced to a logically neat and simple system, which is intellectually satisfying, whereas using different arithmetics and geometries, we should find our physics full of very complicated *ad hoc* hypotheses. But what we find neat, simple, easy, and intellectually satisfying surely depends rather on our psychological make-up, than on the behaviour of measuring rods, solids and fluids, electrical charges – the 'external world'.

CHAPTER XII

THEORY CONSTRUCTION

By J. J. C. Smart

IN a monograph[1] published in 1939 Dr. J. H. Woodger puts forward some interesting views as to the ideal at which a scientific theory should aim, and illustrates some of the features of this ideal by putting forward a specimen theory which exemplifies them. As I think that Dr. Woodger's conceptions both of what a scientific theory is and of what it ought to be are mistaken, and as they are in some quarters very fashionable conceptions, I think that it is worth while to consider Dr. Woodger's monograph in some detail.

In the opening pages of the monograph Woodger puts forward reasons for inventing an artificial language for scientific purposes. He says that the richness of the vocabularies of natural languages such as English or French makes them unsuitable for scientific purposes, because 'the process of calculation is not possible in a natural language'. Another objection to the natural languages is that since 'we learn them during the most impressionable period of our lives, they become to such an extent part of ourselves that we come to use them without ever being aware of their conventional and arbitrary character, and thus of certain of their properties which are least admirable from the point of view of science' (p. 2). I shall try to argue that the whole conception of an artificial language is extremely confused; and that the reasons given by Woodger for constructing one are bad reasons; and that his programme acquires a specious plausibility on account of our liability to confuse it with a very different one which he mentions on p. 3. Here he says something which is true and important, namely that 'in so far as the *direction* of the development of mathematics has been given a bias by the special requirements of the problems of physics ... it may, in some of its most fully deve-

---

[1] *The Technique of Theory Construction*, by J. H. Woodger (International Encyclopedia of Unified Science, Vol. II, No. 5), University of Chicago, 1939.

loped branches, be unsuitable for the use of other sciences, e.g.
for the biological sciences'. It is indeed possible that some parts of
Principia Mathematica, such as the calculus of relations, or similar
branches of mathematics, may turn out to be valuable in biological
theory. 'We require a technique for constructing new kinds of
mathematics as well as for constructing new languages for scientific purposes', says Woodger, and I do not in the least want to
argue that new kinds of mathematics may not be highly desirable,
though whether there could be a *technique* for producing them
seems doubtful, for surely new branches of mathematics are the
products of genius. What I want to object to is the alleged programme of constructing new *languages*. My argument will be
in two parts. In the first place I shall try to point out that it is
misleading to call the artificial language a 'language' at all. In
the second place I shall argue that whatever it is, language or
not a language, it is not a desirable thing to incorporate in a
science.

It is logically possible that a person might know how to use a
language without ever having been taught it. It is logically
possible, though of course it never happens, that a baby might be
born talking Latin or English. Nevertheless if we suppose that a
language has been acquired by being *taught* it is a logical impossibility that certain expressions should have been learnt before
certain other expressions have been learnt. A child cannot learn
how to use 'or' as in 'my brother or my sister is crying' until it
has learnt words like 'brother' and 'sister'. A consideration of
how a language might be taught to a child thus sheds light on
some of its logical features; it enables us to classify concepts in
layers of sophistication. It is worth noting that the layers of
sophistication have a bottom layer; this is equivalent to the
platitude that it is possible to teach a natural language to someone,
e.g. a baby, who knows no language whatsoever. Let us examine
whether this feature is shared by Woodger's 'language'. This
consists partly of various logical expressions such as 'not', 'and',
'or', 'asym'. Logical expressions, however, belong to a higher
level of sophistication than certain non-logical ones; they can
never form a bottom layer of sophistication. So we must look to
Woodger's non-logical expressions. These are 'cell', 'part of',
and 'before in time'. Let us concentrate on 'cell'. How could we

teach a person how to use this word? A cell, we might say, is the smallest form of living thing. There would not be much precision in this. Can we precisely explain what is meant by 'living'? Perhaps 'cell' could be explained ostensively? Should we show the person a cell through a microscope? This by itself would hardly do. How would he know that we weren't trying to show him *protoplasm*, for example? Again, we should have to make it clear that he had to look through a microscope. This would involve teaching him something about optics, for clearly looking through a tube with flat plates of glass instead of lenses would not do. Again, suppose that he did look through a tube with flat plates of glass and saw a freak which looked just as a cell looks through a microscope. Is he to call *this* a cell? Should *we* call it a cell, a monstrously huge cell, but still a cell, or should we call it something else? We should have. to observe it and see if its functioning was similar enough to that of cells to make it *convenient* to call it a cell. All sorts of considerations might be relevant. For example the word 'cell' as actually used by biologists gets much of its meaning from the role it plays in cell theory. Now if a cell were very large the ratio of its surface area to its volume would be very much less than for small cells. This might upset cell theory considerably and make us very reluctant to recognize very large cell-like things as cells. We see from all the above considerations that the use of a word like 'cell' is a complicated thing and that quite a lot of talk would be required to teach a person how to use the word.

Woodger would almost certainly agree that it would be impossible to teach his artificial language to a person who knew no language whatever. The explanation of the use of his language, he might say, would be done in a metalanguage, which would be the natural language of the person concerned. The trouble is that this sort of terminology misleads by suggesting that the artificial language and its metalanguage have the sort of independence which two real languages such as English and French have. It tends to make us minimize or even totally ignore the extent to which the artificial language has its roots in ordinary language and to which it draws almost its whole life from ordinary language. In the monograph Woodger says hardly anything about how the use of the word 'cell' is to be explained, and yet if biology consisted entirely of his theory and the evidence for it then this explanation of the use of 'cell' would be the most important thing in biology. This shows how misleading it is to talk of 'a new language for scientific purposes', for the most important scientific purposes would be subserved by something outside the 'language'.

Woodger constructs his 'language' by introducing a few 'meaty' (or not purely logical) words into a logical calculus. Now a logical calculus is not a language but is part of the mathematical theory of languages, to which certain parts of actual languages more or less conform. Thus the axioms of the propositional calculus may be *interpreted* as a set of suggested rules (not quite the actual ones) for the use of words like 'and', 'or', 'not'. (They may also be given an *arithmetical* interpretation. To propound a paradox: there is nothing specially logical about logic.) Now the mathematical theory of languages no more lends itself to being turned into a language than the mathematical theory of games can be made into a game.

Physical theory makes use of various branches of mathematics, and similarly a biological theory might make use of a logical calculus. In neither case, however, would the branch of mathematics or the logical calculus be coextensive with the theory. Thus in a physical theory some of the mathematical expressions must correspond to measurable magnitudes, and it must be explicitly stated that they do. This correlation with measurable magnitudes must involve the description of processes of measurement, and hence a descent from the high language of theory to the often technical but nevertheless 'earthy' language of the laboratory. We must not say, therefore, that a theory can be written 'in mathematics' as you or I could write a story in English or French.

The thesis that an artificial language is desirable for scientific purposes, then, will not seem plausible even if we confuse 'scientific purposes' with 'theoretical purposes'. The thesis begins to take on quite a fantastic air when we pay attention to the great part of scientific literature which consists in reports of experimental and observational work. A great deal of the vocabulary of this part of the literature of science is technical, but a great deal, which is quite indispensable, is taken from the vocabulary

Q

of ordinary life. Consider this short extract from Millikan's *The Electron* (Cambridge University Press, 1935), p. 67, which is the beginning of a description of the experiment which proved the atomic nature of electricity: 'In order to compare the charges on different ions, the procedure adopted was to blow with an ordinary commercial atomizer an oil spray into the chamber C. The air with which this spray was blown was first rendered dust-free by passage through a tube containing glass wool. The minute droplets of oil constituting the spray . . .' Here we have homely words like 'oil', 'spray', 'chamber', 'air', 'dust', 'tube', 'glass', 'droplet'. What could be meant by saying that this sort of language is unsuitable for science? What could do the job better? There is nothing that could do the job better. Ordinary language just is something whose use cannot be distilled into strict rules, and experimenters, even in atomic physics, cannot get along without this sort of language. It is quite beside the point to say that here 'the process of calculation is not possible' or that the language is not completely precise. Whoever wanted to calculate in this instance? Again if the language is precise *enough* we do not want it to be any *more* precise. If we were not perfectly satisfied with Millikan's description we should ask for a *fuller* description. We should not ask him to stop writing in English.

Woodger might concede all this. He might agree that it is highly misleading to call his system 'a language', and that at some vital points it is rooted in ordinary language, and also that it is totally inapplicable to the experimental and observational literature of science. He might nevertheless stick to the assertion that *theories* would be much better if constructed according to his model. This is the assertion which we must now consider. Of course the theory which Woodger develops in the monograph is only meant to be an illustrative one, and we must not complain because it is not *in fact* a good or useful one. If on the other hand we consider as a specimen a theory which is admitted to be both well-established and fertile and we find that it contains features without which it could only be trivial and which an axiomatized theory just could not possess, and if we find that the axiomatic method conduces only to the development of those features which are of little value in a theory, then the matter will be quite different. For then there would be strong reason to suspect that not only the illustrative theory but *any* theory of the sort that Woodger tries to illustrate would be valueless. This is the point for which I shall argue, and the people I shall try to convert are logicians, for I shall be trying to point out certain features of language. I shall not be trying to convert scientists, for if biologists, for example, ever agree among themselves that a theory similar to Woodger's illustrative one is of genuine value, then there will clearly be something wrong, either by omission or commission, with what I say. It would be arrant scholasticism to lay down criteria for judging theories to a consensus of working biologists. Even if I show that there are errors in Woodger's conception of scientific language, this will not prove that there is not also something of positive value as well. All I want to do is to draw attention to what seem to me to be the errors.

In order to form a just estimate of the value of Woodger's method we must state his theory T as simply as possible, and consider what, if anything, is gained by stating it in his more detailed or 'rigorous' way. We must also see whether T has the characteristics of a good theory: we must see what, if anything, it is supposed to explain, and whether it is able to explain it. To do this I shall also state in outline another theory, which I shall call 'U'. This is the Kinetic Theory of Gases. It will be agreed that U is a good theory, for there are certain things (mainly the gas laws) which it was invented to explain, and it is successful in explaining them. We shall find that U is genuinely explanatory, while T is not, simply in virtue of certain features of U which could not be incorporated in a completely axiomatized theory.

DIAGRAMMATIC VERSION OF THE THEORY T

Regard cells as 4-dimensional solids. (This corresponds to Woodger's propositions 1.1 to 3.13.)[1]

Then the situations in which two cells have a part in common[2] are (a) and (b), and (a) and (b) alone:

---

[1] *Technique of Theory Construction*, pp. 33-40.
[2] Woodger uses 'part' in such a way that being contiguous in time counts as having a part in common.

Q*

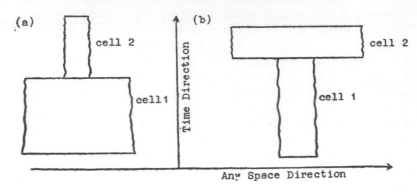

COROLLARY

The following do not represent possible situations:—

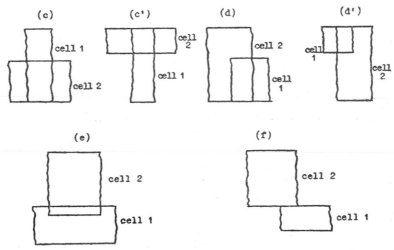

(a) and (b) constitute a picture mainly of Woodger's proposition 3.14.

In situation (a) we say that cell 2 is derived from cell 1 by division. In situation (b) we say that cell 2 is derived from cell 1 by fusion. (These are Woodger's propositions 3.5 and 3.6.)

(My diagrams look a little unnatural because they are designed to say neither more nor less than the propositions of the theory T.

Thus we should expect a picture of division to look not like (a) but like (a¹):—

(a¹)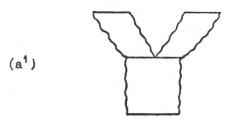

This, however, would be to state more than is actually contained in T. (a¹) is of course compatible with the theory but is not actually entailed by it. I have mentioned this point simply to remove possible misunderstanding; it is not in the least a criticism, for it is highly desirable that an illustrative theory should be simpler than it might have been.)

We can now 'read off' from the diagrams (a) and (b) any of the propositions about division and fusion in Woodger's theory and in particular —

3.52. The relation of division is one-many and asymmetrical.
3.62. The relation of fusion is many-one and asymmetrical.
3.71. No cell both divides and fuses with another cell.
3.72. No cell arises both by division and fusion.

This 'reading off' is very easy and involves no more than our simplest spatial intuitions. I cannot imagine two people ever disagreeing about whether 3.71, for example, can be 'read off' from the diagrams. Now one of the avowed aims of the axiomatic method is to avoid unnecessary controversy. If, however, there is likely to be no controversy, what is the point of stating 'rigorously' in 40 closely packed pages what can be put diagrammatically in about one page? If Woodger had invented a theory of complexity comparable to that of an actual biological theory it would have taken a whole library to state it according to his method, and his simple example, at any rate, has not shown that anything important would have been gained.

The next thing to note is this: most of the things we normally call 'theories' were invented in order to explain certain laws, and in the case of any such theory there would be no difficulty in pointing to the facts which were to be explained. This does not seem to be the case with the theory T. All its propositions appear to be much on a level. Let us contrast the Kinetic Theory of Gases, U.[1] There is no difficulty in pointing to the propositions which U is meant to explain. For example U explains Boyle's Law, '$P \propto \frac{1}{V}$', where P and V are the pressure and volume of a gas. The propositions of the theory itself involve some quite new ideas, for example that of a molecule or a gas particle. When we go from the experimental facts, such as that $P \propto \frac{1}{V}$, to the propositions of the theory, we rise to a totally new level of language. A word like 'molecule' cannot be strictly defined, and the properties of molecules are logically different from measurable properties. 'Find out the velocity of a molecule' makes no sense as does 'Find out the velocity of a billiard ball'. 'Velocity' as it occurs in 'velocity of a molecule' is logically different from 'velocity' as it occurs in 'velocity of a billiard ball'. The latter is an empirical or measurable property, while the former is a purely theoretical concept. If we consider U we shall see how this fact, that the propositions of U are on a different level of language from the laws it is called upon to explain, is an indispensable condition of the fact that U *does* explain those laws, and also of something else which is hardly less important, that U suggests new experiments and new laws which it will explain. Let us therefore consider a very much simplified version of U and examine some of its logical features.

THE THEORY U

The laws to be explained are the following:

(1) At constant temperature PV = constant, where P and V are the pressure and volume of a given mass of a gas. (Boyle's Law.)

[1] N. R. Campbell, in *Physics. The Elements* (Cambridge University Press, 1920), pp. 127 ff. discusses the Kinetic Theory of Gases as an instructive example of a physical theory, and what I shall say about it derives very largely from his ideas. Of course the element of *analogy* is present in varying degrees in different theories. In quantum mechanics, for example, Hamilton equations with operators are modelled on Hamilton equations in analogous systems in classical mechanics. In Newtonian dynamics itself there is very little of the element of analogy. I think, however, that it is possible to show that in the non-analogous type of theory also there is not a tight logical connection between propositions of theory and propositions of observation, that here also the theory and the statements of observational fact are on different levels of language.

(2) If several gases occupy a vessel of volume V then their combined pressure is equal to the sum of the pressures which each gas by itself (and at the same temperature) would have in a vessel of volume V. (Dalton's Law of Partial Pressures.)

It is also tempting to say that the theory should explain the law that if V is constant then $P \propto T$, where T is the absolute temperature, or to rewrite the law in the form 'PV = RT', when R is a constant. This would be a mistake. The equation 'PV = RT' does not state a law over and above Boyle's Law but *defines* the gas scale of temperature. We may reasonably expect of the kinetic theory of gases, however, that it should give a plausible physical meaning to 'temperature' as so defined, and this would be in some ways analogous to explanation of a law. We shall see that the theory does give a plausible physical meaning to 'temperature' as defined on the gas scale.

The situation is that we have some laws crying out for an explanation which cannot be given unless we move outside the limited range of ideas within which the laws are framed. Here the theory U differs considerably from T. In T we do not feel quite sure what explains what, and T never moves outside the range of the experiential ideas about cells which are its basis. In U we proceed to connect the gas laws with ideas, roughly speaking, of the behaviour of things like billiard balls. We introduce the quite new idea of a swarm of very minute perfectly elastic particles moving with very large velocities inside a box in accordance with the laws of dynamics. We investigate whether there would be anything in such a system analogous to the known behaviour of gases.

The following is an extremely simplified form of the investigation. It will make use only of the very easiest algebra and a correct presentation would of course be very much more complicated. It will, however, suffice to make clear the principles involved. (Also, in order to save space I shall only give that part of it which is the deduction of the analogue to Boyle's Law.)

Consider a box in the form of a cube of side *l*, three of whose edges lie along the axes OX, OY, OZ. Let ABCD and OEFG be the faces perpendicular to OX. Suppose that the box contains

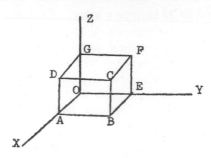

a very large number n of very minute perfectly elastic particles $P_1, P_2, \ldots P_n$, each being of mass M and let u_r, v_r, w_r be the components of the velocity of P_r. If we disregard the possibility of collisions between the particles, u_r, v_r, w_r will remain constant except that they will change sign when P_r hits the walls of the box perpendicular to OX, OY, OZ. (It is extremely plausible to suppose that our conclusions will remain unaffected if we disregard collisions between the particles, as any momentum lost by one of two colliding particles will be gained by the other, but the actual proof of this would involve us in more complicated considerations than are necessary for our present purposes.)

The time taken for the particle P_r to go from the wall ABCD to OEFG and back to ABCD again is obviously $\frac{2l}{u_r}$.

The change of momentum of P_r at each impact on ABCD is $2mu_r$

since it changes its velocity parallel to OX from u_r to $-u_r$

Hence the average rate of change of momentum of P_r at the face ABCD is $\dfrac{2mu_r}{\dfrac{2l}{u_r}} = \frac{1}{l}mu_r^2$

Hence the total rate of change of momentum on ABCD due to all the particles, and hence the force on ABCD is $\dfrac{m}{l} \sum_{r=1}^{n} u_r^2$

By symmetry we may take it that

$$\sum_{r=1}^{n} u_r^2 = \sum_{r=1}^{n} v_r^2 = \sum_{r=1}^{n} w_r^2$$

So the force on ABCD is

$$\frac{1}{3} \frac{m}{l} \sum_{r=1}^{n} (u_r{}^2 + v_r{}^2 + w_r{}^2)$$

$$= \frac{1}{3} \frac{m}{l} \sum_{r=1}^{n} c_r{}^2$$

where c_r is the magnitude of the velocity of the particle P_r, that is,

$$\frac{1}{3} \frac{mn}{l} \overline{c}^2$$

where $\overline{c}^2$ is the mean square velocity of the particles.

The pressure P is clearly equal to the last quantity divided by the area of ABCD, which is l^2.

That is,

$$P = \frac{1}{3} \frac{mn}{l^3} \overline{c}^2$$

Now l^3 is the volume V of the box.

$$\text{So } P = \frac{1}{3} mn \, \overline{c}^2 . \frac{1}{V}$$

$$\text{or } PV = \frac{1}{3} mn \, \overline{c}^2.$$

But $\frac{1}{2} mn \, \overline{c}^2$ is the total kinetic energy of the particles, and so

$$PV = \frac{2}{3} \times \text{ total kinetic energy of the particles.}$$

If two gases are at the same temperature no heat flows between them. So if we identify the heat energy of the gas with the kinetic energy of our particles we may take it that if the temperature is constant the kinetic energy is constant, that is

PV = constant, which corresponds to Boyle's Law.

It is also very easy to derive a law corresponding to Dalton's Law of Partial Pressures, and also to give a plausible physical meaning to 'temperature' as defined by the gas scale of temperature (i.e. by the equation PV = RT), namely as corresponding to the average kinetic energy of a particle of the gas.

We see, then, that if we think of a gas as a swarm of particles the gas laws become more intelligible; we feel that they have been explained, for we see that the laws of the behaviour of a swarm of perfectly elastic particles would be similar. The theory is explanatory because it shows the analogy between a gas and a swarm of particles, and in putting forward the analogy it has created some entirely new ideas, such as that of a gas particle. It is important to see that this is the case and that if we use 'particle' in the sense of 'molecule' or 'gas-particle' and if we use it in the original dynamical sense (roughly speaking in such a sense as that in which we might call a billiard ball a particle), we are using language in two different ways, and have created a new systematic ambiguity[1] in the use of 'particle'. For example a billiard ball must be either white, black, coloured, or transparent, but it would be absolutely without sense to apply any of these predicates to a molecule. Again, when we talk of the mass or velocity of a billiard ball we are talking about an experimental magnitude which might be determined by weighing or by clocking, whereas 'mass' and 'velocity' as applied to a molecule only have meaning within the theory. If told to measure the velocity of a billiard ball I might say 'No, it's too difficult', but if you told me to measure the velocity of an air molecule I would not say that it was too difficult but that I did not know what you wanted me to do. Again, we can talk about the history and distinguishing marks of an individual billiard ball, but we have given no meaning to talk about an individual molecule. Such talk would be quite in the air and without possibility of test. If asked to measure the root mean square velocity of a set of billiard balls I might do it by measuring their individual velocities and taking the root mean square, whereas if asked to find out the root mean square velocity of the molecules of the air in this room I should do quite a different sort of thing, such as to measure the barometric pressure and the temperature and, by connecting my measurements up with the kinetic theory, say what the root mean square velocity was. 'Velocity of a billiard ball' is an experimental concept, a magnitude that can be determined prior to all theory whatsoever, whereas 'velocity of a molecule' is a theoretical concept which if connected up with experiment would be connected up *via* the theory to experimental magnitudes quite different from velocities.

---

[1] [See Vol II, Ch. I, pp. 16 ff. for an explanation of this expression. — EDITOR.

In these and other ways we can see that the logical grammar of 'molecule' differs in important respects from that of 'billiard ball'.

It thus follows that unless we recognize the difference of language level between the various uses of 'particle' it might be misleading to say that a gas consists of particles. On the other hand it would not do to retain the use of 'particle' for things like billiard balls and to refuse to say that a gas consists of particles. How else can we bring out the analogy on which the explanatory power of the theory consists?

'All right', a semantic philosopher might say, 'we'll lay down a set of strict syntactical rules for "particle" = "molecule" and for "particle" = "billiard ball" and we will bring out the analogy[1] required for the theory by showing which rules are similar for the two cases, and also show where the analogy breaks down, by showing where the rules do not correspond'. This would not be a good idea, comforting though it is to our love for tidiness. *It would destroy the fertility of the theory*. All that it would be possible to derive from the theory would be the laws it was originally invented to explain.

In the first place *Avogadro's hypothesis* that all gases at the same temperature and pressure contain the same number of molecules in a given volume is a simple deduction from the theory if we identify his 'molecules' with the hypothetical gas particles of the kinetic theory. Avogadro's hypothesis was invented as an explanation of certain chemical facts, and the concept of a molecule was originally a chemical concept. We have now to attribute to our particles the property of being able to enter into combination with one another, a property quite unlike any property of a particle, in the sense in which a billiard ball is a particle. That is, we have to keep the logical grammar of an expression like 'gas particle' fairly fluid, so that we are ready to introduce modifications of the concept which will link our theory up with other theories and with laws of different sorts from those which it was first called upon to explain.

Secondly, it is eminently desirable to think in a fairly crude

---

[1] If the theory is to be explanatory some device for bringing out the analogy is required, even though we do not wish to use the very convenient and (so long as we are aware of what we are doing) perfectly harmless one of systematic ambiguity.

way and to press the analogy further than it will go. (The axiomatic method is expressly designed to prevent us from pressing analogies further than they will go.) The following example will show why this over-pressing of analogies may be a good thing. In the case of dynamical particles like small billiard balls the condition of perfect elasticity is never fulfilled, and some of the kinetic energy of the particles is not transferred on collision but is dissipated as heat and sound radiation and as internal vibration within the particles. The kinetic theory will not work if we attribute these properties to the gas particles. Why not? A logician whose ideal of a language is that it should everywhere proceed in accordance with rigid rules would have to say that from his point of view the question is a silly question, that 'particle' in the sense of 'billiard ball' and 'particle' in the sense of 'molecule' are two different words, and that some questions which, according to his rules, can be asked with the one, cannot, according to his rules, be asked with the other. I want to point out that a great deal of vital importance would be liable to be lost if we were to adopt such an attitude. Physicists rightly tried to press the analogy in the direction of asking why the energy of the gas particles was not dissipated in the way it could be expected to be on the analogy, and when it was eventually found that there were reasons, drawn from quantum theory (which itself was derived from a realm of observations quite different from those which led up to the kinetic theory of gases), why the analogy could not be expected to work in this respect, this constituted a triumph not only for the quantum theory of radiation but also for the kinetic theory of gases.

In the third place it is not true that we say that a theory has to be given up, or even 'modified', if its predictions are not always closely confirmed. A failure to fit the facts may in certain circumstances be additional reason for accepting the theory as being essentially sound. This is the case with the theory of gases, for at high pressures the laws predicted by the theory are not closely obeyed. Now on the analogy on which the theory was based we can see that we could have expected that this would be so. We failed to consider the *volumes* and the *mutual attractions* of the particles of the gas. Even without working the thing out in detail we can see from a general consideration of the rough outline of the kinetic theory that in cases where the particles are so near one another that the above two factors cannot be neglected the modification of Boyle's Law called 'Van der Waal's Equation' would be extremely plausible. Hence our confidence in the general soundness of the theory and the accuracy of its predictions in the cases in which we should expect it to work is not diminished but enhanced.

We may note some of the linguistic expressions which occurred in the last paragraph — 'can be neglected', 'might have expected', 'failed to consider'. Such expressions are very characteristic of much actual scientific language but could find no place in a formalized language. Strict rules for 'what we might expect' cannot be laid down; we use such an expression when we are using our judgment.

It might be retorted that all this applies only to the growing stages of a theory, but that when a theory is in its final and perfect stage it can then be formalized. My reply to this would be that when a theory is in its final and perfect stage it is dead and of no further use, for, as I have tried to show, if a theory is to have any valuable explanatory, predictive, and unifying function, it must contain linguistic features which are present only in a living language, and which could not be present in a formalized system. It would be patently absurd to construct a 'language' for 'scientific purposes' if the only theories which could be put into the 'language' are fossilized theories, theories with no surviving scientific purpose.

Consideration of the above theory U, and comparison with theory T, have, I hope, shown that U possesses features which are indispensable and which no theory of the axiomatized sort could possess. It is perhaps superfluous, therefore, to claim that any of the supposed virtues of T are not really virtues, if it be agreed that T lacks an *indispensable* virtue. Nevertheless it may help to persuade a reader who is as yet unconvinced if I say a few words about what is supposed to be the chief virtue of T, namely *rigour*. I want to point out that 'rigour', in the sense in which it is pursued in pure mathematics is not an ideal in applied mathematics (or physics). The conception of 'rigour' involved in physics is that whereby it makes sense to say 'rigorous enough', and if enough *is* enough there is no point in making our proofs *more* rigorous. In any case rigour is not the all-important thing.[1]

Rigour, in the pure mathematician's sense of the word, is an ideal which only does apply to pure mathematics. Pure mathematics can be made into a calculus, and theorems may be derived from the axioms in accordance with strict rules. The axioms really are axioms (postulates), and they are not in any way to be tested by experience in the way that some of Woodger's 'postulates' are supposed to be. If a theorem can be proved it can be strictly proved, and if the proof is accepted there is no further question. Science is not like this. Even if the steps within a theory are formalized, the important steps, which are those from the theory to the experimental facts, are of quite a different sort. We saw this in the theory U when, for example, we identified the theoretical concept of the average pressure exerted by a swarm of minute particles with the empirical concept of the pressure we measure with a barometer tube. It is in this step from the theoretical to the empirical, and in the converse step from the empirical to the theoretical, that 'judgment' characteristically enters into science. An experimenter has often to judge, on the basis of his general 'feel' for the subject, whether a new phenomenon has entered into his experiments or whether something has just gone wrong. Thus Millikan's oil drop experiment might give results which at first sight might be thought to falsify the theory of discrete electronic charges, but then the anomalous way in which the rate of fall of an oil drop changed would be attributed by the experimenter to some such cause as the evaporation of the drop. It ought to be obvious that no strict rules can be invented for telling the experimenter what he ought to say in such cases; for one thing there is no finite set of types of experimental apparatus, and so there is no knowing from what range of experience the experimenter will have to extract his 'excuses' for an apparent anomaly. Again, it is often only genius, which works according to no rules, which spots the apparent anomaly which it is important to recognize as a real anomaly.

We thus see that the step from theory to fact is not like the

[1] In the preface to his 'Introduction to the Kinetic Theory of Gases' (Cambridge University Press, 1940) Sir James Jeans, who was a lover of pure theory if ever there was one, speaks of 'the physicist's need for clearness and directness of treatment rather than the mathematician's need for rigorous general proofs'.

step from one proposition to another in a calculus; roughly speaking, we may say that within a theory or within the description of fact we are on one level of language, but when we step from the level of theory to the level of fact or vice versa, we are in a region where expressions like 'make more plausible', 'lead us to expect that', or 'strongly suggest' apply, but where the logical relations of implication and contradiction do not strictly apply.[1] If, then, some of the most important and quite indispensable steps which a scientist makes cannot be reduced to strict rule, why bother about absolutely strict rules within a theory either? So long as our rules are strict enough to prevent us getting into trouble, or so long as we watch our step in those deductions where it is relatively easy to commit an important fallacy, why do any more towards making our theoretical deductions rigorous? To suggest that it is desirable to formalize a theory in the way that pure mathematics is formalized is like suggesting that holes in the side of a bottomless bucket should be stopped up. However carefully we seal the sides of the bucket it still will not hold water. (This analogy must not be taken too seriously, for I am far from wanting to suggest that science is somehow defective as a bottomless bucket would be. The ideal of a bucket with a bottom is not a logically absurd ideal, whereas the ideal of a science for which the canons of criticism are everywhere those of strict deduction is a logically absurd ideal.) As I have said, the conception of 'rigour' in physics is that in which it makes sense to say 'rigorous enough'. My statement of U, for example, would certainly not be regarded by physicists as rigorous enough. This does not mean, however, that the standard of rigour required is that of the pure mathematician.

My statement of Woodger's theory T, with the aid of diagrams, was not rigorous, i.e. not formalized, but surely it is far easier to understand than Woodger's version, and it enables us to grasp the properties of cells which are described (though not explained) by it. Rigour would only be useful to the extent that it would

---

[1] I owe this idea to Dr. F. Waismann. As a rough analogy, compare the way in which one chess rule may be incompatible with another, or one move may be incompatible with another, but a move cannot contradict a rule, though it may be a breach of it. Logic, in the sense of *Principia Mathematica*, Dr. Waismann has said, is not coextensive with language, but at most with a given level of language. [See his *Language Strata* now published as Vol. II, Ch. I. — EDITOR.]

prevent avoidable controversies, but what controversy could there be about the conclusions of the theory T?

In pure mathematics it is proved rigorously that if $f(x)$ is a continuous function which has a derivative $f^1(x)$ for all values of x, then if $f(x) = 0$ for $x = a$ and $x = b$ then $f^1(\xi) = 0$ for some values ξ of x where $a < \xi < b$. This corresponds to the proposition that if we draw a smooth curve which cuts the line OX at two points A and B then there is some point in between A and B where the tangent to the curve is parallel to OX. We get the feeling that if we were to connect up the proposition about drawn curves with the proof of the proposition in pure mathematics we would put the proposition about drawn curves on a sounder basis. This feeling is quite wrong. It comes from the failure to see that the strict idea of continuity which is applicable in mathematical analysis is quite inapplicable to the realm of talk about drawn curves, trajectories of rifle bullets, and so on. For example if $f(x)$ is a continuous function then between any two values of $f(x)$ we can find a third, but when we say that a trajectory

is continuous we do not mean that between two points $\dfrac{1}{10^{\frac{1}{10}}}$

millimetres apart we could find a third. No possible measurement or observation would be in the least relevant to such an assertion; no possible experiences could verify or falsify it, and consequently it can do no work and is quite pointless. Of course we do represent trajectories by continuous functions, e.g. by $y = x^2$, rather than by very subtly discontinuous ones. It is clearly far more convenient to do so, for continuous functions are easier to handle mathematically — for example they can usually be differentiated. This, however, is all there is to the matter, and should not blind us to the change in the use of 'continuous' which occurs when we pass from the use of this word in physics or in ordinary life to its use within pure mathematics. Even if the mathematical ideal of rigour were applicable to scientific language it would not be worth striving after. A physicist would be just silly if he were to put axioms about continuity, etc., into his talk about trajectories, so as to model his talk on rigorous pure mathematical talk about functions, quite apart from the fact that his axioms would have no physical meaning or possibility of test. What would be the good of constructing a strict derivation of the proposition that if a projectile moves in a smooth curve from A to B, where A and B are at sea-level, then at some point between A and B its motion will be momentarily in a horizontal direction? Who could doubt it? What controversy could there be? The ordinary crude ideas of continuity are good enough for physical purposes, nor is there anything better for those purposes, and the sort of activity the pure mathematician goes in for would have no point.

In any case it is worth asking ourselves, in the light of the actual development of science, just how true it is that by making our derivations more rigorous we shall materially reduce the chance of controversy about our theories.[1] Controversies in physics, at any rate, do not seem normally to hinge on the strict rigour of derivations. They hinge on other things, such as the satisfactoriness of the analogy displayed; for example on whether pressing the analogy further does not lead us to deduce all sorts of false laws, and as to whether anything can be said as to why the analogy should not be pressed in these directions. I suggest that Woodger in constructing his theory T is doing in biology what a physicist would be doing if he included in a theory of ballistics proofs of things such as the proposition about trajectories discussed above, that are everywhere, outside pure mathematics where the position is different, quite rightly allowed to pass without question. His method conduces to what is misplaced in a theory, namely rigour (in the pure mathematician's sense) of derivations, and leaves out something which is incompatible with strict rigour (in this sense), namely the features of scientific language which are not present in a calculus and which give a theory the power to explain. The only language which can be used in an explanatory way is language with what Dr. Waismann has called 'a many-level structure'. Dr. Woodger's monograph is an ingenious and admirable exercise in pure logic, but as a

---

[1] On p. 34 proposition 1.25 Woodger claims to have cleared up, or at least avoided, a controversy. He has defined 'sum' so that it becomes analytical to say that a thing is the sum of its parts. This, however, is to miss the point of the controversy in question, which is something like this: as to whether after doing sufficient experiments on the parts of an organism we can predict the laws of its behaviour as a whole. This is surely a real question, though it may also be a muddled one, and remains unaffected by Woodger's treatment.

contribution to the philosophy of science it seems to me to be one more case of the tendency, so common in modern philosophy, to carry over into other realms of language ideals and conceptions which have their place only in pure mathematics.

N